# Aesop's Fables

## in Latin

# Aesop's Fables
## in Latin

Ancient Wit and Wisdom from
the Animal Kingdom

Laura Gibbs

Bolchazy-Carducci Publishers, Inc.
Mundelein, Illinois USA

*Editor:* Laurie Haight Keenan
*Contributing Editor:* Gary Varney
*Cover & Book Design:* Adam Phillip Velez

**Aesop's Fables in Latin**
**Ancient Wit and Wisdom from the Animal Kingdom**

Laura Gibbs

Reprinted with corrections 2010, 2014

**Bolchazy-Carducci Publishers, Inc.**
1570 Baskin Road
Mundelein, Illinois 60060
www.bolchazy.com

Printed in the United States of America
**2014**
by United Graphics

ISBN 978-0-86516-695-0

---

Library of Congress Cataloging-in-Publication Data

Aesop's fables. Latin.
  Aesop's fables in Latin : ancient wit and wisdom from the animal kingdom / Laura Gibbs.
      p. cm.
  ISBN 978-0-86516-695-0 (pbk. : alk. paper)  1.  Fables, Greek--Translations into Latin. 2.  Aesop's fables--Translations into Latin.
I. Aesop. II. Gibbs, Laura. III. Title.

  PA3855.A2 2008
  398.24'52--dc22

                                                                                                        2008052405

# CONTENTS

# LIST OF ILLUSTRATIONS

# PREFACE

In this book, you will find eighty Aesop's fables in Latin prose, with individual vocabulary and notes for each fable. These little stories are an ideal way to start reading Latin on your own after you have completed a basic Latin course. First and foremost, the fables are short, often just a few sentences in length. The characters are creatures who are already familiar to you: lions, foxes, roosters, donkeys, cats and dogs, and so on. Some of the stories will be familiar, too, such as the fable of *The Tortoise and The Hare*, *The Boy Who Cried "Wolf!"* or *The Goose Who Laid the Golden Eggs.* You may be surprised to find out that the famous English phrases "sour grapes" and "the lion's share" actually got their start as Aesop's fables. You will also meet some fables that are probably entirely new to you, such as the story of *The Vipers and The Hedgehogs,* or the sad affair of *The Amorous Lion.*

These Latin texts come from a collection of Aesop's fables published in 1687 by Francis Barlow, who was one of the most renowned nature artists of seventeenth-century England. Barlow created a series of beautiful illustrations to accompany the Latin fables, and you will find forty of those illustrations included with the fables in this book. The author of the Latin texts was Robert Codrington (d. 1665), a prolific writer and translator who was well known in his day, although he is now largely forgotten. Codrington would no doubt be delighted to discover that his fables have gained a new lease on life after a quietus that has lasted over three hundred years. You can read more about Codrington's classical sources in the notes about the fable tradition, which you will find at the end of the *Introduction* to this book.

You may be familiar with a way of telling Aesop's fables that ends with the formulaic phrase, "And the moral of the story is . . ." While you will not find this formulaic phrase used in the Latin texts in this book, the stories do have a moral—that is, they have a message for you, a meaning that extends beyond the tiny world of the fable itself. Sometimes you will see that one of the characters in the fable expresses the moral in the closing words of the story. At other times, it is up to you to supply the moral, deciding just what lesson you will take away from the fable that you could apply to your own life. As you embark on your journey through these Latin fables, keep an eye out for the morals of the stories, because they just might lead you to an unexpected destination. I myself have been journeying in the land of Latin fables for close to twenty years now, and I continue to find new meanings and messages in the fables at every turn; I hope your journey through the fables will likewise be a rewarding experience!

*Mutato nomine, de te fabula narratur.*

With the name changed, the fable is talking about you.
Horace, *Satires* I.1

# ACKNOWLEDGEMENTS

This book got its start thanks to the poetry of Coleman Barks, especially his book *We Are Three*, which first prompted me to start studying the history of Aesop's fables and their extraordinary diffusion over space and time. For introducing me to the 1687 edition of Barlow's Aesop, I am indebted to Peter Berg and the Special Collections staff in the Michigan State University Library; the illustrations in this book are reproduced with their kind permission. Laurie Keenan, Andrew Reinhard, and Gary Varney at Bolchazy-Carducci have been wonderful to work with, and I am grateful for their help with this unusual project. I would also like to thank my friends Nancy Diven, Lynne Levy and Nina Livesey for their language enthusiasm in both Latin and Greek. Most importantly, I would like to dedicate this book to my husband, Anderson White, *fidelis usque ad finem*, who has somehow survived another book project with his marvelous sense of humor miraculously intact.

## ACKNOWLEDGMENTS

# INTRODUCTION

## Organization of the Book

In this *Introduction*, you will find a guide to the materials contained in this book, along with study tips and strategies, plus some basic background information about the genre of Aesop's fables itself—almost three thousand years old, and still going strong! You will also find information about the *Fables.MythFolklore.net* website, an online source for additional learning materials related to the fables in this book.

Following the *Introduction* is the *List of Most Frequently Used Words*. These are the words that occur so frequently in Latin and/or in these particular fables that they are not included in the fable-by-fable word lists. You will probably want to memorize the words on this list that are not already familiar to you, or perhaps make a photocopy of the list to keep handy when you are reading the fables.

The *Fables* then follow, eighty in number, arranged in order of difficulty, more or less. Gauging the difficulty of a story is highly subjective, but based on overall length, vocabulary, and syntactic features, the fables progress from easier stories (shorter, simpler) to more difficult stories (longer, more complex).

At the end of the book, you will find a complete *Glossary* containing entries for all the words used in the fables, as well as any other Latin words used in the book. You will also find the *Index* at the back of the book, listing proper names, grammar terms, as well as the characters in the fables.

Interspersed throughout the book, you will find some *Latin Proverbs*. Sometimes the proverbs provide a moral you might apply to the fable, and sometimes the proverbs are about one of the characters in the story. For help with the vocabulary in these proverbs, see the *Glossary* in the back of the book.

## The Fables

For each fable, you will find the following materials: *Introduction, Grammar Overview, Latin Text, Grammar Notes,* and *Word Lists*. In addition, forty of the fables are accompanied by Francis Barlow's original illustrations.

### Introduction

The *Introduction* to each fable provides you with some questions to keep in mind as you read the story, based on the various ways in which the fable has been interpreted and retold over the centuries. You might find information about ancient Greek or Roman versions of the story, or possibly some reference to the great authors of the English fable tradition, such as the pioneering printer William Caxton (d. 1492), the renowned politician Sir Roger L'Estrange (d. 1704), the Reverend George Fyler Townsend (d. 1900) or the great folklorist Joseph Jacobs (d. 1916). You will probably want to read the *Introduction* one time before you work through the Latin text of the fable, and then return to it again after you finish the story, comparing your impression of the fable to the traditional interpretations.

In addition, the *Introduction* to each fable contains several cross-references to other, similar fables in the book. These might be fables with the same moral or theme, or fables with the same type of plot, or fables about the same animal characters. Given that there is nothing sacrosanct about the sequencing of the fables in this book, you can build your own pathway through the fables by pursuing these cross-references from fable to fable.

## Grammar Overview

The *Grammar Overview* section for each fable provides information about an item of Latin grammar or style that pertains to that specific fable. How you use the *Grammar Overview* is up to you. If your interest is strictly in reading Latin and not in the formal study of Latin grammar and style, you may choose to skip over the *Grammar Overview* and proceed directly to the fable text.

In general, the topics I have addressed in the *Grammar Overview* sections fall into these broad categories:

- **unusual verb forms,** such as the gerund, gerundive, supine, future imperative, and future periphrastics
- **syntax topics,** such as subjunctive versus indicative, direct and indirect speech, and predication
- **"little" words,** such as postpositive particles, correlatives, and relative pronouns
- **word formation,** such as diminutives, frequentative and inchoative verbs, intensified and negated adjectives, and compound words
- **stylistic questions,** such as emphasis and word order, finite verbs versus participles, and active versus passive voice

The topics in the *Grammar Overview* sections are driven by the contents of the individual fables and do not follow any particular order. If you are looking for a specific grammar topic, check the *Index* to the book, which includes listings for all the topics covered in the *Grammar Overview* sections.

The *Grammar Overview* sections often contain questions for you to answer in order to test and expand your knowledge. Some of these are open-ended questions, while others are questions with a particular answer in mind (such questions are usually accompanied by a good hint or two). To find out more about the answers to these questions and to study these grammar topics in further depth, visit the *Fables.MythFolklore.net* website.

Because Latin to English translation is still a widely used method in the teaching of Latin, I have included comments in the *Grammar Overview* sections regarding the different English translation options you might use for various Latin constructions.

At the same time, I would strongly encourage you to find other ways to engage with the Latin, rather than limiting yourself to English translation. For specific suggestions about alternatives to English translation in deepening your understanding of the Latin stories, see the *Study Tips and Strategies* section below.

## Latin Text

In editing the Latin text, I have modernized the punctuation and capitalization. Perhaps most importantly, I have not included the moral supplied for each story in Barlow's 1687 edition of the book; instead, I have left the fables open-ended to encourage you to formulate your own morals as you see fit. If you are curious about the specific morals included with the fables in Barlow's 1687 edition of the book, you can find them listed at the *Fables.MythFolklore.net* website.

## Grammar Notes

Following the Latin text of each fable is a list of *Grammar Notes*. As a general rule, all difficult or unusual forms are provided with a note. This includes all gerunds and gerundives, future imperatives, and future periphrastic expressions, as well as all uses of relative pronouns where the referent of the pronoun appears in the previous sentence. I have also indicated any infinitive that is used in indirect statement, along with all ablative absolute constructions. As regards the subjunctive, I have not labeled subjunctives following *ut* and *ne* or following *si* and *nisi*, but all other uses of the subjunctive have been noted.

As with the *Grammar Overviews* for each fable, how you use the *Grammar Notes* is up to you. If you are not particularly interested in the formal study of Latin grammar and style, you might choose to ignore the notes, using them only when you need some help in understanding a difficult passage in the reading. If, however, you are interested in the formal study of Latin grammar and style for its own sake, you may find it helpful to read all the notes, even when the meaning of the Latin text is already clear to you.

## Vocabulary

Each fable is accompanied by *Vocabulary* for all words in the fable that do not appear in the *List of Most Frequently Used Words*. Long marks have not been included, but you can find long marks in the *Glossary* in the back of the book. As you will see, the word lists are organized by functional groups: nouns, adjectives, verbs, and "other" (prepositions, adverbs, interjections, etc.). This method of presentation is intended to help reinforce your understanding of the basic grammatical structures that govern the Latin language.

**Nouns.** For each noun, you will find the dictionary form, the genitive form, as well as the gender of the noun. These are the essential elements you need to analyze each instance of a Latin noun as it is used in a Latin sentence. These are also the elements you need to memorize as you build your Latin vocabulary.

**Adjectives.** For each adjective, you will find the dictionary form by gender. If you see three forms, they are masculine, feminine and neuter (e.g., *altus, alta, altum*), in that order. If you see only two forms (e.g., *mollis, molle*), that means they are masculine/feminine and neuter, in that order. If you see only one form (e.g., *ingens*), that means it is valid for all three genders. If the adjective belongs to the third declension, the genitive form is also supplied in parentheses.

**Verbs.** For each verb, the first and second parts are provided so that you can identify the conjugation of the verb and all forms found in the present system. In addition, if there is a perfect form of the verb that appears in the fable, the third and fourth parts (the perfect system) are also supplied in the word list. If a verb listing does not include the third and fourth parts, it does not mean that the verb is lacking a perfect system. Rather, it simply means that the forms of the verb that you will find in the fable belong to the present system and can be identified from the first and second parts of the verb alone. You will find the third and fourth parts of all the verbs included in the *Glossary* at the back of the book.

**Other.** The prepositions, adverbs, interjections and other parts of speech in Latin do not decline, so only the dictionary form is provided in this listing. You should be able to identify the type of speech from context, but if you are not sure, you can find that information in the *Glossary* at the back of the book.

**Definitions.** For each word, you will find a very brief English definition, usually just one or two words. You will find these same definitions in the *Glossary* in the back of the book. For more complete definitions, make sure you consult a good Latin dictionary (Traupman's *New College Latin & English Dictionary* is an excellent and affordable paperback dictionary). Please remember that all English equivalents for Latin are rough at best. The English words are there to help you start learning the Latin vocabulary, but the only way to truly learn Latin is through reading Latin—reading lots of Latin—so that you can get a feel for how the words are actually used to create meaningful expressions in the Latin language itself.

## Study Tips and Strategies for Reading Latin

Reading the fables in Latin, without translating into English, is the best thing you can do to increase your reading confidence. Even if you plan to do an English translation, make sure you read the entire fable in Latin first, enjoying each and every Latin word and phrase, before you do any translating. Once you get used to reading Latin without translating, you will find that the reading goes much more smoothly than if you try to translate while you read. English translation often slows you down unnecessarily, without really improving your understanding of the Latin itself. Try to make it your goal to read these Latin fables with a sense of fun and confidence, enjoying the Latin for its own sake, without making English translation the benchmark of your success.

## *Latin Reading Checklist*

People all read Latin in their own ways, based on their own strengths, weaknesses and motivations. It's a good idea to come up with a reading procedure or checklist of some kind to help ensure that you are being thorough and consistent when you read something new in Latin. In order to give you some ideas for how to develop a reading strategy of your own, I've outlined below the reading procedure I use when I am working through a fable for the first time.

Given that I've been studying Latin for many years, I've developed a pretty large Latin vocabulary, so dictionary use is not a critical element for me (although I certainly do consult the dictionary whenever I am in doubt about the form or meaning of a word). If you are a beginning Latin student, vocabulary will be a bigger challenge for you, and you will want to come up with some good strategies for keeping track of new words as you read and identifying which new words you should commit to memory. For example, when reading the fables in this book, pay special attention to the *List of Most Frequently Used Words*, mastering each of those words as you encounter them, since you are likely to meet those words again soon!

1. **Ready to Read.** First, I get a copy of the Latin text that I can mark up. If the Latin text is online, I print out a copy. If it is in a book, I make a photocopy of the page or write out a copy by hand (transcribing the Latin text by hand is very good practice, if the text is not too long). Since I make a lot of noise reading the Latin out loud, I usually close my study door so that I don't frighten innocent bystanders.

2. **First Read-Through.** If the fable is short, as most fables are, I read through the whole thing, out loud, very slowly. My goal is to see just how many words I recognize and how much of the main idea I can piece together on my own as I read through the whole story.

3. **Sentence by Sentence.** I now start working through the text sentence by sentence.

   a. I read the current sentence out loud, slowly, doing my best to understand what I am reading, while pausing at the phrase boundaries and penciling them in. (For the fables in this book, you can find a phrase-by-phrase presentation of each fable at the *Fables.MythFolklore.net* website.)

   b. Next, I read through the current sentence again, looking up any unfamiliar words in the dictionary. I do not write any English definitions on the page with the text, although I sometimes keep a vocabulary list on a separate page and/or underline words in the passage that puzzle me.

   c. If there are notes or commentary provided, I consult those notes to see if they can give me some help, either by confirming my understanding of the Latin or by giving me additional information.

d.  If something in the current sentence is still really confusing to me, I read through the whole fable again, keeping my eyes and ears open for any clues that might help me to understand the current sentence.

e.  When I have done my best with the current sentence, I then go on to the next sentence, knowing that as I work my way through the fable, things will continue to become more clear.

4.  **Review**. By the time I have worked through the whole fable this way, sentence by sentence, I should be in pretty good shape. I then read through the fable again, one last time, checking to make sure that I am confident in my understanding of all the Latin expressions.

Of course, it sometimes happens that after working carefully on a fable, I am still not sure about something. If I still have questions, these are some of the strategies I use to find the answers:

• To get more help in understanding the form of a word, I use a morphology program, such as Whitaker's Words. For help in understanding the meaning of a word, I look it up in an even bigger Latin dictionary, such as the online Latin dictionaries at the Perseus website. (You can find tips on how to use these tools at the *Fables.MythFolklore.net* website.)

• I ask somebody to help me. A great way to get help from others is to work together in a study group, so that you can pool your collective knowledge!

• If I am really stuck, I try to find some English translations to help me. The more English translations I can find, the better, since no English translation can perfectly reflect the Latin. (For the fables in this book, you can find rough-and-ready English translations at the *Fables.MythFolklore.net* website.)

• Finally, I sleep on it. There is nothing like putting something aside and looking at it again the next day.

Most importantly, I never give up! If something has me really puzzled, I'll read a few more fables and come back to the problem again later. For an Aesop's fable that will encourage you to be patient and persistent in your studies, consider the story of the crow and the urn (Fable 5). Just like the crow who raised the water level in the pot by dropping in one small stone after another, you need to keep adding to your Latin knowledge with every new text you read, bit by bit, until the meaning of the Latin is at last within your reach.

## Parsing and Reading Comprehension

As you are reading, you will probably want some way to test your reading comprehension. Of course, the best way to measure reading comprehension is from the sheer joy of reading; if you are reading well, you will know it, because you will be able to understand and appreciate the meaning of the Latin. Still, you might also want to do some monitoring, just to make sure you are really reading the Latin and not relying too much on the power of the lucky guess. To distinguish between reading and guessing, you need to parse. While parsing is not the same as reading, it offers a reliable method for checking to make sure that you understand the grammatical structures of Latin that make meaning possible, word by word.

*Nota bene:* **Parsing does not involve English translation of any kind.** Unlike translation, which is an art (and an extremely subjective one at that), parsing is a science, an objective grammatical analysis of Latin words used in the context of a Latin sentence. Parsing has nothing to do with English at all; it is about how the Latin sentence is put together, word by word. If you have learned Latin using a Latin-only method, so much the better! It does not matter whether you use the word genitive or *genitivus* when you parse; the results are exactly the same whether you use English or Latin parsing terms to label your results.

**Parsing in context.** When you were first learning Latin, you might have been asked to memorize paradigms in order to learn the different forms of words in Latin. When you parse, you are also identifying the forms of words, but you are doing that in the meaningful context of a Latin sentence. Is *boni* masculine genitive singular, neuter genitive singular, or masculine nominative plural? A paradigm tells you that all three forms are possible, but in a given Latin sentence, only one form will be correct. You cannot just look at the isolated Latin word as in a paradigm; to parse correctly, you have to read and understand the word in the context of a Latin sentence.

**Parsing nouns.** If the word is a noun, you need to be able to identify its *case* and *number*. Ideally, you should know the gender of the noun, too—but it's okay if you are not 100% sure about the gender, because you can always just look up the gender of a noun in the dictionary. For parsing a noun, what is essential is that you understand, from context, the case and number of the noun as it is being used in the passage you are reading.

**Parsing adjectives.** For every adjective, you need to be able to identify its *case* and *number*, and also its *gender*. Unlike a noun, you cannot look up the gender of an adjective in the dictionary; you can only determine the gender of an adjective based on the way the adjective is being used in a sentence.

**Parsing verbs.** With verbs, you first have to determine what part of speech you are dealing with: a finite verb, a verbal noun (such as an infinitive), or a verbal adjective (such as a participle). Here are some general guidelines for parsing the most common verb forms you will find:

> **Finite Verbs**: *person - number - tense - voice - mood*
>
> **Infinitives**: *tense - voice*
>
> **Participles**: *tense - voice - case - number - gender*

Don't worry about the more rare verb forms you might find, such as future imperatives, for example; these rare forms are identified for you in the *Grammar Notes* for each fable.

## Why Translate When You Can Innovate?

After you are confident about the meaning of a Latin fable, you are ready to work with that fable to make it your own. You may want to do this simply by writing out your own English translation, but there are also some much more challenging, and much more satisfying, exercises you can use to enrich your Latin experience of the fables. Here are some suggestions:

**Reading out loud, with feeling.** One of the best ways to develop your Latin language skills is to work on oral performance, practicing each fable so that you can read it out loud with real feeling. You might even memorize the fable so that you are able to declaim it in Latin. Try to read with feeling and enthusiasm, and with a clear and sure intonation that shows you fully understand the meaning of what you are saying. There is no one "right" way to perform a fable, and the way you choose to read—your use of emphasis, dramatic pauses, tone of voice, and so on—will demonstrate your own unique interpretation of the story.

**Let's put on a play!** As you will see, most of the fables are based on a confrontation between two characters, involving both action and dialogue. That makes it easy to rewrite the fables as tiny theater scripts. Not only can you rewrite the fables as plays, you can perform them! If you are shy about acting out the story yourself, or if you are a solo student, don't worry: with a small investment in finger puppets made from paper or cloth, you can put on a play all by yourself, without even having to get up on the stage.

**Point of view.** The plot of a fable looks very different depending on just who is telling the story. For a great composition exercise, you can pretend you are one of the characters in the story, and write out the story in first-person style from the point of view of that character. The story of *The Tortoise and The Hare*, just to take one example, would sound very different based on whether the tortoise is the storyteller, or the hare. Writing the fable in first-person style is not only a great way to get inside the mind of one of the characters, it is also an excellent way to practice different Latin verb forms as well.

**Sequels and alternate endings.** Sometimes the fable ends with the death of the main character, but if any of your characters are still left alive at the end of the story, you can take a cue from Hollywood and write a sequel. For example, Fable 37, the story of the mouse's marriage, is actually a sequel to the story of the mouse and the lion, Fable 67. Or, instead of writing a sequel, maybe you want to change the ending. If you are not happy with the fact that the wolf eats the lamb in Fable 53, for example, or if you want the ant in Fable 16 to show some sympathy to the cricket after all, then you can compose your own version of the fable with the ending of your choice.

**Morals, morals, morals.** Adding new morals to the fables is part of the great Aesopic tradition—a tradition you can contribute to by adding morals of your own. A moral can come before or after the fable, or it can be spoken by a character inside the story. Morals can also take a variety of grammatical forms, so you can test your grammatical skills by writing out the morals using different constructions, such as comparisons, imperatives, conditionals, etc. Plus, you can write different morals directed towards different audiences: a story might convey one message when applied to students, another message when applied to parents and children, yet another message for politicians, and so on. Taking advantage of all these different options, see how many of your own morals you can add to each fable!

### The Bestiaria Latina Blog: Fables and More

In addition to using the materials printed here in this book, I hope you will also visit the *Bestiaria Latina Blog*, which you can find at *BestLatin.net*. The *Bestiaria Latina Blog*, in continuous publication since 2007, features an abundance of Latin fables and proverbs that you can use to work on your Latin and also to expand your knowledge of the Latin wit and wisdom tradition

## The Aesop Fable Tradition

Now for a few words about the fables themselves. The fables of Aesop go back a long way. . . a very long way! The ancient Greek historian Herodotus, writing around the year 430 BCE, tells us that Aesop was famous as a "maker of stories," a *logopoios* (from the Greek words *logos*, "story" and *poios*, "maker"). Was there really a historical storyteller named Aesop? It's hard to say. Herodotus reports that Aesop was a former slave who was murdered by the people of Delphi, an incident that is also reported in Aristophanes's comedy, *The Wasps*. Even more intriguing is the notice in Plato's *Phaedo* that Socrates was putting Aesop's fables into verse before his own death. While we cannot know for sure whether or not there really was a storyteller named Aesop who died in Delphi, there is abundant evidence that the fables attributed to Aesop and the legends about Aesop's own life and death were well known in ancient Greece and also in Rome. Altogether, there are approximately 600 Aesop's fables preserved in ancient Greek and Roman writers, with the more popular fables attested in multiple sources.

In addition to the fables preserved in written form, there were doubtless hundreds more fables that circulated in oral form, passing from person to person. As with other types of folklore, such as jokes and riddles, the fables do not have just one standard version. Instead, the "same" story appears in many different versions. Each time the story is told to an audience (even if it is just an audience of one person), the storyteller has a chance to make up a new version, changing the cast of characters, adding a new twist to the plot, or perhaps inventing a moral specifically suited for that particular audience on that particular storytelling occasion.

As you will see from the stories included in this book, the fables are short, sometimes only a few sentences in length. Yet even the shortest fable has a point, a lesson to be learned—in other words, a "moral" to the story. Sometimes the moral is expressed by means of a positive exemplum, a character who gives us a model of behavior to imitate. It is far more common, however, for the fable to present a negative exemplum, a foolish character who makes a mistake, often a fatal mistake, that shows us the kind of behavior we should avoid. Usually, but not always, the main characters in Aesop's fables are talking animals, although you will also find fables about human beings, as well as fables about the Olympian gods.

The first written collection of Aesop's fables seems to have been made in the third century BCE by Demetrius of Phalerum. That collection has not survived, but there are numerous later collections of fables in Greek prose, as well as a large collection of fables in Greek verse attributed to an otherwise unknown poet, Babrius, who probably lived sometime in the third century CE (although not even that much is certain about this mysterious Greek poet).

Meanwhile, in Rome, the poet Phaedrus (a freed slave from the household of the Emperor Augustus) composed several books of verse fables in the first century CE, which makes Phaedrus's poems the oldest surviving ancient collection of fables. Another famous collection of Latin verse fables is attributed to Avianus, a shadowy figure who seems to have lived in the fourth or fifth century CE. Because they are in verse form, the fables of Phaedrus and Avianus are harder to read than fables written in prose, but after you have become familiar with the Latin prose fables in this book, you will probably want to try reading some Latin verse fables, too.

Unlike other genres of ancient Latin literature, Aesop's fables are attested in an unbroken stream throughout the Middle Ages; while other great works of Roman literature vanished from sight for centuries, Aesop's fables kept on going strong. Then, with the advent of printing in the fifteenth century, Aesop's fables started to circulate widely not just in Latin, but also in the vernacular languages. The first printed edition of Aesop's fables in English was published by William Caxton in 1484. Many other editions of Aesop's fables were published in England during the sixteenth and seventeenth centuries, including the 1687 edition of Aesop's fables on which this book is based. Meanwhile, Renaissance scholars throughout Europe, such as Abstemius, Hieronymus Osius and Caspar Barth, to name just a few, continued to invent new fables in Latin, based on the ancient tradition.

You might be surprised to learn that throughout the classical, medieval and Renaissance periods, Aesop's fables were not considered to be children's literature at all. Rather, the fables were humorous stories told by adults, for adults—sometimes with some rather adult themes. In more recent times, however, Aesop's fables have come to be regarded as children's literature. Today, most of the books of Aesop's fables that you will find in a bookstore are written specifically for children, without the sharp social criticism that is so characteristic of the ancient fables.

There are many editions of Aesop's fables that you can find online, including the English versions by Sir Roger L'Estrange, George Fyler Townsend and Joseph Jacobs. You can also find some beautifully illustrated editions online. I've collected the online editions of Aesop in both English and Latin at the *Aesopica.net* website, where you will find literally thousands of fables at your fingertips. If you are interested in learning more about the fables, I've also provided a list of useful books below, emphasizing materials in English translation as well as illustrated editions of the fables.

## *Select Bibliography*

Duff, J. W., and A. M. Duff. *Minor Latin Poets: II* (Loeb Library). Cambridge: Harvard University Press, 1982. [The verse fables of Avianus, with facing-text English translations.]

Gibbs, Laura. *Aesop's Fables: A New Translation*. Oxford: Oxford University Press, 2002. [English translations of fables from the ancient Greek and Latin sources, organized thematically.]

Hansen, William F. *Anthology of Ancient Greek Popular Literature*. Bloomington: Indiana University Press, 1998. [The best source for an English translation of the ancient *Life of Aesop*.]

Jacobs, John C. *The Fables of Odo of Cheriton*. Syracuse: Syracuse University Press, 1985. [English translation of the Latin fables of Odo of Cheriton, a medieval English preacher.]

Lenaghan, Robert. *William Caxton's Translation of The Subtyl Historyes and Fables of Esope*. Cambridge: Harvard University Press: Cambridge, 1967. [Includes both Caxton's text and the woodcut illustrations.]

L'Estrange, Roger. *Aesop—Fables* (Everyman's Library Children's Classics). New York: Knopf, 1992. [A seventeenth-century English translation with modern illustrations.]

McTigue, Bernard. *The Medici Aesop*. New York: Abrams, 1989. [Beautiful facsimile edition of a fifteenth-century illuminated manuscript of the fables in Greek.]

Perry, Benjamin E. *Babrius and Phaedrus* (Loeb Library). Cambridge: Harvard University Press, 1965. [The fables of Babrius and Phaedrus with facing-text English translations, along with an invaluable appendix that lists all the ancient Greek and Latin fables.]

## About the Author

I began studying Latin as an undergraduate student at UC Berkeley, where I received my BA in 1986 with a double-major in both Classical Languages (Latin and Greek) and Slavic Languages (Polish and Russian). I continued my studies at Oxford University, where I completed an MPhil in European Literature in 1988, writing a thesis on the Latin elegies of the Polish poet Jan Kochanowski. After several years of travel, research, and odd jobs, I returned to UC Berkeley, where I completed a PhD in Comparative Literature in 1999, with a dissertation on Aesop's fables. Since 1999, I have been an instructor at the University of Oklahoma, where I teach online courses in mythology and folklore, ancient Indian epics, and world literature. You can find the materials for my online courses at the *MythFolklore.net* website.

In addition to the Aesop book you now hold in your hands, I have published a complete English translation of Aesop's fables with Oxford University Press in the Oxford World's Classics series: *Aesop's Fables: A New Translation* (2002). I've also published two books specifically for Latin students and teachers: *Latin Via Proverbs: 4000 Proverbs, Mottoes and Sayings* (2006) and *Vulgate Verses: 4000 Sayings from the Bible* (2007). Most recently, I have published *Mille Fabulae et Una: 1001 Aesop's Fables in Latin* (2010) and *Brevissima: 1001 Tiny Latin Poems* (2012). You can find out more about my teaching and web publications at *MythFolklore.net*. You can find my Latin teaching materials online at the *Fables.MythFolklore.net* website, and also at the "Bestiaria Latina" website, *BestLatin.net*.

# List of Most Frequently Used Words

These frequently used words are included in the *Glossary* in the back of the book, but you will not find them in the individual fable-by-fable word lists. This list is based on the actual frequency in the fables themselves (as indicated by an asterisk), supplemented by the list of the 300 most frequently used words in Latin from Paul Bernard Diederich's booklet, *The Frequency of Latin Words and Their Endings* (1939).

## *Nouns*

**accipiter (accipitris,** *m.***):** hawk*
**aetas (aetatis,** *f.***):** age, stage of life
**amicus (amici,** *m.***):** friend*
**animal (animalis,** *n.***):** animal, living being
**animus (animi,** *m.***):** mind, spirit
**aqua (aquae,** *f.***):** water
**aquila (aquilae,** *f.***):** eagle*
**arbor (arboris,** *f.***):** tree*
**ars (artis,** *f.***):** art, skill
**asinus (asini,** *m.***):** donkey*
**avis (avis,** *f.***):** bird*

**bellum (belli,** *n.***):** war, combat
**bos (bovis,** *m.***):** ox, bull*

**caelum (caeli,** *n.***):** sky, heaven
**canis (canis,** *m/f.***):** dog*
**caput (capitis,** *n.***):** head, person, life
**cattus (catti,** *m.***):** cat*
**causa (causae,** *f.***):** reason, cause
**cervus (cervi,** *m.***):** deer, stag*
**columba (columbae,** *f.***):** dove, pigeon*
**consilium (consilii,** *n.***):** advice, suggestion
**corpus (corporis,** *n.***):** body

**deus (dei,** *m.***):** god
**dies (diei,** *m.***):** day
**dominus (domini,** *m.***):** master, owner
**domus (domus,** *f.***):** home, house*
**dux (ducis,** *m.***):** leader, commander

**equus (equi,** *m.***):** horse*
**fides (fidei,** *f.***):** faith, trust, security
**filius (filii,** *m.***):** son
**finis (finis,** *m.***):** end, limit

**formica (formicae,** *f.***):** ant*
**fortuna (fortunae,** *f.***):** luck, fortune

**gallus (galli,** *m.***):** rooster*
**gens (gentis,** *f.***):** tribe, nation
**genus (generis,** *n.***):** kind, type
**gratia (gratiae,** *f.***):** favor, thanks
**grus (gruis,** *f.***):** crane*

**herus (heri,** *m.***):** master, owner*
**homo (hominis,** *m.***):** person, man
**hostis (hostis,** *m/f.***):** enemy, stranger

**ignis (ignis,** *m.***):** fire
**iter (itineris,** *n.***):** journey, path
**iuvenis (iuvenis,** *m.***):** young man, youth

**labor (laboris,** *m.***):** effort, work
**laus (laudis,** *f.***):** praise, glory
**leo (leonis,** *m.***):** lion*
**locus (loci,** *m.***):** place*
**lupus (lupi,** *m.***):** wolf*

**manus (manus,** *f.***):** hand
**mater (matris,** *f.***):** mother*
**mens (mentis,** *f.***):** mind, brain
**milvus (milvi,** *m.***):** kite [a bird]*
**modus (modi,** *m.***):** means, measure
**mons (montis,** *m.***):** mountain
**mors (mortis,** *f.***):** death
**mos (moris,** *m.***):** habit; (*pl.*) character
**mus (muris,** *m/f.***):** mouse*

**natura (naturae,** *f.***):** nature, birth
**natus (nati,** *m.***):** son, child
**nox (noctis,** *f.***):** night

**oculus (oculi,** *m.***):** eye

**opus (operis,** *n.***):** work, deed
**os (oris,** *n.***):** mouth
**ovis (ovis,** *f.***):** sheep*

**parens (parentis,** *m/f.***):** parent
**pars (partis,** *f.***):** part, portion
**pater (patris,** *m.***):** father
**pectus (pectoris,** *n.***):** chest, heart
**periculum (periculi,** *n.***):** danger, hazard, trial*
**pes (pedis,** *m.***):** foot*
**praeda (praedae,** *f.***):** prey, plunder*
**puella (puellae,** *f.***):** girl
**puer (pueri,** *m.***):** boy

**rana (ranae,** *f.***):** frog*
**res (rei,** *f.***):** thing, business*
**rex (regis,** *m.***):** king*
**rusticus (rustici,** *m.***):** peasant, country-man*

**silva (silvae,** *f.***):** woods, forest*
**sol (solis,** *m.***):** sun
**spes (spei,** *f.***):** hope*
**studium (studii,** *n.***):** eager pursuit, dedication

**tempus (temporis,** *n.***):** time
**testudo (testudinis,** *f.***):** tortoise, turtle*

**urbs (urbis,** *f.***):** city
**ursus (ursi,** *m.***):** bear*

**verbum (verbi,** *n.***):** word*
**via (viae,** *f.***):** way, road
**viator (viatoris,** *m.***):** wayfarer, traveler*
**vir (viri,** *m.***):** man, husband
**virtus (virtutis,** *f.***):** worth, excellence
**vis (***abl.* **vi,** *acc.* **vim,** *pl.* **vires,** *f.***):** force, strength*
**vita (vitae,** *f.***):** life
**vox (vocis,** *f.***):** voice
**vulpes (vulpis,** *f.***):** fox*

## Adjectives - Pronouns

**aliquis, aliquid (alicuius):** somebody, some
**alius, alia, aliud (alius):** other, another
**alter, altera, alterum (alterius):** other, another
**altus, alta, altum:** high, tall

**bonus, bona, bonum:** good

**certus, certa, certum:** fixed, sure
**ceterus, cetera, ceterum:** rest, other

**dignus, digna, dignum:** worthy, deserving
**dulcis, dulce (dulcis):** sweet
**duo, duae, duo:** two

**ego** (personal pronoun): I*

**fortis, forte (fortis):** strong

**gravis, grave (gravis):** weighty, serious

**hic, haec, hoc (huius):** this; he/she/it*

**idem, eadem, idem (eiusdem):** the same
**ille, illa, illud (illius):** that; he/she/it*
**ipse, ipsa, ipsum (ipsius):** the very one; he/she/it*
**is, ea, id (eius):** he/she/it; this, the*
**iste, ista, istud (istius):** that, that there of yours

**magnus, magna, magnum:** great, large
**maior, maius (maioris):** greater
**malus, mala, malum:** bad, unlucky
**medius, media, medium:** middle, medium
**melior, melius (melioris):** better
**meus, mea, meum:** my, mine*
**miser, misera, miserum:** wretched, unfortunate*
**multus, multa, multum:** much, many, great*

**noster, nostra, nostrum:** our, ours

**novus, nova, novum:** new

**nullus, nulla, nullum (nullius):** none, not any*

**omnis, omne (omnis):** all, every*

**plenus, plena, plenum:** full

**prior, prius (prioris):** preceding, previous

**quantus, quanta, quantum:** how much, how great

**qui, quae, quod (cuius):** which, that*

**quidam, quaedam, quiddam (cuiusdam):** a certain*

**quis, quid (cuius):** who, what*

**quisque, quidque (cuiusque):** everybody, each person

**sacer, sacra, sacrum:** sacred, holy

**se** (*personal pronoun*): himself, herself, itself*

**senex (senis):** aged, old

**suus, sua, suum:** his/hers/its (*reflexive*)*

**tantus, tanta, tantum:** of such size, so great*

**totus, tota, totum (totius):** all, whole*

**tres, tria (trium):** three

**tu** (*personal pronoun*): you (*singular*)*

**tuus, tua, tuum:** yours (*singular*)*

**unus, una, unum (unius):** one, sole*

**uterque, utraque, utrumque (utriusque):** each of two

**vester, vestra, vestrum:** your, yours (*pl.*)

## Verbs

**accedo (accedere), accessi, accessus:** come near, approach*

**adsum (adesse), affui:** be present, attend

**ago (agere), egi, actus:** do, carry out the role

**aio:** say; **aiunt:** they say

**amo (amare), amavi, amatus:** love

**audio (audire), audivi, auditus:** hear*

**capio (capere), cepi, captus:** get, seize*

**coepi (coepisse):** begin, start

**credo (credere), credidi, creditus:** believe, think

**debeo (debere), debui, debitus:** owe, ought

**dico (dicere), dixi, dictus:** say*

**do (dare), dedi, datum:** give*

**doceo (docere), docui, doctus:** teach

**duco (ducere), duxi, ductus:** lead, bring

**eo (ire), ii, itus:** go*

**facio (facere), feci, factus:** make, do*

**fero (ferre), tuli, latus:** carry, bear*

**fio (fieri), factus sum:** become, happen

**fugio (fugere), fugi, fugitus:** run away, flee

**gero (gerere), gessi, gestus:** carry on, manage

**habeo (habere), habui, habitus:** have*

**inquam:** I say; **inquit:** he says; **inquiunt:** they say*

**invenio (invenire), inveni, inventus:** find, discover

**iubeo (iubere), iussi, iussus:** command, order

**lego (legere), legi, lectus:** gather, collect

**mitto (mittere), misi, missus:** send

**morior (mori), mortuus sum:** die*

**nosco (noscere), novi, notus:** get to know, be familiar with

**oro (orare), oravi, oratus:** ask, pray*

**peto (petere), petivi, petitus:** ask, request

**pono (ponere), posui, positus:** place, put

**possum (posse), potui:** be able, can*

**puto (putare), putavi, putatus:** think, reckon

**quaero (quaerere), quaesivi, quaesitus:** search out, seek

**reddo (reddere), reddidi, redditus:** return, give back

**redeo (redire), redii, reditus:** return, go back*

**refero (referre), retuli / rettuli, relatus:** return, carry back

**relinquo (relinquere), reliqui, relictus:** leave, abandon

**respondeo (respondere), respondi, responsus:** reply*

**rogo (rogare), rogavi, rogatus:** ask*

**scio (scire), scivi, scitus:** know

**sequor (sequi), secutus sum:** follow, pursue

**soleo (solere), solitus sum:** be in the habit of

**sto (stare), steti, status:** stand, stay

**sum (esse), fui:** be*

**timeo (timere), timui:** fear, be afraid

**valeo (valere), valui:** be well, be strong

**venio (venire), veni, ventus:** come*

**video (videre), vidi, visus:** see*

**vinco (vincere), vici, victus:** conquer, win

**vivo (vivere), vixi:** live

**voco (vocare), vocavi, vocatus:** call

**volo (velle), volui:** want, will

## *Other*

**ab:** from; by (*agent*)*

**ad:** to, towards*

**ante:** before, in front of

**at:** but, but yet

**atque (ac):** and, and moreover

**aut:** or

**autem:** but, moreover*

**cum:** when, since, because; with*

**de:** down from, about*

**deinde:** afterwards, then

**dum:** while*

**enim:** for, that is to say*

**ergo:** therefore, then

**et:** and; even also*

**etiam:** even, also

**ex:** out, from*

**iam:** already, now*

**ibi:** there

**igitur:** therefore*

**in:** in, into*

**inde:** from there, thence

**inter:** between, among, during*

**ita:** thus, therefore

**longe:** far, at length, greatly*

**mox:** soon, then*

**nam:** for, for instance

**ne:** in order not to, so that not*

**nec (neque):** nor, neither, and not*

**nihil:** nothing*

**nisi:** unless, except

**non:** not*

**nunc:** now

**nunquam:** never, not ever

**o:** o, oh

**per:** through, by, by way of*

**plus:** more

**post:** after, behind

**pro:** in exchange for

**quam:** how, how much, as; than*

**quasi:** as if

**~que:** and*

**quia:** because

**quidem:** indeed*

**saepe:** often
**satis:** enough, satisfactory
**sed:** but*
**semper:** always
**si:** if*
**sic:** thus, in this way
**simul:** at the same time
**sine:** without
**sub:** under, beneath
**super:** above, over and above

**tam:** so, so much, to such an extent*
**tamen:** however, but
**tandem:** finally*
**tum:** then, next
**tunc:** then, at that time

**ubi:** where, when
**unde:** from where, whereupon
**ut:** as; so, in order to*

**vel:** or
**vero:** in fact, indeed

# Aesop's Fables

# Fables

## in Latin

# Fable 1.
# DE LEAENA ET VULPE
## (Barlow 32)

## Introduction
### *The Lioness and The Fox*

There are various versions of this Aesop's fable in which the animals debate about the quantity and the quality of their litters. Sometimes it is a pig who debates with the lioness, which makes sense because the sow is notorious for having many piglets in each of her litters. In this version of the fable, however, it is a fox who insults the lioness for the size of her litter. The fox is Aesop's favorite trickster, a character who is often a bit too sly for her own good. In this story, who do you think wins the debate: the fox or the lion?

For another story about the fox and her cubs, see the fable of the fox and the eagle (Fable 31), and for another story about an animal mother, see the fable of the sow in labor (Fable 26). For another encounter between a fox and a lion, see the fable of the lion in the cave (Fable 46).

## Grammar Overview
### *Direct and Indirect Speech*

You will see two different kinds of speech in this fable: direct and indirect. The words of the lioness are quoted directly, inside quotation marks. The words of the fox, however, are not quoted in quotation marks, but are reported indirectly. If the words of the fox were quoted directly, they would be, *"O Leaena, quolibet partu, unum dumtaxat catulum parturis!"* ("O Lioness, with each litter, you give birth to one cub only!"). As you read through the fables, pay attention to whether a given fable contains direct quoted speech, or whether it relies on indirect speech, or a mixture of both, as in this fable. How do you think storytellers decide between using direct and indirect speech when they craft a story? Why do you think it is the lioness who has the special distinction of being quoted directly in this fable, when the fox's words are reported only indirectly? (For more information about indirect speech in Latin, see the notes to Fable 7.)

## Vocabulary

### Nouns

**catulus (catuli,** *m.***):** puppy, whelp
**leaena (leaenae,** *f.***):** lioness
**partus (partus,** *m.***):** birth, labor

### Adjectives

**quilibet, quaelibet, quodlibet (cuiuslibet):** whatever, every

### Verbs

**exprobro (exprobrare):** reproach, criticize
**parturio (parturire):** give birth, be in labor

### Other

**dumtaxat:** only, precisely
**pol:** by Pollux, really!
**quod:** because, that
**sane:** truly, surely

*Noli irritare leones.*

# DE LEAENA ET VULPE

## Dramatis Personae

*Leaena*, the lioness, and *Vulpes*, the fox.

Leaena, cum a Vulpe saepe exprobraretur quod, quolibet partu, unum dumtaxat catulum parturiret, respondit, "Unum sane, at pol Leonem!"

## Grammar Notes

**cum a vulpe exprobraretur.** The subjunctive, introduced by **cum**, gives causal background information; this is why the lioness made her reply to the fox.

**quod parturiret.** The subjunctive, introduced by **quod** ("because"), gives causal background information; according to the fox, this is why the lioness should be criticized.

**quolibet partu.** The word **quolibet** is from **quilibet**, a compound of two words, **qui + libet,** of which only the first word declines (see Fable 3 and Fable 44 for similar compounds). The sense is "with each birth" or "every time she goes into labor."

**unum sane.** The accusative case implies a verb, which can be supplied from the verb **parturiret** in the preceding statement: **unum sane (parturio)**.

*Multum, non multa.*

Canis, confestim sese erigens, tota voce elatravit.

# Fable 2.
# DE CANE ET BOVE
## (Barlow 29)

## Introduction
### The Dog and The Ox

This is the story of the proverbial "dog in the manger," a mean-spirited animal who will not let the other animals enjoy the food that is properly theirs. Sir Roger L'Estrange, in his seventeenth-century version of the fable, explains the moral as follows: "Envy pretends to no other happiness than what it derives from the misery of other people." Joseph Jacobs puts it more simply: "People often grudge others what they cannot enjoy themselves." In the illustration to this fable, you can see a rooster along with a hen and her chicks who also happen to be in the stable at the time: what words do you think the hen might use to express the moral of the story, based on the events she has witnessed?

For another story about a vicious dog, see the fable of the dog and the bell (Fable 28); for a greedy dog, see the fable of the dog at the stream (Fable 55). For a completely different kind of adventure that takes place in the ox's stable, see the fable of the stag hiding in the straw (Fable 34).

## Grammar Overview
### The Postpositive Particle, Enim

Latin prose relies heavily on "postpositive particles." These are words that must be placed after the first word of the sentence, clause, or phrase in which they appear ("post-positive" = placed after). These little words tell you how the new statement is connected to the preceding statement. Unlike a conjunction such as *et*, however, these particles are not grammatical connectors, and they can be deleted from a sentence with no harm done to the grammar. Instead, what these particles do is show you how the meaning flows from one sentence to the next. For example, the postpositive particle you will see in this fable is *enim*, which tells you that the next sentence is going to provide an explanation of the preceding sentence. If you want, you can think about the postpositive *enim* as a kind of colon mark in verbal form. When you see the particle *enim*, you know that an explanation is forthcoming—which is the same thing you expect when you see a colon mark in English. The Romans did not use the punctuation marks that we use today, but in a sense they did not need them; in the absence of punctuation marks, the Romans could rely on *enim* and the other postpositive particles to indicate where sentences started and stopped, and how they fit together. (To learn more about postpositive particles in Latin, see the notes to Fable 16.)

## Vocabulary

### Nouns

**faenum (faeni,** *n.***):** hay
**invidia (invidiae,** *f.***):** envy, grudge
**praesepe (praesepis,** *n.***):** manger, stall

### Verbs

**comedo (comedere):** eat, consume
**decumbo (decumbere):** lie, lie down
**elatro (elatrare), elatravi, elatratus:** bark, bark out
**erigo (erigere):** raise, erect
**perdo (perdere):** lose, destroy
**sino (sinere):** allow, permit
**vescor (vesci):** eat, feed on

### Other

**confestim:** immediately, at once

*Invidus a propria roditur invidia.*

# DE CANE ET BOVE

## Dramatis Personae

*Canis*, the dog, and *Bos*, the ox.

In praesepi faeni pleno decumbebat Canis. Venit Bos ut comedat faenum, cum Canis, confestim sese erigens, tota voce elatravit. Cui Bos: "Dii te, cum ista tua invidia, perdant (inquit): nec enim faeno ipse vesceris, nec me vesci sines."

## Grammar Notes

**faeni pleno.** The adjective **pleno** here takes a genitive complement ("full of").

**cum canis elatravit.** Note the use of **cum** plus an indicative verb (see Fable 22).

**cui bos inquit.** The referent of the relative pronoun **cui** is **canis** in the previous sentence (see Fable 4): **cui (cani) bos inquit.**

**dii perdant.** The subjunctive is used independently here, expressing a wish or command; it expresses the result that the ox would like to see happen.

**nec enim.** Note the postpositive particle **enim** in second position (see the *Grammar Overview* for this fable).

**nec faeno ipse vesceris.** The verb **vesceris** takes an ablative complement ("feed on"), and **ipse** modifies the implied subject of the verb: **nec faeno (tu) ipse vesceris.**

**nec . . . nec.** This double use of **nec** is equivalent to the English "neither . . . nor" (see Fable 65). You can replace **nec** with **et non** as follows: **et faeno ipse non vesceris, et me vesci non sines** (see Fable 18).

*Invidia dolor animi est ex alienis commodis.*

*Parva leves capiunt animos.*

*Parturient montes, nascetur ridiculus mus.*

# Fable 3.
# DE PARTU MONTIUM
## (Barlow 73)

## Introduction
### *The Mountains in Labor*

You've probably heard the English expression "making a mountain out of a molehill." For the Romans, this fable about "mountains giving birth to a mouse" expressed a similar idea. In *The Art of Poetry*, Horace remarks: *Parturient montes, nascetur ridiculus mus,* "The mountains are going to give birth, and a ridiculous mouse will be born." In other words, there will be all kinds of ominous rumblings, but nothing much will happen in the end. The Roman poet Phaedrus applied this moral to his version of the fable: "This is a fable written for people who make serious-sounding threats but who actually accomplish nothing." In his English version of the fable, Sir Roger L'Estrange comments simply, "Much ado about nothing." The folklorist Joseph Jacobs provides this moral: "Much outcry, little outcome." If one of the human on-lookers in this Latin version of the fable were to give a moral to the story, what do you think he would say?

For another story about being misled by gossip and rumor, see the fable of the wolf and the nanny (Fable 70). For more stories about a tiny mouse, see the fable of the lion and the mouse (Fable 67), or the fable of the mouse's marriage (Fable 37).

## Grammar Overview
### *The Compound Word, Quid + Piam*

Watch out for the little word *quidpiam* in this story, because it is actually a compound word, with *quid-* as the first part of the compound. This first part, *quid*, declines just as you would expect: *quid, cuius* (genitive), *cui* (dative), and so on, but the second part, *piam,* does not decline, resulting in the forms *quidpiam, cuiuspiam* (genitive), *cuipiam* (dative), and so on. This may seem a bit strange, but in English we also have compound words where the first part of the word changes but the second part does not. For example, you might have one sister-in-law, but if you have several, they are your sisters-in-law (not your sister-in-laws). Can you think of some other compound Latin words in which the first part of the compound declines, but the second part does not change? (Hint: Who was the head of the Roman household?)

## Vocabulary

### Nouns

**monstrum (monstri,** *n.***):** portent, unnatural thing
**partus (partus,** *m.***):** birth, labor
**pavor (pavoris,** *m.***):** terror, panic
**rumor (rumoris,** *m.***):** rumor, gossip

### Adjectives - Pronouns

**quispiam, quidpiam (cuiuspiam):** something, anything
**ridiculus, ridicula, ridiculum:** silly, laughable

### Verbs

**accurro (accurrere):** run to, run up
**circumsto (circumstare):** surround, stand around
**exeo (exire):** go out, come out
**expecto (expectare):** await, anticipate
**parturio (parturire):** give birth, be in labor

### Other

**undique:** on all sides, from all sides

*Ad omnia trepidat, licet
vel mus movet.*

# DE PARTU MONTIUM

## Dramatis Personae

*Montes*, the mountains, *Homines*, the people, and *Mus*, the mouse.

> Rumor erat parturire Montes. Homines undique accurrunt et circumstant, monstri quidpiam non sine pavore expectantes. Montes tandem parturiunt; exit ridiculus Mus.

*[handwritten annotations: the people all ran / stood a certain / at last gave birth and out came the the mysterious mouse / expecting]*

## Grammar Notes

**rumor erat parturire montes.** Accusative plus infinitive construction in indirect statement (see Fable 7), introduced by **rumor erat**, "there was a rumor (that) . . ."

**monstri quidpiam.** The word **monstri** is a partitive genitive (see Fable 30): **quidpiam** (something) **monstri** (of an unnatural thing) = "something unnatural." The word **quidpiam** is a compound, **quid** + **piam**, of which only the first part declines (see the *Grammar Overview* for this fable).

> *Mons parturibat, deinde murem prodidit.*

*Ex parvo satis.*

*Crescentem sequitur cura pecuniam.*

# Fable 4.
# DE MURE URBANO ET MURE RUSTICO
## (Barlow 17)

## Introduction
### The City Mouse and The Country Mouse

The story of the city mouse and the country mouse is a famous Aesop's fable, one that is still well known today. Horace tells an elaborate version of the story in one of his *Satires*, using the contrast between the two mice to explain his own preference for the simple life. In an English version of the fable, V. S. Vernon Jones has the country mouse explain to the city mouse: "You live in the lap of luxury, but you are surrounded by dangers; whereas at home I can enjoy my simple dinner of roots and corn in peace." Joseph Jacobs has the country mouse say simply: "Better beans and bacon in peace than cakes and ale in fear." In the Latin version you are about to read, the country mouse expresses his opinion with the rhyming words *mel* and *fel*, "honey" and "bile." The use of rhyme is a good way to come up with a catchy, memorable moral. Can you think of a rhyming moral for this fable, either in English or in Latin?

For another story about the perils of luxurious living, see the fable of the wolf and the dog (Fable 80), or the horse and the donkey (Fable 21). For a story about the daily dangers faced by mice, see the fable of the old mouse and the cat (Fable 69).

## Grammar Overview
### Relative Pronouns and the Previous Sentence

In English, you rarely find a relative pronoun as the first word in a sentence, but in Latin this is a common occurrence, often with the referent of the pronoun in the previous sentence. This creates a wonderful flow from one sentence to the next in Latin, but it can be very awkward to translate into English. So, for example, in the following fable, there is a sentence that begins: *Qui dixit Urbano Muri* . . . Translated literally (and awkwardly) into English, this means: "Which said to the City Mouse . . ." To make this easier to render in English, you can replace the relative pronoun with the referent noun, making sure to put the referent noun into the case of the pronoun. So, if you look for the referent of this relative pronoun, you will discover that it is the Country Mouse, *Rusticum Murem*, in the previous sentence. Next, put *Rusticum Murem* into the case of the relative pronoun *qui* (nominative), and you get the following result: *Rusticus Mus dixit Urbano Muri*, "The Country Mouse said to the City Mouse . . ." That sounds much better! You can use this substitution technique wherever you find a confusing relative pronoun in Latin—and it is usually the relative pronouns that come first in a sentence that are the most confusing of all. (For more information about relative pronouns in Latin, see the notes to Fable 10.)

— 15 —

# Vocabulary
## *Nouns*

**anxietas (anxietatis,** *f.***):** worry, anxiety
**cena (cenae,** *f.***):** dinner, meal
**clamor (clamoris,** *m.***):** shouting, outcry
**copia (copiae,** *f.***):** abundance, plenty
**daps (dapis,** *f.***):** feast, meal
**fel (fellis,** *n.***):** gall, bile
**hospes (hospitis,** *m.***):** host, guest, visitor
**inopia (inopiae,** *f.***):** lack, poverty
**lautitia (lautitiae,** *f.***):** luxurious lifestyle, elegance
**mel (mellis,** *n.***):** honey
**penum (peni,** *n.***):** provisions, food
**rus (ruris,** *n.***):** countryside, farm

## *Adjectives*

**dives (divitis):** rich, wealthy
**insolitus, insolita, insolitum:** unusual, unaccustomed
**quotidianus, quotidiana, quotidianum:** daily, each day's
**securus, secura, securum:** safe, untroubled
**urbanus, urbana, urbanum:** urban, city

## *Verbs*

**attono (attonare), attonui, attonitus:** daze, strike with lightning
**damno (damnare):** find guilty, condemn
**deambulo (deambulare):** go for a walk, walk around
**depromo (depromere):** fetch, bring out
**epulor (epulari):** feast, dine lavishly
**expleo (explere):** satisfy, fulfill
**intellego (intellegere), intellexi, intellectus:** understand, realize
**invito (invitare):** invite
**laudo (laudare):** praise
**malo (malle):** prefer, want more

# DE MURE URBANO ET MURE RUSTICO

## Dramatis Personae

*Mus Rusticus*, the country mouse, and *Mus Urbanus*, the city mouse.

Mus Rusticus, videns Urbanum Murem rus deambulantem,
invitat ad cenam depromitque omne penum, ut tanti hospitis
expleat lautitiam. Urbanus Mus ruris damnat inopiam urbisque
copiam laudat, secumque in urbem ducit Rusticum. Qui, inter
epulandum attonitus insolitis clamoribus, cum intellexerat
periculum quotidianum esse, dixit Urbano Muri, "Tuae dapes
plus fellis quam mellis habent. Malo securus esse cum mea
inopia quam dives esse cum tua anxietate."

## Grammar Notes

**secumque.** This is a compound word, in inverted order: **secumque** = **et cum se**.

**qui . . . dixit urbano muri.** The referent of the relative pronoun **qui** is **rusticum (murem)** in the previous sentence (see the *Grammar Overview* for this fable): **qui (rusticus mus) dixit urbano muri.**

**inter epulandum.** The gerund with the preposition **inter** means "while" (see Fable 47).

**cum intellexerat.** Note the use of **cum** plus an indicative verb (see Fable 22).

**periculum quotidianum esse.** Accusative plus infinitive construction in indirect statement (see Fable 7); **periculum** is the accusative subject of the infinitive, and **quotidianum** is a predicate adjective.

**plus fellis.** Partitive genitive (see Fable 30): **plus** (more) **fellis** (of bile) = "more bile."

**plus fellis quam mellis.** The word **quam** coordinates a comparison introduced by **plus**, with **mellis** parallel to **fellis**.

**malo securus esse quam dives esse.** The word **quam** coordinates a comparison introduced by **malo** (= **magis** + **volo**), with the infinitive phrases as the objects being compared.

Sitibunda cornix reperit urnam aqua plenam.

# Fable 5.
# DE CORNICE ET URNA
## (Barlow 39)

## Introduction
### *The Crow and The Pot*

The ancient Greeks and Romans were fascinated by animal tricks and anything that the animals did that seemed to suggest that the "dumb beasts" were, after all, intelligent. We share the same fascination, of course, as shown by the endless supply of animal trick videos on YouTube. The fable you are about to read is very much like a YouTube animal video. The crow in this story does not speak, and instead we just watch her ingenious behavior, step by step, as she discovers a way to raise the level of water in a pot so that she can take a drink. Of course, since this is an Aesop's fable, the story also has a moral we can learn from. Joseph Jacobs expressed the moral of the story as "Little by little does the trick." For Townsend, the moral of the story is that "Necessity is the mother of invention." If the little crow spoke a few words at the end of the fable, how do you think she would express the moral of the story?

For other stories about intelligent birds, see the fable of the swallow and the flax seed (Fable 59), the dove who rescued the ant (Fable 43), or the lark who watched the farmer (Fable 49).

## Grammar Overview
### *Passive and Active Verbs in Translation*

Whenever you find a passive participle in Latin, you are faced with a double dilemma. First, what to do about the passive voice? The Latin passive system is extremely rich and flexible, but English passive verbs often convey a sense of vagueness. Next, what to do about the participle? Again, the Latin participle system is well developed, much more so than in English. So, when you see a Latin passive participle, you might try rendering the Latin passive participle as an active finite verb in English in order to make your English sound more like English and less like Latin. Here's an example from the fable you are about to read: *Cornix lectos ex arena lapillulos iniectat*, "The crow tosses in pebbles gathered from the sand." If you change the Latin participle to an active verb in English, you can actually stay closer to the Latin word order, in addition to creating a more lively sentence: "The crow gathers little stones from the sand and tosses them in." The difference is stylistic, based on your goals and preferences as a translator. The key is to understand the Latin grammar fully, so that you can then make well-informed stylistic choices as you translate. (See the notes to Fable 8 for the closely related problem of how to translate Latin ablative absolutes into English.)

## Vocabulary
### Nouns
**arena** (**arenae,** *f.*): sand
**cornix** (**cornicis,** *f.*): crow, she-crow
**lapillulus** (**lapilluli,** *m.*): pebble, tiny stone
**molimen** (**moliminis,** *n.*): effort, vehemence
**urna** (**urnae,** *f.*): pot, urn

### Adjectives
**profundus, profunda, profundum:** deep
**sitibundus, sitibunda, sitibundum:** thirsty
**vanus, vana, vanum:** meaningless, useless

### Verbs
**bibo** (**bibere**): drink
**conor** (**conari**): attempt, endeavor
**effundo** (**effundere**): pour out
**exhaurio** (**exhaurire**): drain, drink up
**iniecto** (**iniectare**): lay on, put in
**levo** (**levare**): lift up, elevate
**reperio** (**reperire**): find, discover

*Ex granis acervus.*

# DE CORNICE ET URNA

## Dramatis Persona

*Cornix*, the crow.

Sitibunda Cornix reperit urnam aqua plenam, sed erat urna profundior quam ut exhauri a Cornice possit. Conatur igitur vano molimine aquam effundere, sed non valet. Lectos igitur ex arena lapillulos iniectat. Hoc modo aqua levatur et Cornix bibit.

*[Handwritten annotations above the Latin text: "thirsty crow find pot water plenty but was pot deep and let drink crow able attempt therefor useless effort water pour out but not valid bed therefore out sand thru stone puts thru this now water elevated and the crow drinks"]*

## Grammar Notes

**aqua plenam.** The adjective **plenam** here takes an ablative complement ("filled with").

**profundior quam ut exhauri a cornice possit.** The word **quam** coordinates a comparison introduced by the comparative adjective **profundior** ("deeper than what could be drunk by the crow").

**conatur igitur.** For the postpositive particle **igitur,** see Fable 32.

**lectos lapillulos iniectat.** You might translate the passive participle with an active verb (see the *Grammar Overview* for this fable): the crow gathered the little stones (**lectos**) and then tosses them in (**iniectat**).

> *Omnium rerum principia parva sunt.*

*Avis a cantu dignoscitur.*

*Est avis in dextra melior quam quattuor extra.*

# Fable 6.
# DE ACCIPITRE ET LUSCINIA
## (Barlow 76)

## Introduction
### The Hawk and The Nightingale

The story of the hawk and the nightingale is one of the oldest Aesop's fables in existence, dating back to the archaic Greek poet Hesiod who lived around the year 700 BCE. It is a typical Aesop's fable about the "big guy" and the "little guy" in a potentially deadly confrontation. The nightingale is a tiny bird, but with a beautiful song. The hawk, on the other hand, is a perfect embodiment of greed and of violence, caring nothing for the nightingale's musical art. Is there a lesson to be learned here? What do you think the moral of this fable could be?

For a story where the hawk manages to get himself into trouble, see the fable of the hawk who chased a dove (Fable 18). For another story about a musician pleading for mercy, see the fable of the trumpeteer who became a prisoner of war (Fable 52). For another little creature held captive, see the fable of the fisherman and the fish (Fable 50).

## Grammar Overview
### Word Wraps

Unlike English word order, which is very strictly regulated by grammar, Latin word order is mostly a matter of style, not grammar. One favorite style of Latin word order is "wrapping," where a compound phrase consisting of two or more words is split into two pieces and wrapped around another word or phrase. In the fable you are about to read, for example, the noun phrase *clamosas querimonias*, "noisy complaints," wraps around the verb of which it is the direct object: *clamosas cies querimonias*, "you are producing noisy complaints," as the hawk says to the nightingale. Grammatically, any word order is possible here, and there are actually six different ways that these three words could be arranged (try it and you'll see!). The particular choice that the author has made yields two nice stylistic effects: the wrapped word order lends a quality of unity to the phrase as a whole, and it puts *clamosas* in the emphatic first position, thus calling attention to just how noisy the nightingale is.

## Vocabulary
### Nouns
**avicula (aviculae,** *f.*): bird, little bird
**luscinia (lusciniae,** *f.*): nightingale
**querimonia (querimoniae,** *f.*): complaint, grievance
**unguis (unguis,** *m.*): claw, talon

### Adjectives
**captivus, captiva, captivum:** imprisoned, caught
**clamosus, clamosa, clamosum:** shouting, noisy

### Verbs
**cieo (ciere):** set in motion, produce
**clamo (clamare):** shout, exclaim
**commoveo (commovere), commovi, commotus:** provoke, disturb
**comprehendo (comprehendere), comprehendi, comprehensus:** grasp, seize
**demitto (demittere):** let go, send away
**libero (liberare):** set free, release

### Other
**frustra:** in vain, unsuccessfully
**licet:** even if, although
**misere:** sadly, wretchedly

*Nutrit et accipiter pullos suos.*

# DE ACCIPITRE ET LUSCINIA

## Dramatis Personae

*Luscinia*, the nightingale, and *Accipiter*, the hawk.

Comprehenderat Lusciniam Accipiter, quae misere clamabat ut
se captivam demitteret. Cui Accipiter: "Frustra clamosas cies
querimonias, nam licet omnes silvarum commoveris aviculas, non
ab unguibus meis liberabunt."

## Grammar Notes

**quae clamabat.** The referent of the relative pronoun **quae** is **luscinia**, the nightingale: **quae (luscinia) clamabat.**

**ut se demitteret.** The reflexive pronoun **se** refers back to the nightingale: **(luscinia) clamabat ut se (lusciniam) demitteret**.

**se captivam.** The adjective **captivam** agrees with the pronoun **se** in gender, number and case; it is feminine because it refers back to the nightingale.

**cui accipiter.** The referent of the relative pronoun **cui** is **lusciniam** in the previous sentence (see Fable 4), with an implied verb of speaking: **cui (lusciniae) accipiter (inquit).**

**clamosas cies querimonias.** The phrase **clamosas querimonias** wraps around the verb (see the *Grammar Overview* for this fable).

**licet omnes silvarum commoveris aviculas.** The phrase **omnes silvarum aviculas** wraps around the verb, with the hypothetical subjunctive introduced by **licet,** meaning "even if, although" (see Fable 38).

*Ne ad pugnam vocet
aquilam luscinia.*

Sine pennis volare haud facile est.

Homo ad laborem natus est et avis ad volatum.

# Fable 7.
# DE PAVONE ET GRUE
## (Barlow 44)

## Introduction
### The Peacock and The Crane

There are several Aesop's fables about the "proud peacock." In one story, the peacock is proud of his feathers, but he is also ashamed that he does not have a good singing voice; the peacock's voice is, in fact, an ugly screech compared to the songs of birds with truly beautiful voices, such as the nightingale. This story focuses on another of the peacock's defects: the peacock's feathers may be beautiful, but they are not very good for flying. In an ancient Greek version of this fable, the wise crane states the moral of the story as follows: "I would prefer to be admired while dressed in my well-worn clothes than to live without honor, no matter how fine my clothes might be." What are the words that you would choose to express the moral of this story?

For another debate about animal beauty, see the fable of the fox and the leopard (Fable 9). For another creature who is foolish and proud, consider the puffed-up frog (Fable 14). For another story about animals dining together, see the fable of the fox and the stork (Fable 19).

## Grammar Overview
### Accusative Plus Infinitive

One of the distinctive features of Latin is the use of the infinitive with an accusative subject to express indirect speech. In the fable you are about to read, you will see an example of this "accusative plus infinitive" construction in Latin, introduced by the verb *fatetur*, "admits." The crane admits that the peacock is more beautiful: *fatetur pavonem formosiorem esse.* The accusative *pavonem* serves as the subject of the infinitive *esse*, and the predicative adjective, *formosiorem*, agrees with the subject in gender, number, and case (accusative). This accusative plus infinitive construction can also be found in English, but it sounds very stilted and old-fashioned: "the crane confesses the peacock to be more beautiful." Even if you decide you want to imitate Latin participles in your English translations (see Fable 5), you probably do not want to try to imitate the Latin accusative plus infinitive construction too often in English! Of course, there can be a kind of formal grandeur to this construction in English, precisely because it is so rarely used. Can you think of a famous line from the Declaration of Independence that features a lofty example of the accusative plus infinitive in English? (Hint: Does the phrase "we hold these truths" ring a bell?)

# Vocabulary
## *Nouns*

**cauda** (**caudae,** *f.*): tail
**foedus** (**foederis,** *n.*): treaty, agreement
**hospes** (**hospitis,** *m.*): host, guest, visitor
**nobilitas** (**nobilitatis,** *f.*): respectability, excellence
**nubis** (**nubis,** *m.*): cloud
**pavo** (**pavonis,** *m.*): peacock
**penna** (**pennae,** *f.*): feather, wing
**tectum** (**tecti,** *n.*): roof, ceiling
**volatus** (**volatus,** *m.*): flight

## *Adjectives*

**animosus, animosa, animosum:** courageous, energetic
**formosus, formosa, formosum:** shapely, lovely

## *Verbs*

**ceno** (**cenare**): dine, eat
**contemno** (**contemnere**): scorn, disparage
**fateor** (**fateri**): admit, confess
**iacto** (**iactare**): boast about, brandish
**ineo** (**inire**): go in, enter into
**ostento** (**ostentare**): show, display
**penetro** (**penetrare**): enter, penetrate
**supervolito** (**supervolitare**): flutter over, fly above

## *Other*

**una:** together
**vix:** scarcely, hardly

# DE PAVONE ET GRUE

## Dramatis Personae

*Pavo*, the peacock, and *Grus*, the crane.

Pavo et Grus foedus inter se ineunt unaque cenant. Inter
cenandum, Pavo nobilitatem suam iactat, formosam ostentat
caudam, Gruemque hospitem contemnit. Grus fatetur Pavonem
formosiorem esse pennis; se tamen, cum vix tectis supervolitat
Pavo, animoso volatu penetrare nubes.

## Grammar Notes

**inter cenandum.** The gerund with the preposition **inter** means "while" (see Fable 47).

**formosam ostentat caudam.** The phrase **formosam caudam** wraps around the verb (see Fable 6).

**gruem hospitem contemnit.** The nouns **gruem** and **hospitem** are in apposition to one another.

**pavonem formosiorem esse.** Accusative plus infinitive construction in indirect statement (see the *Grammar Overview* for this fable), with **pavonem** as the accusative subject, and **formosiorem** as a predicate adjective.

**formosiorem esse pennis.** The ablative **pennis** expresses the way in which the peacock was more beautiful, "with his feathers," "because of his feathers."

**cum vix tectis supervolitat pavo.** Note the use of **cum** plus an indicative verb (see Fable 22); the verb **supervolitat** here takes a dative complement, **tectis.**

**se tamen penetrare nubes.** This accusative plus infinitive construction continues the indirect statement, with **se** as the accusative subject and **nubes** as the object of the infinitive; for the postpositive particle **tamen,** see Fable 66.

Avibus cum bestiis asperrima pugna erat.

# Fable 8.
# DE AVIBUS ET QUADRUPEDIBUS
## (Barlow 30)

## Introduction
### The Birds and The Beasts

The bat is an ambiguous creature. He has wings like a bird, but he also has fur like an animal. In this story, the bat attempts to take advantage of this ambiguity, but his plan does not succeed, and as a result the bat now only comes out at night, never during the day. The bat's nocturnal nature is reflected in the bat's own name in Latin, *vespertilio*, from the word *vesper*, meaning "evening." This type of story, one that explains the origin of an animal trait, is called an "aetiological tale," from the Greek word *aetion*, meaning "cause" or "origin." Of course, in addition to providing an explanation of the bat's nature, the story also has a moral to teach as well. If the bat were to add some words to the end of the story, explaining the lesson that he has learned, what do you think he would say?

For another story about an animal war, check out the battle of the mouse and the frog (Fable 44). For another "double nature," see the fable of the satyr and the man in the snow (Fable 64). For another aetiological story, see the fable of the swallow and the flax seed (Fable 59).

## Grammar Overview
### The Ablative Absolute

One of the most common constructions in Latin is the ablative absolute. English also has an absolute construction, but it is rarely used and almost always sounds somewhat formal and stilted. So, if you are translating a Latin ablative absolute into English, you might want to use a finite verb instead of an absolute construction. Consider, for example, this sentence from the fable you are about to read: *Vespertilio, relictis sociis, ad hostem defecit.* You could render this sentence very literally with a passive absolute in English: "The bat, his allies having been abandoned, went over to the enemy." Adopting a more idiomatic English style, however, you could choose to use two finite verbs instead: "The bat abandoned his allies and went over to the enemy." You could even subordinate one clause to the other: "After the bat abandoned his allies, he went over to the enemy." As always with translation, the choice is yours, so you need to be aware of the choices you are making and be able to explain those choices when asked. (For more information about participles and finite verbs in English translation, see the notes to Fable 72.)

# Vocabulary

## *Nouns*

**auspex (auspicis,** *m.***):** seer, guide
**bestia (bestiae,** *f.***):** beast, animal
**lux (lucis,** *f.***):** light
**metus (metus,** *m.***):** fear, dread
**pugna (pugnae,** *f.***):** fight, battle
**quadrupes (quadrupedis,** *m/f.***):** animal, four-footed beast
**socius (socii,** *m.***):** ally, partner
**transfuga (transfugae,** *m.***):** deserter, renegade
**vespertilio (vespertilionis,** *m.***):** bat

## *Adjectives*

**asper, aspera, asperum:** violent, rough
**ingens (ingentis):** huge, enormous
**postremus, postrema, postremum:** last, endmost

## *Verbs*

**damno (damnare):** find guilty, condemn
**deficio (deficere), defeci, defectus:** falter, defect
**numero (numerare):** number, count
**volo (volare):** fly

## *Other*

**amplius:** more, any more
**cur:** why
**iterum:** again, a second time
**utrimque:** on both sides

# DE AVIBUS ET QUADRUPEDIBUS

## Dramatis Personae

*Aves*, the birds (led by *Aquila*, the eagle), *Bestiae*, the beasts, and *Vespertilio*, the bat.

Avibus cum Bestiis asperrima pugna erat, utrimque spes, utrimque ingens metus, utrimque periculum, cum Vespertilio, relictis sociis, ad hostem defecit. Ad postremum vincunt Aves, duce et auspice Aquila. Transfugam vero Vespertilionem damnant, ut nunquam iterum inter Aves numeretur, nec amplius in luce videatur. Et haec causa est cur Vespertilio nunquam, nisi nocte, volat.

## Grammar Notes

**avibus pugna erat.** The dative expresses what we might consider possession in English ("the birds were having a fight"); see Fable 64 for information about the dative of possession.

**asperrima pugna.** For this use of the superlative, see Fable 39.

**utrimque spes.** As often in Latin, the verb "to be" is omitted: **utrimque (erat) spes,** "there was hope for both sides," i.e., "both sides were hopeful" (see Fable 13 for the omitted copula).

**cum vespertilio defecit.** Note the use of **cum** plus an indicative verb (see Fable 22).

**relictis sociis.** Ablative absolute construction (see the *Grammar Overview* for this fable).

**ad postremum.** This idiomatic phrase means "at last."

**duce et auspice aquila.** The words **duce** and **auspice** are predicate nouns in an ablative absolute construction, with the verb "to be" omitted.

**transfugam vero vespertilionem damnant.** The nouns **transfugam** and **vespertilionem** are a double predicate (see Fable 71): "they condemn the bat (as) a traitor." For the postpositive particle **vero,** see Fable 60.

> *Pardus maculas non deponit.*

> *Non formosus erat, sed erat facundus Ulixes.*

# Fable 9.
# DE VULPE ET PARDO
## (Barlow 58)

## Introduction
### The Fox and The Leopard

You may be familiar with the Biblical saying, "The leopard cannot change its spots," meaning that people cannot change their fundamental nature. In this fable, the leopard does not want to change his spots; instead, he is extremely proud of his beautiful coat. The fox, however, is not impressed, and insists that the beauty of the mind or soul, *animus*, far exceeds the beauty of the physical body, *corpus*. As you look at the way the fox describes the beauty of her own mind, what kind of beauty is she praising? What exactly does it mean, according to the fox, to have a beautiful mind?

For another story in which the fox boasts about her special qualities, see the fable of the fox and the cat (Fable 72). For a story where the fox is on the losing side of a debate, see the fox and the lioness (Fable 1). For a story about an animal who tries to change her appearance, see the fable of Venus and the cat (Fable 75).

## Grammar Overview
### Transitive Deponent Verbs

As you know, the "deponent verbs" in Latin have passive forms only, with no active finite forms. Unlike other passive verbs, however, deponent verbs are active in meaning and there are even some deponent verbs that are transitive, able to take a direct object in the accusative case (unlike passive verbs which, by definition, cannot take an object). You will see an example of a transitive deponent verb in the following fable, where the fox says that she is glad that she obtained a remarkable mind: *animum insignem sortita est*. Even though the deponent verb is passive in form, *sortita est*, it takes a direct object in the accusative case, *animum insignem*. While the number of transitive deponent verbs is not large, some of the most commonly used deponent verbs fall into this category, such as the verb *sequi*, "to follow." Consider, for example, this famous saying from Horace: *Crescentem sequitur cura pecuniam*, "Worry follows wealth as it increases." (For another example of Horace's praise of the simple life, see Fable 4).

## Vocabulary

### *Nouns*

**nota (notae,** *f.***):** mark, sign
**pardus (pardi,** *m.***):** panther, leopard
**pellis (pellis,** *f.***):** skin, hide
**pulchritudo (pulchritudinis,** *f.***):** beauty

### *Adjectives*

**formosus, formosa, formosum:** shapely, lovely
**insignis, insigne (insignis):** conspicuous, remarkable
**speciosus, speciosa, speciosum:** attractive, appealing
**varius, varia, varium:** different, diverse
**versicolor (versicoloris):** changing color, varicolored

### *Verbs*

**concerto (concertare):** fight over, argue
**extollo (extollere):** raise up, praise
**praepono (praeponere):** put in front, prefer
**sortior (sortiri), sortitus sum:** win by lot, obtain

*Forma bonum fragile est.*

# DE VULPE ET PARDO

## Dramatis Personae

*Vulpes*, the fox, and *Pardus*, the leopard.

Vulpes et Pardus de pulchritudine concertabant et, Pardo suam pellem versicolorem extollente, Vulpes, cum suam praeponere non possit, dicebat Pardo, "At quanto ego sum speciosior, et quam longe formosior, quae non corpus, sed animum versicolorem et variis notis insignem sortita sum?"

## Grammar Notes

**pardo pellem extollente.** Ablative absolute construction (see Fable 8).

**cum non possit.** The subjunctive, introduced by **cum**, gives causal background information; this is why the fox replied as she did to the leopard.

**quanto ego sum speciosior.** The ablative **quanto** is used to express the degree of difference in a comparison, "(by) how much more attractive." For the emphatic use of the personal pronoun, see Fable 40.

**quam longe formosior.** The adverbial phrase **quam longe** modifies the comparative adjective: "how far more beautiful."

**non corpus sed animum sortita sum.** The deponent verb **sortita sum** is transitive and takes a direct object in the accusative (see the *Grammar Overview* for this fable).

*Quaelibet vulpes caudam suam laudat.*

*Parva securi prosternitur quercus.*

*Qui leviter credit, deceptus saepe redit.*

# Fable 10.
# DE RUSTICO ET SILVA
## (Barlow 98)

## Introduction
### *The Peasant and The Woods*

Sometimes in Aesop's fables, it is not only the animals who act and think like human beings; there are some fables in which the trees, too, are able to interact with humans, as you will see in this story about the peasant who persuades the trees to give him some wood with which to make a handle for his axe. As you can imagine, it is not a very good idea for trees to be helping someone to make an axe! William Caxton's fifteenth-century version of the fable includes this very pointed moral: "Men ought not to gyue the staf by whiche they may be beten with," in other words, "Men ought not to supply the staff with which they may be beaten." As you read the Latin version of the story, try to imagine just what the trees might say when they realize the terrible mistake they have made. What words would they use to express the moral of this story?

For some other stories about misguided generosity, see the fable of the peasant and the frozen snake (Fable 35), or the crane who rescued the wolf (Fable 30). For another story about a tree, see the fable of the reed and the oak tree (Fable 58).

## Grammar Overview
### *Prepositions and Relative Pronouns*

Although Latin word order is remarkably free, especially compared to English (see Fable 6), there is one strict rule of Latin word order: a preposition wants to come before its noun. The term "preposition" itself alerts you that the preposition wants to come first: it is "pre-positioned" before its noun. This rule is so strong that even a relative pronoun, which likes very much to stand first in its clause, follows the preposition. So, when a preposition is involved, the relative clause does not start with the relative pronoun; instead, the preposition is the first word in the relative clause. You will see an example of this word order in the following fable, which refers to *lignum, ex quo ansam fabricaret*, "wood from which (*ex quo*) the man could make a handle." The preposition *ex* is the first word in the relative clause, followed by the relative pronoun *quo*. There's a famous Latin phrase that is still used in English that features a preposition in first place: *sine qua non* (less commonly found in the plural form, *sine quibus non*). Are you familiar with the way this phrase is used in English? If not, look it up in an English dictionary and see what you can discover. (For more information about relative pronouns in Latin, see the notes to Fable 19.)

## Vocabulary
### *Nouns*
**ansa (ansae,** *f.*): handle
**lignum (ligni,** *n.*): wood, timber
**securis (securis,** *f.*): axe, hatchet

### *Verbs*
**adapto (adaptare), adaptavi, adaptatus:** modify, fit to
**concedo (concedere):** give up, grant
**deporto (deportare):** bring to, carry along
**detrunco (detruncare):** cut down, lop off
**fabrico (fabricare):** make, fashion

*Nihil inimicius quam sibi ipse.*

# DE RUSTICO ET SILVA

## Dramatis Personae

*Rusticus*, the peasant, and *Arbores*, the trees.

Accedebat silvam Rusticus et rogabat Arbores ut sibi lignum concederent, ex quo ansam securis fabricaret. Concedebant lignum illi Arbores, quod ad domum deportabat. Quo mox ad securim adaptato, ad silvam redibat et omnes Arbores ad unum detruncabat.

## Grammar Notes

**ex quo.** The relative pronoun **quo** comes after the preposition **ex**, which stands as the first word in the relative clause (see the *Grammar Overview* for this fable).

**ansam fabricaret.** The subjunctive explains the purpose to which the man will put the wood.

**quo adaptato.** Ablative absolute expression; the referent of the relative pronoun **quo** is **lignum** in the previous sentence: **quo (ligno) adaptato.**

**ad unum.** The phrase means "to the (last) one."

*Serum est cavendi tempus in mediis malis.*

Rusticus Herculem implorat, cum statim vox a caelo auditur.

# Fable 11.
# DE RUSTICO ET ARATRO SUO
## (Barlow 53)

## Introduction
### The Peasant and His Plow

You have probably heard the famous saying, "God helps them that help themselves," an English motto that dates to the year 1757, when it first appeared in Benjamin Franklin's *Poor Richard's Almanac*. You could adapt this saying slightly and apply it to the fable you are about to read: "Hercules helps them that help themselves." Throughout the ancient Greek and Roman worlds, Hercules was a divine helper whom you could call on in a moment of need. In the Forum Boarium in Rome, for example, you can find the remains of a temple of Hercules (*Victoris Herculis aedes*, "The Temple of Hercules the Victor"). Yet when the man in this fable calls on the divine Hercules for help, he does not get the answer he expects. Based on the answer the man receives to his prayers, how would you express the moral of the story?

For another story about praying for supernatural help, see the fable of the old man and Death (Fable 33), or the fable of the kite and his mother (Fable 27). For another story about the dangers of being idle, see the fable of the heifer and the ox (Fable 24).

## Grammar Overview
### The Future Imperative

This fable contains a form of the Latin imperative that you might not have encountered before in your studies, the so-called "future" imperative. Don't let the name fool you! The future imperative is not an order you can put off till some time in the future—the future imperative is just as much of a command as the present imperative. The most important difference between the present imperative and the future imperative is that the present imperative can be used only in the second person, while the future imperative can be second person or third person. Take the future imperative *esto,* for example. This is the second person singular future imperative of *esse,* "to be," and it is commonly found in Latin mottoes, such as *Ut ameris, amabilis esto,* "To be loved, be lovable," or *Esto fidelis usque ad finem,* "Be faithful unto the end." But be careful: *esto* is also the third person singular future imperative form, as you can see in the motto of the state of Missouri: *Salus populi suprema lex esto,* "Let the welfare of the people be the highest law." Now, if *esto* is the same form in both second person and third person, how can you be certain that the state motto of Missouri contains a third person future imperative? (Hint: What is the grammatical role of the word *salus* in that sentence?)

## Vocabulary

### *Nouns*

**aratrum (aratri,** *n.***):** plow
**Hercules (Herculis,** *m.***):** Hercules
**lutum (luti,** *n.***):** mud, clay
**rota (rotae,** *f.***):** wheel
**umerus (umeri,** *m.***):** shoulder, upper arm

### *Adjectives*

**ineptus, inepta, ineptum:** foolish, silly
**profundus, profunda, profundum:** deep
**propitius, propitia, propitium:** favorable, well-disposed

### *Verbs*

**annitor (anniti):** lean upon, strive
**flagello (flagellare), flagellavi, flagellatus:** whip, flog
**haereo (haerere):** stick, cling
**imploro (implorare):** call for, call upon
**invoco (invocare):** call upon, beg for
**prosterno (prosternere), prostravi, prostratus:** stretch out, lay low

### *Other*

**statim:** immediately, at once

*Sine labore non erit panis in ore.*

# DE RUSTICO ET ARATRO SUO

## Dramatis Personae

*Rusticus*, the peasant, and *Hercules*, the god.

Rustici aratrum haeret in profundo luto. Mox prostratus, Herculem implorat, cum statim vox a caelo auditur: "Inepte, flagellato equos et ipse totis viribus umerisque annitere rotis! Et deinde Herculem invocato! Tunc enim tibi propitius Hercules aderit."

## Grammar Notes

**cum vox auditur.** Note the use of **cum** plus an indicative verb (see Fable 22).

**flagellato.** Future imperative (see the *Grammar Overview* for this fable), second person singular.

**ipse annitere rotis.** The word **ipse** modifies the implied subject of the imperative: **(tu) ipse annitere;** the verb takes a dative complement, **rotis**.

**invocato.** Future imperative, second person singular.

**tunc enim.** For the postpositive particle **enim,** see Fable 2.

*Ora et labora, deus adest sine mora.*

Dum puero auxilium imploranti non subveniunt, fiunt oves praeda lupo.

# Fable 12.
# DE PASTORIS PUERO ET AGRICOLIS
## (Barlow 59)

## Introduction
### The Shepherd's Boy and The Farmers

The story of the boy who cried "Wolf!" is one of the most famous of Aesop's fables. In his fifteenth-century version of the story, William Caxton supplies this moral: "Men bileue not lyghtly hym whiche is knowen for a lyer," in other words, "Men do not easily believe someone who is known to be a liar." In the English version of the fable by Joseph Jacobs, the moral of the story is that "A liar will not be believed, even when he speaks the truth." Of course, herding sheep is no longer a central part of our lives, as it used to be in days gone by, yet this story continues to be one of the best known of Aesop's fables, even in the modern age. What do you think are some of the reasons why this fable continues to be so popular?

For some other stories about the dangers posed by the wolf, see the fable of the wolf in sheep's clothing (Fable 23), or the sheep who made a treaty with the wolves (Fable 13). For a story where the wolf himself is fooled by some words spoken in jest, see the fable of the nanny and the wolf (Fable 70).

## Grammar Overview
### Semel-Bis-Ter

There are several types of numerical expressions in Latin, including the cardinal numbers for counting (*unus, duo, tres, quattuor,* etc.), the ordinal numbers for ordering (*primus, secundus, tertius, quartus,* etc.), and also a series of words that are referred to as "numerical adverbs," which describe the number of times that something happens: *semel* (once), *bis* (twice), and *ter* (thrice). After "thrice" in English, the series stops, but the Latin series continues ever onwards: *quater* (four times), *quinquies* (five times), *sexies* (six times), and so on. In this fable, you will see the Latin words *ter* and *quater* used to describe the way that the little boy cried "Wolf!" over and over and over again, *lupum terque quaterque adesse clamitans.* So, just for fun, if you had to make up some new English words meaning "four times" and "five times" and "six times" and so on, based on the once-twice-thrice pattern in English, what forms would you propose? (For more information about counting in Latin, see Fable 73.)

## Vocabulary

### Nouns

**agricola (agricolae,** *m.***)**: farmer
**auxilium (auxilii,** *n.***)**: help
**iocus (ioci,** *m.***)**: jest, joke
**pastor (pastoris,** *m.***)**: shepherd
**pratum (prati,** *n.***)**: meadow, meadow grass

### Adjectives

**editus, edita, editum:** high, rising

### Verbs

**clamito (clamitare)**: shout repeatedly, yell loudly
**excieo (exciere)**: rouse, summon
**illudo (illudere), illusi, illusus:** fool, dupe
**imploro (implorare)**: beg for, call for
**pasco (pascere)**: graze, feed
**subvenio (subvenire)**: come to the aid of, rescue

### Other

**quater:** four times
**ter:** three times, thrice
**undique:** on all sides, everywhere

*Lupus in fabula.*

# DE PASTORIS PUERO ET AGRICOLIS

## Dramatis Personae

*Puer*, the boy, and *Agricolae*, the farmers.

Puer editiore prato oves pascebat atque, per iocum, lupum
terque quaterque adesse clamitans, Agricolas undique exciebat.
Illi, saepius illusi, dum auxilium imploranti non subveniunt,
fiunt oves praeda lupo.

## Grammar Notes

**editiore prato.** The comparative **editiore** indicates that the grassy pasture was "very high up, rather high up," without an explicit term of comparison (see Fable 28).

**prato oves pascebat.** The ablative **prato** indicates the means by which the boy was feeding his sheep (i.e., the sheep were feeding on the meadow grass).

**lupum adesse.** Accusative plus infinitive construction in indirect statement (see Fable 7).

**illi . . . non subveniunt.** The pronoun refers to the farmers, **illi (agricolae)**.

**auxilium imploranti.** The participle refers to the boy, **imploranti (puero)**, and it takes a direct object, **auxilium**.

**imploranti non subveniunt.** The verb **subveniunt** takes a dative complement.

**fiunt oves praeda.** The word **praeda** is a predicate noun.

*Lupus non curat
numerum ovium.*

*Ovium nullus usus, si pastor absit.*

*Vae miseris ovibus, iudex lupus est.*

# Fable 13.
# DE LUPIS ET OVIBUS
## (Barlow 9)

## Introduction
### *The Wolves and The Sheep*

This is a fable made famous by the ancient Greek orator, Demosthenes. He supposedly used this fable to warn the Athenians to beware of Alexander the Great. When Alexander conquered Athens in 335 BCE, he insisted that the Athenians turn Demosthenes over to him as a prisoner, but Demosthenes persuaded the Athenians not to do what Alexander asked; according to Demosthenes, Alexander was like the wolf in the story, the Athenians were the sheep, and he, Demosthenes, was like a loyal sheepdog, trying to defend the Athenians from their enemies. What kind of situation, political or otherwise, do you think this fable could be applied to in the modern world?

For another story about a misguided alliance, see the doves who elected the hawk as their king (Fable 32), or the frogs who asked Jupiter to give them a king (Fable 77). For another story about wolves and sheep, see the fable of the lamb at the stream (Fable 53).

## Grammar Overview
### *The Omitted Copula*

In Latin, every sentence must have a subject and a predicate, either expressed or implied (for the implied subject, see the notes to Fable 75). The predicate usually contains a verb, but not always. For example, consider this sentence: *Scientia potentia,* "Knowledge is power." The Latin sentence has a subject, *scientia,* and a predicate, *potentia,* but there is no verb expressed. This is because the form of the verb that you would expect, *est,* has disappeared. In Latin, unlike English, forms of the verb "to be" often disappear. The technical term for this phenomenon is the "omitted copula," because "to be" is a copula, a linking verb that joins the subject of the sentence to the predicate. Since the copula does not actually describe any specific verbal action, forms of the verb "to be" often disappear in Latin. Usually, the missing form is *est,* although other forms of the verb "to be" can disappear. In the following fable, for example, the perfect passive infinitive, *solutam esse,* appears as *solutam,* with the *esse* omitted. As a result of the vanishing verb, there can be some pithy little Latin sayings that consist of just two or three words. Take, for example, this Latin proverb: *Medium certum.* What do you think this saying could mean? (Hint: Think about the phrase "the Golden Mean.")

## Vocabulary
### *Nouns*
**catulus (catuli,** *m.***):** puppy, whelp
**custodia (custodiae,** *f.***):** guard, protection
**desiderium (desiderii,** *n.***):** longing, desire
**discordia (discordiae):** disagreement, dispute
**foedus (foederis,** *n.***):** treaty, agreement
**lupulus (lupuli,** *m.***):** wolf-cub, little wolf
**obses (obsidis,** *m.***):** hostage, guarantee
**praesidium (praesidii,** *n.***):** protection, defense
**ululatus (ululatus,** *m.***):** howl, yell

### *Adjectives*
**vigil (vigilis):** alert, watchful

### *Verbs*
**clamito (clamitare):** shout repeatedly, yell loudly
**destituo (destituere), destitui, destitutus:** leave without, desert
**edo (edere), edidi, editus:** bring forth, put out
**irruo (irruere):** rush in, rush into
**lanio (laniare):** mangle, tear to pieces
**pasco (pascere):** graze, feed
**quiesco (quiescere), quievi, quietus:** rest, be inactive
**solvo (solvere), solvi, solutus:** unbind, dissolve
**trado (tradere), tradidi, traditus:** hand over, bestow

### *Other*
**aliquando:** sometime, sometime or other
**utrimque:** on both sides

# DE LUPIS ET OVIBUS

## Dramatis Personae

*Lupi*, the wolves, and *Oves*, the sheep.

Foedus aliquando fuit inter Lupos et Oves, quibus natura discordia
est. Obsides utrimque tradebantur. Oves, in suam partem, vigilem
canum custodiam, Lupi suos catulos tradiderunt. Quietis Ovibus
ac pascentibus, lupuli matrum desiderio ululatus edunt. Tum Lupi
irruentes foedus fidemque solutam clamitant, Ovesque, canum
praesidio destitutas, laniant.

## Grammar Notes

**quibus natura discordia est.** The relative pronoun **quibus** has both **lupos** and **oves** as its
referent, with **natura** in the ablative case ("naturally, by nature").

**tradiderunt.** The verb is part of a parallel construction: **oves custodiam (tradiderunt) . . .
lupi catulos tradiderunt.**

**quietis ovibus ac pascentibus.** Ablative absolute construction (see Fable 8).

**matrum desiderio.** The word **matrum** is an objective genitive, expressing the object of the
longing in **desiderio:** "because of a longing for their mothers."

**ululatus edunt.** The word **ululatus** is accusative plural (for more about this type of verbal
noun, called the supine, see Fable 27).

**foedus fidemque solutam.** Accusative plus infinitive construction in indirect statement
(see Fable 7), with **esse** omitted (see the *Grammar Overview* for this fable), and the infinitive agreeing with the nearest of the two subjects: **fidem solutam (esse).**

**praesidio destitutas.** The participle **destitutas** ("left without, bereft of") takes an ablative
complement.

*Fuge magna.*

*Suam quisque pellem portat.*

# Fable 14.
# DE RANA ET BOVE
## (Barlow 26)

## Introduction
### The Frog and The Ox

This fable takes the idea of being "puffed up with pride" and applies the idea literally to a frog who is so puffed up with pride that she thinks she can equal an ox in size! Sir Roger L'Estrange concludes his English version of the fable with this moral: "Betwixt pride, envy and ambition, men fancy themselves to be bigger than they are, and other people to be less." Joseph Jacobs observes that "Self-conceit may lead to self-destruction." As you will see in this Latin version of the fable, the frog's son is standing by, and tries to give his mother some good advice. If the frog's son were to express the moral at the end of the story, what words do you think he would use?

For another story about a foolish frog, see the fable of the frog physician (Fable 78). For another story about an animal puffed up with pride, see the fable of the peacock and the crane (Fable 7), or the fable of the fox and the cat (Fable 72).

## Grammar Overview
### Gerunds

In this fable, you will see an example of the Latin gerund, a verbal noun that is very similar in form to the future passive participle. Don't be fooled, though! There is nothing passive in meaning about the gerund, which is an active verbal noun, able to take a direct object in the accusative case, as you will see here. When the fable tells you that the frog is *cupida aequandi bovem*, it means she is "desirous of equaling the ox" in size. The gerund is *aequandum*, which can be translated with the English verbal noun, "equaling." The noun *bovem* is in the accusative case, because it is the object of the gerund: "equaling the ox." The gerund is put into the genitive case because of the adjective *cupidus*, which takes a genitive complement: *cupida aequandi bovem*, "desirous of equaling the ox." There is nothing passive about this business of *aequandum*: the frog is determined that she is going to equal that ox in size, very actively indeed! (For more information about the uses of the Latin gerund, see the notes to Fable 47 and Fable 48.)

## Vocabulary
### *Adjectives*
**cupidus, cupida, cupidum:** desiring, longing for
**tertius, tertia, tertium:** third

### *Verbs*
**aequo (aequare):** equal, level
**clamito (clamitare):** shout repeatedly, yell loudly
**crepo (crepare), crepui, crepitus:** burst, snap
**desisto (desistere):** stop, cease
**distendo (distendere):** spread out, extend
**hortor (hortari):** encourage, urge
**intumesco (intumescere), intumui:** swell up, puff up
**posthabeo (posthabere), posthabui, posthabitus:** disregard, think unimportant

### *Other*
**licet:** even if, although
**secundum:** afterwards, a second time

*Infra tuam pelliculam te contine.*

# DE RANA ET BOVE

## Dramatis Personae

*Rana*, the frog, and *Bos*, the ox.

Rana, cupida aequandi Bovem, se distendebat. Filius hortabatur
Matrem coepto desistere; nihil enim esse Ranam ad Bovem. Illa
autem, posthabito consilio, secundum intumuit. Clamitat Natus:
"Crepes licet, Mater, Bovem nunquam vinces." Tertium autem cum
intumuisset, crepuit.

## Grammar Notes

**cupida aequandi bovem.** The adjective **cupida** ("desirous of") takes a genitive complement,
**aequandi,** a gerund that has **bovem** as its direct object (see the *Grammar Overview* for
this fable).

**coepto desistere.** The infinitive **desistere** ("cease from, give up on") takes an ablative
complement, while the participle **coeptum** is being used substantively here to mean "the
thing begun, the project embarked upon."

**nihil esse ranam.** Accusative plus infinitive construction in indirect statement (see Fable
7), with an implied verb of speaking, **(dicens) nihil esse ranam**; the accusative subject is
**ranam**, and **nihil** is the predicate noun.

**ad bovem.** The prepositional phrase expresses the idea of comparison: "(in comparison) to
an ox."

**illa autem.** For the postpositive particle **autem,** see Fable 16.

**posthabito consilio.** Ablative absolute construction (see Fable 8).

**crepes licet.** The hypothetical force of the subjunctive is explained by **licet,** meaning "even
if, although" (see Fable 38).

**tertium autem cum intumuisset.** The subjunctive, introduced by **cum**, gives causal background information; this is why the frog finally exploded. The word **tertium** is in the
emphatic first position in the **cum** clause, with the postpositive particle **autem** in second
position.

Auceps, dum insidias molitur, premit forte calcibus anguem.

# Fable 15.
# DE AUCUPE ET PALUMBE
## (Barlow 12)

## Introduction
### The Birdcatcher and The Dove

The words spoken by the birdcatcher at the end of this story echo a lesson found in the *Book of Proverbs* in the Bible: *Qui fodit foveam incidet in eam, et qui volvit lapidem revertetur ad eum*, "He who digs a pit will fall into it, and if someone rolls a stone, it will roll back upon him." This is indeed what happens to the birdcatcher in this story, when he suffers a fatal accident as a result of trying to catch a dove. What do you think about the snake who suddenly appears at the end of the story: is the snake's arrival just a random event, or is this "accident" really the result of some kind of Aesopic karma?

For another story about the birdcatcher, see the fable of the ant and the dove (Fable 43), or the fable of the partridge in the snare (Fable 25). For another story about the danger posed by snakes, see the fable of the peasant who rescued the snake in the snow (Fable 35).

## Grammar Overview
### The Accusative of Exclamation

In this fable, you will see an example of the so-called "accusative of exclamation" in which a noun phrase is put into the accusative case independent of a verb or other word that would explain the use of the accusative. *Me miserum*, shouts the birdcatcher when he realizes he is dying, "Me wretched." Or, in less Tarzan-like English, "I'm in big trouble!" There are actually some examples of the accusative of exclamation in English, too. Just think about the grammar of English exclamations such as "Lucky me!" or "Dear me!" or "Silly me!" The use of the distinct English accusative form "me" in these phrases shows that they are quite similar to the Latin accusative of exclamation. In English usage, however, these are frozen, fixed expressions, and you cannot just make up new accusatives of exclamation in English the way that you can in Latin. In Latin, the accusative of exclamation is a productive form of speech; you can just put whatever noun phrase you want into the accusative case, and exclaim! (To learn more about the accusative of exclamation in Latin, see the notes to Fable 42.)

## Vocabulary

### Nouns

**anguis (anguis,** *m.***):** snake, serpent
**auceps (aucupis,** *m.***):** fowler, birdcatcher
**calx (calcis,** *f.***):** heel, foot
**insidiae (insidiarum,** *f.***):** ambush, snare
**palumbes (palumbis,** *m.***):** ringdove, wood-pigeon

### Adjectives

**exanimatus, exanimata, exanimatum:** deprived of air, deprived of life
**improvisus, improvisa, improvisum:** unexpected, unforeseen
**nidulans (nidulantis):** nesting
**subitus, subita, subitum:** sudden, unexpected

### Verbs

**adpropero (adproperare):** hasten, hurry towards
**dispereo (disperire):** perish, be lost
**insidior (insidiari):** lie in wait, ambush
**molior (moliri):** construct, build
**mordeo (mordere):** bite
**premo (premere):** press, press upon

### Other

**foras:** out, out of doors
**forte:** by chance, accidentally
**procul:** far off, at a distance

*Latet anguis in herba.*

# DE AUCUPE ET PALUMBE

## Dramatis Personae

*Auceps*, the birdcatcher, and *Palumbes*, the dove.

It foras Auceps; videt nidulantem procul in altissima arbore Palumbem. Adproperat et, dum insidias molitur, premit forte calcibus Anguem, qui ex improviso mordebat. Auceps, subito exanimatus malo: "Me miserum! (inquit) Dum alteri insidior, ipse dispereo."

## Grammar Notes

**insidias molitur.** The deponent verb **molitur** is transitive and takes a direct object in the accusative (see Fable 9).

**qui mordebat.** The referent of the relative pronoun **qui** is the snake, and the implied object of the verb is the birdcatcher: **qui (anguis) mordebat (aucupem).**

**subito exanimatus malo.** The ablative phrase **subito malo** wraps around the participle (see Fable 6).

**me miserum.** An exclamation using the accusative (see the *Grammar Overview* for this fable).

**alteri insidior**. The verb **insidior** takes a dative complement.

**ipse dispereo.** The word **ipse** refers to the implied subject: **(ego) ipse dispereo.**

*Sibi parat malum,*
*qui alteri parat.*

Famelica cicada venit ad formicam et mendicat victum.

# Fable 16.
# DE CICADA ET FORMICA
## (Barlow 49)

## Introduction
### The Cricket and The Ant

In this famous fable, the ant spends the summer working hard, unlike the cricket, who spends all her time singing. What is the cricket going to do when winter finally comes? In a Greek version of the fable, the ant says to the cricket: "Since you sang like a fool in the summer, you better be prepared to dance the winter away!" For Joseph Jacobs, the moral of the story is simply that "It is best to prepare for the days of necessity." If you place the ant and the cricket at opposite ends of a behavior scale, where would you rank yourself on that scale: more like the cricket, or more like the ant?

For some more stories about what dangers lie ahead when winter comes, see the fable of the drunken man who sold his clothes (Fable 42), the hedgehogs who needed a home (Fable 76), or the story of the satyr who rescued a man in the snow (Fable 64).

## Grammar Overview
### The Postpositive Particle, Autem

In Fable 2, you learned about the postpositive particle *enim*, which indicates an explanatory connection between two clauses or sentences. In this fable you will see a different postpositive particle, *autem*, which signals an adversative relationship to the preceding sentence. So, when you see *autem*, it means that something contradictory is coming up, something that goes against what you just learned in the preceding sentence. In the fable you are about to read, for example, you will see that *autem* signals the onset of winter after the summer is over: *saeviente autem bruma*. The particle *autem* is not required by the grammar of the sentence; it is just used to emphasize that there is something new and different coming up in the next sentence, a change in the weather from summer to winter. You could omit the word *autem* without doing any damage to the grammar of the sentence, but you would no longer see as clearly the specific relationship between this new sentence and the sentence that came before it. (For another postpositive particle that signals an element of change or surprise, see the comments about *tamen* in the notes to Fable 66.)

## Vocabulary

### Nouns

**aestas (aestatis,** *f.***):** summer, summer heat
**antrum (antri,** *n.***):** cave, hollow place
**bruma (brumae,** *f.***):** winter weather, cold
**cicada (cicadae,** *f.***):** cricket
**granum (grani,** *n.***):** grain, seed
**hiems (hiemis,** *f.***):** winter, winter time
**messis (messis,** *f.***):** harvest, crop
**victus (victus,** *m.***):** food, sustenance

### Adjectives

**famelicus, famelica, famelicum:** starving, hungry

### Verbs

**canto (cantare):** sing
**dictito (dictitare):** say, repeat
**exerceo (exercere):** conduct, carry out
**laboro (laborare), laboravi, laboratus:** work, exert effort
**mendico (mendicare):** beg, be a beggar
**renuo (renuere):** refuse, shake head no
**repono (reponere):** store, put up
**saevio (saevire):** rage, rave
**traho (trahere):** drag, haul

*Ignavis semper feriae sunt.*

# DE CICADA ET FORMICA

## Dramatis Personae

*Cicada*, the cricket, and *Formica*, the ant.

> Dum per aestatem Cicada cantat, Formica suam exercet
> *[handwritten: When summer cricket sing ant himself carry out]*
> messem, trahendo in antra grana et in hiemem reponendo.
> *[handwritten: crop drag cave seed and winter store]*
> Saeviente autem bruma, famelica Cicada venit ad Formicam
> *[handwritten: rage cold criclet go ant]*
> et mendicat victum; renuebat autem Formica, dictitans sese
> *[handwritten: and begger food refuse ant say himself]*
> laborasse, dum illa cantabat.
> *[handwritten: work then sing]*

## Grammar Notes

**suam exercet messem.** The phrase **suam messem** wraps around the verb (see Fable 6).

**trahendo et reponendo.** For the use of gerunds in the ablative case, see Fable 48.

**saeviente autem bruma.** Ablative absolute construction (see Fable 8), with the postpositive particle **autem** in second position (see the *Grammar Overview* for this fable).

**sese laborasse.** Accusative plus infinitive construction in indirect statement (see Fable 7); **sese** is an alternate form of **se**, and **laborasse** is an alternate form of **laboravisse**.

*[handwritten: While the cricket sings through the summer the ant carries out his crops, by draging the seeds into the cave and storing them in the winter. With raging however, the stawy cricket goes to the Ant and begs him for food; the ant refused however, saying that he had worked, while the cricket sang]*

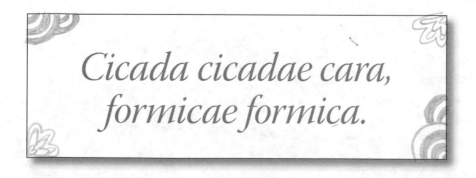

*Cicada cicadae cara,*
*formicae formica.*

Laqueum praetendit rusticus gruibus anseribusque; capitur et ciconia.

# Fable 17.
# DE AGRICOLA ET CICONIA
## (Barlow 56)

## Introduction
### The Farmer and The Stork

You may have heard the legend that babies are delivered by storks. This is not a belief found in ancient Greece or Rome, but the Greeks and Romans did consider the stork to be a bird with a strong sense of family values. Supposedly the storks took good care of their young and then, when those young storks grew up, they in turn took good care of their aged parents. The stork in this fable hopes that this admirable reputation will save her life when she is caught in a trap together with some birds of other species. As you will see, however, the peasant is not persuaded by the stork's good reputation. What approach would you take to this kind of dilemma: do you think the man should let the stork go, or not?

For another story about a bird pleading for its life, see the fable of the birdcatcher and the partridge (Fable 25). For some other stories about storks, see the fable about the frogs and their king (Fable 77), or the fox who invited the stork to dinner (Fable 19).

## Grammar Overview
### Adverbial Et

The most common use of the Latin word *et* is as a conjunction, linking two things together in a sequence, much like the English conjunction "and." In Latin, however, the word *et* can also function as an adverb, meaning something like "also," "too" or "even." So, whenever you meet with *et* in a sentence, you should check to see if it is coordinating two equal things. If it is coordinating two equal things, it is a conjunction—if not, you are dealing with an adverbial *et*. Consider this sentence from the fable you are about to read: *Capitur et ciconia.* It might look like the word *et* is joining the words *capitur* and *ciconia*, but that cannot be, because *capitur* is a verb while *ciconia* is a noun, and the conjunction *et* can only connect things that play an equal role in the sentence (two adjectives, two nouns, two verbs, two clauses, etc.). So, the *et* here must be adverbial: *Capitur et ciconia*, "A stork is captured, too." Probably the most famous adverbial *et* in Latin is in the statement: *Et tu, Brute?* (the words spoken by the dying Julius Caesar in Shakespeare's play). How can you tell that the *et* in this famous sentence is adverbial and not a conjunction?

# Vocabulary

## Nouns

**agricola (agricolae,** *m.***):** farmer
**anser (anseris,** *m.***):** goose
**ciconia (ciconiae,** *f.***):** stork
**laqueus (laquei,** *m.***):** snare, trap
**nocens (nocentis,** *m.***):** criminal, guilty person
**senium (senii,** *n.***):** old age

## Adjectives

**innocens (innocentis):** harmless, innocent
**optimus, optima, optimum:** best

## Verbs

**alo (alere):** nourish, raise
**clamito (clamitare):** shout repeatedly, yell loudly
**conficio (conficere), confeci, confectus:** consume, exhaust
**consuesco (consuescere), consuevi, consuetus:** be in the habit of, get used to
**depascor (depasci):** graze on, eat up
**inservio (inservire):** look after, take care of
**praetendo (praetendere):** stretch out, spread
**sero (serere), sevi, satus:** sow, plant
**supplico (supplicare):** plead, beg

## Other

**postquam:** after, since
**quippe:** obviously, inasmuch
**sedulo:** carefully, attentively
**verum:** the fact is, truth be told

# DE AGRICOLA ET CICONIA

## Dramatis Personae

*Rusticus*, the peasant, and *Ciconia*, the stork.

Laqueum praetendit Rusticus gruibus anseribusque, sata
depascentibus. Capitur et Ciconia. Supplicat illa et innocentem
sese clamitat, nec gruem nec anserem esse, sed avium omnium
optimam, quippe quae parentibus sedulo inservire eundemque
senio confectum alere consueverat. Agricola: "Horum (inquit)
nihil me fugit; verum cum nocentibus postquam te cepi, cum
nocentibus morieris."

## Grammar Notes

**sata depascentibus.** The participle **sata** is used substantively, meaning "crops, things sown
in the fields."

**capitur et ciconia.** Note the adverbial use of **et,** meaning "also" (see the *Grammar Overview*
for this fable).

**innocentem sese.** Accusative plus infinitive constructions in indirect statement (see Fable
7), with **sese** (alternate form of **se**) as the subject, and **innocentem** as a predicate adjective:
**innocentem sese (esse).**

**nec gruem nec anserem esse.** Continuation of the accusative plus infinitive construction,
with the accusative subject implied, and **gruem** and **anserem** as predicate nouns: **(se) nec
gruem nec anserem esse**; note the double use of **nec,** meaning "neither . . . nor" (see Fable
65).

**avium omnium optimam.** Continuation of the accusative plus infinitive construction,
with the subject and the infinitive implied, and **optimam** as a predicate adjective: **avium
omnium optimam (se esse).**

**quippe quae.** The particle **quippe** can be often used with the relative pronoun to mean
"inasmuch as (she is) someone who . . ."

**parentibus inservire.** The verb **inservire** takes a dative complement.

**inservire . . . alere consueverat.** The infinitives **inservire** and **alere** are complements to
**consueverat.**

**eundem senio confectum.** The word **eundem** (masculine accusative singular of **idem**)
refers to the stork's aforementioned parent: **eundem (parentem) senio confectum.**

**horum nihil.** Partitive genitive (see Fable 30): **nihil** (nothing) **horum** (of these things) =
"none of these things."

Accipiter, cum columbam praecipiti insequeretur volatu, a rustico captus est.

# Fable 18.
# DE ACCIPITRE COLUMBAM INSEQUENTE
## (Barlow 68)

## Introduction
### The Hawk Pursuing The Dove

This fable is an example of what is called the "Golden Rule" in English: Do unto others as you would have them do unto you. This saying goes back to the Bible, as in this Latin version from the Gospel of Matthew: *Omnia quaecumque vultis ut faciant vobis homines, et vos facite illis,* "Everything whatsoever you want people to do for you, do you also for them." After you read this story, see how the Golden Rule could be applied to this fable. What is the message of the Golden Rule for the hawk? And what about the man who captures the hawk: according to the Golden Rule, what do you think the man should do with his prisoner?

For some other stories about the predatory hawk, see the fable of the hawk and the nightingale (Fable 6), or the hawk and the doves (Fable 32). For a story about another bird caught by a man, see the fable of the partridge in the snare (Fable 25).

## Grammar Overview
### Nec and Neque

Although the Latin word *nec* appears more commonly than the fuller form *neque,* you can understand the word *nec* more easily if you think about *neque.* As you can see, the word *neque* is a compound of the negating word *ne-* and the suffix *-que,* which is equivalent to *et.* So, every time you see the word *neque* or the word *nec* in Latin, you are really dealing with two words, "not" (*ne-*) and "and" (*-que*). As a result, you can safely replace the word *neque* or *nec* in any Latin sentence with the words *et non* if that will help you to understand the sentence more clearly. Although you may have memorized an English definition such as "nor" or "neither" to use in rendering the words *neque* and *nec,* you might find it much easier to take this "and not" approach, rather than trying to use words like "neither" or "nor"—words that are probably not part of your own everyday English vocabulary. So, keep that "and not" option in mind as you read the last words of this fable, where the farmer rebukes the hawk with the words, *Nec haec te laeserat.* (For a similar style dilemma in English, see the comments about *huc* and *illuc* in Fable 34.)

## Vocabulary

### *Nouns*

**villa (villae,** *f.*): farm, country home
**volatus (volatus,** *m.*): flight

### *Adjectives*

**praeceps (praecipitis)**: headlong, precipitous

### *Verbs*

**dimitto (dimittere)**: let go, send away
**ingredior (ingredi), ingressus sum:** enter, go into
**insequor (insequi)**: pursue, chase after
**laedo (laedere), laesi, laesus:** hurt, injure
**obsecro (obsecrare)**: implore, beseech

### *Other*

**blande:** charmingly, coaxingly
**etenim:** as a matter of fact, because

*Suo ipsius laqueo captus est.*

# DE ACCIPITRE COLUMBAM INSEQUENTE

## Dramatis Personae

*Accipiter*, the hawk, *Columba*, the dove, and *Rusticus*, the peasant.

Cum Accipiter Columbam praecipiti insequeretur volatu, villam
quandam ingressus, a Rustico captus est, quem blande, ut se
dimitteret, obsecrabat. "Non etenim te laesi," dixit. Cui Rusticus:
"Nec haec te laeserat."

## Grammar Notes

**cum accipiter columbam insequeretur.** The subjunctive, introduced by **cum**, gives causal background information as to why the hawk was caught; the deponent verb **insequeretur** is transitive and takes a direct object in the accusative (for transitive deponent verbs, see Fable 9)

**praecipiti insequeretur volatu.** The ablative phrase **praecipiti volatu** wraps around the verb (see Fable 6).

**villam quandam ingressus.** The deponent participle **ingressus** is transitive and takes a direct object in the accusative.

**non etenim te laesi dixit.** See the remarks about the postpositive particle **enim** in Fable 2; the subject of **dixit** is the hawk, and the pronoun **te** refers to the man to whom the hawk is speaking.

**cui rusticus.** The referent of the relative pronoun **cui** is **accipiter**, with an implied verb of speaking: **cui (accipitri) rusticus (inquit).**

**nec haec te laeserat.** You can replace the word **nec** with the words **et non,** as follows: **et haec (columba) te non laeserat** (see the *Grammar Overview* for this fable).

*Adiuvat accipitrem impetus, columbam fuga*

Vulpeculae licuit obsonium videre, gustare non licuit; ciconia rostro facile exhausit.

# Fable 19.
# DE VULPECULA ET CICONIA
## (Barlow 85)

## Introduction
### *The Fox and The Stork*

As you have seen, Aesop's fables are usually short and focus on a single event, but the fable you are about to read has two distinct parts: in the first part, the fox invites the stork to dinner and then, in response, the stork extends an invitation to the fox. The result is a story of the "trickster tricked," because the fox's victory in the first part of the story is undone in the second part, when the clever stork manages to outfox the fox. For the moral of this story, Joseph Jacobs takes the usual saying, "One good turn deserves another," and turns it inside-out: "One bad turn deserves another." If the stork were given the task of pronouncing the moral of the story, what do you think she would say? As for the fox, what lesson do you think she might have learned from attending these two dinner parties?

For another story about the trickster tricked, see the fable of the lion and the horse (Fable 54). For another story about the fox and her tricks, see the fable of the fox who lost her tail in a trap (Fable 51), or the fable of the fox and the goat in the well (Fable 63).

## Grammar Overview
### *Initial Quod*

You have already seen how a relative pronoun at the beginning of a sentence can have its referent noun in the previous sentence (see the notes to Fable 4). Likewise, you will also encounter Latin sentences beginning with the relative pronoun *quod,* a generic neuter pronoun that does not have a specific referent in the preceding statement but that instead refers to the entire situation that has been described. So, for example, in this fable, after the fox gobbles up the liquid food on the flat table, the next clause begins with *quod* in this backward-looking sense: *quod Ciconia frustra rostro tentavit,* "which (thing) the stork tried to do with her beak, unsuccessfully." Or, in more idiomatic English, "The stork tried to do this with her beak, unsuccessfully." This use of the backward-looking relative pronoun at the beginning of the Latin sentence creates a great flow from sentence to sentence in Latin, but it can make for an awkward-sounding English translation. Replacing the generic relative pronoun *quod* with the generic demonstrative pronoun *hoc* ("this") or *illud* ("that") will usually make the sentence much easier to render in English. (For the placement of this backward-looking *quod* as the first word in a *cum* clause, see Fable 37.)

# Vocabulary

## *Nouns*

**cena (cenae,** *f.***):** dinner, meal
**ciconia (ciconiae,** *f.***):** stork
**guttur (gutturis,** *n.***):** throat, gullet
**iniuria (iniuriae,** *f.***):** injury, injustice
**lingua (linguae,** *f.***):** tongue
**mensa (mensae,** *f.***):** table, counter
**obsonium (obsonii,** *n.***):** food
**rostrum (rostri,** *n.***):** beak
**vas (vasis,** *n.***):** vessel, container
**vulpecula (vulpeculae,** *f.***):** fox, vixen

## *Adjectives*

**artus, arta, artum:** narrow, tight
**liquidus, liquida, liquidum:** liquid
**pauci, paucae, pauca:** few, small in number
**situs, sita, situm:** placed, positioned
**vitreus, vitrea, vitreum:** glass, glassy

## *Verbs*

**abeo (abire):** go away, depart
**effundo (effundere):** pour out
**eludo (eludere), elusi, elusus:** frustrate, cheat
**exhaurio (exhaurire), exhausi, exhaustus:** drain, empty
**gusto (gustare):** taste, enjoy
**interlabor (interlabi), interlapsus sum:** glide away, slip by
**invito (invitare):** invite
**licet (licere), licuit:** it is permitted, allowed
**lingo (lingere):** lick
**piget (pigere):** disgusts, irks
**pudet (pudere):** shames, makes ashamed
**tento (tentare), tentavi, tentatus:** attempt, try

## *Other*

**facile:** easily
**frustra:** in vain, unsuccessfully

# DE VULPECULA ET CICONIA

## Dramatis Personae

*Vulpecula*, the fox, and *Ciconia*, the stork.

Vulpecula ad cenam invitavit Ciconiam, obsoniumque in mensam
effundit et, cum liquidum esset, lingua lingebat, quod Ciconia
frustra rostro tentavit. Abit elusa Avis, pudet pigetque iniuriae.
Paucis diebus interlapsis, invitat ad cenam Vulpeculam. Vitreum
vas situm erat, obsonii plenum. Quod cum esset arti gutturis,
Vulpeculae licuit obsonium videre, gustare non licuit. Ciconia
enim rostro facile exhausit.

## Grammar Notes

**cum liquidum esset.** The subjunctive, introduced by **cum**, gives causal background information; this is why the fox licked the food.

**lingua lingebat.** The noun **lingua** is in the ablative case ("with her tongue, by means of her tongue").

**quod ciconia tentavit.** The relative pronoun **quod** connects back to the previous part of the sentence (see the *Grammar Overview* for this fable), referring to the general situation described there, i.e., the fox licking up the liquid food.

**pudet pigetque iniuriae.** The verbs **pudet** and **piget** each take a genitive complement to express the cause of the feeling.

**diebus interlapsis.** Ablative absolute construction (see Fable 8).

**obsonii plenum.** The adjective **plenum** here takes a genitive complement ("full of").

**quod cum esset.** The referent of the relative pronoun **quod** is **vas** in the previous sentence: **quod (vas) cum esset;** the subjunctive, introduced by **cum**, gives causal background information about why the fox could not eat the food (for the placement of **quod** before **cum,** see Fable 37).

**arti gutturis.** The genitive phrase is used like an adjective in the predicate, "of a narrow neck" = "narrow-necked."

**ciconia enim.** For the postpositive particle **enim,** see Fable 2.

*The fox invited the stork to dinner and poured the food out onto the table, which since it was liquid, he was licking it with his tongue which the stork tried to do in vain with his beak. The bird departed having been cheated, shamed and disgusted by the injustice. With a few days having passed, the stork invites the fox to dinner. A glass vase of food was set out. Since it had a narrow throat, it allowed the fox to see but not taste it. For, the stork easily drained it with her beak.*

Passus est leo dentes et ungues evelli ut virgine frueretur.

# Fable 20.
# DE LEONE AMATORIO
## (Barlow 109)

## Introduction
### *The Amorous Lion*

You may be familiar with the fairy tale of *Beauty and The Beast.* Unlike that famous story, however, this fable of the woodsman's daughter and the lion does not have a happily-ever-after ending. The lion is willing to do anything for love, but this turns out to be a big mistake on his part, as you will see. In the ancient Greek version of this story, the poor lion ends up being clubbed to death. In this Latin version, the lion manages to escape with his life, but just barely! If the lion were to add a moral in his own words at the end of this story, what do you think he would say is the lesson he has learned?

For another sad love story, see what happened when the mouse tried to marry a lion (Fable 37), or the fable of the man who was in love with a cat (Fable 75). For a story about a more fierce and formidable lion, see the fable of the lion's share (Fable 73).

## Grammar Overview
### *Words and Word Boundaries*

Although you may take it for granted that everyone knows what a word is, it is not always easy to decide just where words start and stop. In written language, we are used to putting spaces between the words, but this is an innovation: ancient writing did not always put spaces between the words, just as when you speak the words naturally flow into one another without marked breaks. So, in order to learn how the ancient Romans perceived the boundaries between words, we have to rely on indirect clues. In this fable, you will see a clue provided by the postpositive particle *igitur,* which means "therefore" (see Fable 32 for more about the meaning of *igitur*). When this word is used as a postpositive particle, *igitur* cannot come in first position. Usually, that means it is the second word in its clause, but in this fable you will see that *igitur* is actually the third word in its clause: *Passus est igitur.* The placement of *igitur* here gives you an important clue about how the Romans regarded the perfect passive verb forms. Even though we regard *passus est* as two words, those two words were regarded by the Romans as a single word unit, *passus-est,* so that *igitur* is really in second position here, just as you would expect. The placement of postpositive particles like *igitur* is a great way to see just how the Romans themselves thought about words and word boundaries in Latin. Sometimes we are not sure about word boundaries in English, too, of course. Take, for example, this new item in the English language: do you usually write "web page" (two words) or "webpage" (one word)? Over time, there is a strong tendency for languages to develop more and more compound words—this was true in ancient Latin, just as you can see it happening in English today.

# Vocabulary

## Nouns

**dens (dentis,** *m.***):** tooth, fang
**filia (filiae,** *f.***):** daughter
**fustis (fustis,** *m.***):** club, stick
**matrimonium (matrimonii,** *n.***):** marriage
**silvanus (silvani,** *m.***):** woodsman, forester
**unguis (unguis,** *m.***):** claw, talon
**virgo (virginis,** *f.***):** virgin, girl

## Adjectives

**amatorius, amatoria, amatorium:** amorous, in love
**delicatulus, delicatula, delicatulum:** charming, dainty
**hamatus, hamata, hamatum:** hooked
**imbellis, imbelle (imbellis):** unwarlike, defenseless
**tenellus, tenella, tenellum:** tender, delicate

## Verbs

**abigo (abigere):** drive away, expel
**evello (evellere):** pluck, tear out
**fruor (frui):** use, enjoy
**involo (involare):** fly into, rush at
**patior (pati), passus sum:** suffer, undergo
**sollicito (sollicitare):** molest, annoy

## Other

**perdite:** helplessly, hopelessly

# DE LEONE AMATORIO

## Dramatis Personae

*Leo*, the lion, and *Silvanus*, the forester.

Leo Silvani cuiusdam Filiam perdite amavit et Patrem Virginis
sollicitabat ut illi Virgo in matrimonium daretur. Respondebat
Silvanus Filiam esse tenellam et delicatulam Virginem et
nunquam hamatos eius ungues dentesque passuram. Passus est
igitur Leo dentes et ungues evelli ut Virgine frueretur. Quod cum
vidisset Pater, fustibus illi involabat et longius imbellem abigebat.

## Grammar Notes

**ut illi virgo daretur.** The pronoun **illi** refers to the lion: **illi (leoni)**.

**filiam esse tenellam et delicatulam virginem.** Accusative plus infinitive construction in indirect statement (see Fable 7), with **filiam** as the accusative subject.

**nunquam eius ungues dentesque passuram.** Continuation of the accusative plus infinitive construction; the deponent infinitive **passuram (esse)** agrees with **filiam** (the implied accusative subject), and is transitive, taking a direct object in the accusative, **ungues dentesque**, with the pronoun **eius** referring to the lion, **eius (leonis)**.

**passus est igitur.** The placement of the postpositive particle **igitur** shows that **passus est** is regarded as a single word-unit (see the *Grammar Overview* for this fable).

**passus est leo dentes et ungues evelli.** The verb **passus est** takes a complementary infinitive, **evelli**, with **dentes et ungues** as the accusative subjects of the infinitive.

**ut virgine frueretur.** The verb **frueretur** ("make use of, have the pleasure of") takes an ablative complement.

**quod cum vidisset.** The relative pronoun **quod** connects back to the previous sentence (see Fable 4), referring to the general situation described there, i.e., the lion being declawed; the subjunctive, introduced by **cum**, gives causal background information as to why the man was able to attack the lion (for the placement of **quod** before **cum**, see Fable 37).

**fustibus illi involabat.** The verb **involabat** takes a dative complement, with the pronoun **illi** referring to the lion: **fustibus illi (leoni) involabat.**

**longius imbellem abigebat.** The comparative is used here to indicate "very far, quite far," without an explicit comparison (see Fable 28); the adjective **imbellem** refers to the lion: **longius imbellem (leonem) abigebat.**

*Asinus stramen mavult quam aurum.*

*Non faciunt meliorem equum aurei freni.*

# Fable 21.
# DE EQUO ET ASINO
## (Barlow 14)

## Introduction
### The Horse and The Donkey

In some versions of this story, this proud horse is wounded when he goes off to war. In other versions, the horse is injured when he is running in a race. Both versions of the story still express the same idea: "Pride goeth before a fall." William Caxton, in his fifteenth-century version of the fable, invokes the image of the spinning wheel of fortune: "He that is wel fortuned and happy and is atte vpperest of the whele of fortune may wel falle doune," which is to say: "A man who is fortunate and happy and at the top of the wheel of fortune can still fall down." What are some other images, like the wheel of fortune, that could be used to express the "ups and downs" of this horse's life, in contrast to the life of the donkey?

For more stories about the simple life, see the fable of the country mouse and the city mouse (Fable 4), or the fable of the dog and the wolf (Fable 80). For another story in favor of hard-working animals, see the fable of the ox and the heifer (Fable 24).

## Grammar Overview
### Interrogative Quid

The Latin word *quid* is a very important question word, or "interrogative," to use a more technical term. It is the neuter form of the pronoun *quis,* and when it is used as a question word, it usually means "what?" (just as *quis* means "who?"). Yet, you will sometimes see the word *quid* used to ask not only the question "what?" but also the question, "(for) what (reason)?"—in other words, "why?" So, for example, in the fable you are about to read, when the outraged horse confronts the donkey, he asks, *Quid obsistis Equo?* "Why are you standing in the way of a horse?" In addition to *quid*, there are many other ways to ask the question "why?" in Latin. Can you think of some other Latin words that mean "why?" (Hint: Take a look at Fable 76.)

## Vocabulary
### Nouns

**asellus (aselli,** *m.***):** donkey, little donkey
**carrus (carri,** *m.***):** wagon
**cursus (cursus,** *m.***):** running, race
**frenum (freni,** *n.***):** bridle, harness
**hinnitus (hinnitus,** *m.***):** neighing, whinny
**inguen (inguinis,** *n.***):** groin, muscle
**ornamentum (ornamenti,** *n.***):** decoration, trappings
**ornatus (ornatus,** *m.***):** decoration, apparel
**phalerae (phalerarum,** *f.***):** ornaments, decorations
**sella (sellae,** *f.***):** seat, saddle

### Adjectives

**aureus, aurea, aureum:** gold, golden
**fremebundus, fremebunda, fremebundum:** roaring, murmuring
**ignavus, ignava, ignavum:** lazy, useless
**ingens (ingentis):** huge, mighty
**inutilis, inutile (inutilis):** useless
**onustus, onusta, onustum:** laden, burdened
**ornatus, ornata, ornatum:** decorated, adorned
**splendidus, splendida, splendidum:** shining, brilliant
**tacitus, tacita, tacitum:** silent, quiet

### Verbs

**affor (affari):** speak to, address
**audeo (audere), ausus sum:** dare, venture
**cedo (cedere):** yield, give way
**crepo (crepare):** burst, snap
**curro (currere):** run, race
**evenio (evenire):** come forth, turn out
**obsisto (obsistere):** oppose, withstand
**obsto (obstare):** oppose, hinder
**proculco (proculcare):** trample on
**provolo (provolare):** fly forth, dash forward
**rudo (rudere):** bellow, bray
**spolio (spoliare):** rob, strip
**superbio (superbire):** be proud, boastful

### Other

**forte:** by chance, accidentally
**heus:** hey!
**necesse:** necessary, inevitable
**postea:** afterwards
**quid:** why, for what reason

*In quo nascetur asinus corio morietur.*

# DE EQUO ET ASINO

## Dramatis Personae

*Equus*, the horse, and *Asellus*, the donkey.

Equus phaleris sellaque ornatus cum ingenti hinnitu per viam currebat. Currenti onustus Asellus forte obstabat, cui Equus fremebundus: "Quid (inquit), ignave, obsistis Equo? Cede, inquam, aut te proculcabo pedibus!" Asellus, rudere non ausus, cedit tacitus. Equo provolanti crepat inguen. Tum, cursui inutilis, ornamentis spoliatur. Postea cum carro venientem Asinus affatur, "Heus mi Amice! Quis ille ornatus est? Ubi aurea sella? Ubi splendidum frenum? Sic, Amice, necesse fuit evenire superbienti."

## Grammar Notes

**phaleris sellaque ornatus.** The adjective **ornatus** takes an ablative complement ("outfitted with, adorned with").

**currenti asellus obstabat.** The verb **obstabat** takes a dative complement, with the participle referring to the horse: **currenti (equo) asellus obstabat.**

**equus fremebundus inquit.** The adjective **fremebundus** modifies the subject of the verb, so you might want to translate it as an adverb (see Fable 36).

**quid obsistis equo?** The verb **obsistis** takes a dative complement, and the interrogative **quid** here means "why? for what reason?" (see the *Grammar Overview* for this fable).

**equo crepat inguen.** The dative of possession is commonly used with regard to body parts (see Fable 64): "the horse's groin muscle snaps."

**cursui inutilis.** The adjective **inutilis** takes a dative complement.

**ornamentis spoliatur.** The verb **spoliatur** takes an ablative complement ("stripped of").

**cum carro venientem affatur.** The deponent verb **affatur** is transitive and takes a direct object in the accusative (see Fable 9), with the participle referring to the horse: **(equum) cum carro venientem affatur.**

**ille ornatus.** Be careful to distinguish between the adjectival **ornatus** used earlier (**phaleris sellaque ornatus**) and the noun **ornatus** (for more about these ambiguous forms, see Fable 29).

**sic evenire.** The adverbial **sic** modifies the infinitive **evenire**, meaning "to turn out this way."

*Alter alterius auxilio eget.*

*Facta plus valent quam dicta.*

# Fable 22.
# DE VULPE ET LUPO
## (Barlow 42)

## Introduction
### The Fox and The Wolf

In the ancient Greek collection of Aesop's fables, there is a story about a boy who goes swimming in a river and then gets swept away by the current. He calls out for help to a man he sees walking along the riverbank. Instead of helping the boy, however, the man gives him a lecture on how dangerous river currents can be. As far as the drowning boy is concerned, that kind of lecture is no help at all! This Latin version of the fable is very similar to the Greek fable, except that this time the story is about animals: a fox has fallen into a well, and it is a wolf who happens to be passing by. Do you think the meaning of this fable is changed when the story is told with animal characters, instead of human beings?

For another story of the fox in the well, see the fable of the fox and the goat (Fable 63). For stories about animals who really do help one another, see the fable of the mouse and the lion (Fable 67), or the ant and the dove (Fable 43).

## Grammar Overview
### Cum Plus Subjunctive

The Latin conjunction *cum* sometimes introduces an indicative verb and sometimes a subjunctive verb. If *cum* introduces an indicative verb, it has a temporal meaning ("when"), but if *cum* introduces a subjunctive verb it is often causal ("because"). In English, too, we have a word like *cum* that conveys both temporal and causal meanings: "since." Sometimes the word "since" is temporal, without any causal implication: "I have lived in this house since I was born." Yet more commonly the word "since" indicates a causal relationship: "Since you are my best friend, I will tell you a secret." When the Latin word *cum* appears with a subjunctive verb, it has this causal meaning, and can be translated into English as "since" or "because." Another way you might think about a subjunctive *cum* clause is that it describes events that take place offstage, before the curtain rises and the actual dramatic scene begins. It's relevant to the story, but it's not part of the main action. So, in this fable about the fox in the well, we don't actually see the fox fall into the well; that is something that has taken place offstage, before the curtain rises. As the curtain rises on our story, we see the fox after she has fallen accidentally into the well, *cum in puteum fortuito incidisset*, and is now forced to ask the wolf for help. (For notes about the use of *cum* plus indicative verbs, see Fable 24.)

## Vocabulary
### Nouns
**ambages (ambagis,** *f.*): long story, convoluted words
**funis (funis,** *m.*): rope, cord
**infortunium (infortunii,** *n.*): misfortune, bad luck
**ops (opis,** *f.*): help, means
**ordo (ordinis,** *m.*): order, row
**puteus (putei,** *m.*): well, hole
**ripa (ripae,** *f.*): bank, shore

### Verbs
**comparo (comparare):** provide, buy
**condoleo (condolere):** empathize, feel pain with another
**expedio (expedire):** unfold, explain
**extraho (extrahere):** pull out, extract
**incido (incidere), incidi, incasus:** fall into, meet with
**praetereo (praeterire):** go by, pass by
**precor (precari):** entreat, pray

### Other
**fortuito:** accidentally, by chance
**quin:** why not, why don't
**quomodo:** how

*Auxilium peto, non consilium.*

# DE VULPE ET LUPO

## Dramatis Personae

*Vulpes*, the fox, and *Lupus*, the wolf.

*(interlinear gloss: fox when in well by chance fall into wolf in bank)*
Vulpes, cum in puteum fortuito incidisset, Lupum in ripa
*(interlinear gloss: go by see rope provide)*
praetereuntem vidit rogavitque ut funem sibi compararet
*(interlinear gloss: help himself danger extract)*
opemque daret ad se ipsam a tanto periculo extrahendam.
*(interlinear gloss: wicked fox establish bad luck)*
Cui Lupus: "Miserrima Vulpes, condoleo tuum infortunium.
*(interlinear gloss: tell pray how this well fall into respondes)*
Dic, precor: quomodo in hunc puteum incidisti?" Respondebat
*(interlinear gloss: the fox not help does long story why don't you care provide)*
Vulpes, "Non opus est ambagibus. Quin tu funem comparato,
*(interlinear gloss: and after all to you order explain)*
et deinde omnia tibi in ordine expediam."

## Grammar Notes

**cum in puteum incidisset.** The subjunctive, introduced by **cum**, gives causal background information; this is why the fox had to ask the wolf for help (see the *Grammar Overview* for this fable).

**ad se ipsam extrahendam.** The gerundive with the preposition **ad** expresses purpose (see Fable 54); **se ipsam** refers to the fox, hence the feminine gender of the pronoun **se**, with the gerundive agreeing in gender, number and case.

**cui lupus.** The referent of the relative pronoun **cui** is **vulpes**, with an implied verb of speaking: **cui (vulpi) lupus (inquit)**.

**miserrima vulpes.** For this use of the superlative, see Fable 39.

**non opus est ambagibus.** The phrase **opus est** takes an ablative complement ("there is need of").

**quin comparato.** The word **comparato** is a future imperative, second person singular (see Fable 11); the word **quin** plus the imperative expresses the so-called "interrogative imperative," which can be translated as "Why don't you go buy?"

*(handwritten translation at bottom of page:)*
The fox, since she accidentally fell into the well, she saw a wolf going by the bank and asked that he could provide a rope to her and give help in order to pull her out out from such danger. To whom the Lupus said ", Most miserable fox, I empathize with your bad luck. Pray tell: How did you fall into this well?" The fox responds "The long story does not help. Why don't you provide a rope and after I will explain it all to you in order."

Pellis quidem est ovis, opera autem erant lupi.

# Fable 23.
# DE LUPO OVIS PELLE INDUTO
## (Barlow 11)

## Introduction
### *The Wolf Dressed in a Sheep's Skin*

The notion of the "wolf in sheep's clothing" is an old idea that you can find even in the Bible, where Jesus warns his followers: "Beware of false prophets, which come to you in sheep's clothing, but inwardly they are ravening wolves." In this fable first told by the Renaissance Latin author Abstemius, you will see a literal example of a wolf who wears a sheepskin in order to try to trick the shepherds. The disguise is able to fool some of the more simple-minded shepherds, but there is one wise shepherd who detects the hidden wolf. What lesson can we learn from the mistake made by the wolf? And what lesson can we learn from the mistake made by those simple-minded shepherds who cannot see through the wolf's disguise, even when the wolf is dead?

For a quite different story about disguise, see the fable of the donkey in the lion's skin (Fable 40). For more stories about the wolf and the sheep, see the fable of the sheep and the sheepdogs (Fable 13), or the fable of the boy who cried "Wolf!" (Fable 12).

## Grammar Overview
### *The Postpositive Particle, Quidem*

In this fable, you will meet another postpositive particle, *quidem.* This is an emphatic particle, accentuating the word that comes before it, much as we use an exclamation mark in English. The difference, of course, is that we put the exclamation mark at the end of the sentence, but Latin is able to put its verbal exclamation mark, the particle *quidem*, immediately after the word that is being emphasized. Consider this sentence from the fable you are about to read: *Pellis quidem est ovis,* "The skin (!) is that of a sheep." The particle *quidem* does not contribute to the grammar of the sentence; you can remove the word and the sentence still has the same basic meaning: *Pellis est ovis,* "The skin is that of a sheep." What the particle contributes is an emphasis on the word *pellis*. This special emphasis poses a challenge for you in translating the sentence. You might choose to add an English word that throws emphasis on the skin: "The skin in-deed is that of a sheep." You could also try using some special conventions of written English to add emphasis to the word, such as putting the word in capital letters: "The SKIN is that of a sheep." Now imagine that you are reading the Latin out loud: if you want to convey the emphatic quality of *quidem* when you are speaking in Latin, what technique(s) could you use to do that?

## Vocabulary
### Nouns
**grex (gregis,** *m.***):** flock, herd
**pastor (pastoris,** *m.***):** shepherd
**pellis (pellis,** *f.***):** skin, hide

### Verbs
**animadverto (animadvertere), animadverti, animadversus:** notice, pay attention to
**immisceo (immiscere), immiscui, immixtus:** mix in, mingle with
**induo (induere), indui, indutus:** put on, dress in
**interrogo (interrogare):** question, inquire
**occido (occidere):** kill, slaughter
**suspendo (suspendere), suspendi, suspensus:** hang

### Other
**cur:** why
**quotidie:** daily, each day

*Mors lupi, agnis vita.*

# DE LUPO OVIS PELLE INDUTO

## Dramatis Personae

*Lupus*, the wolf, *Oves*, the sheep, and *Pastor*, the shepherd.

Lupus, Ovis pelle indutus, Ovium se immiscuit gregi, quotidieque aliquam ex eis occidebat. Quod cum Pastor animadvertisset, illum in altissima arbore suspendit. Interrogantibus autem ceteris Pastoribus cur Ovem suspendisset, respondebat, "Pellis quidem est Ovis, opera autem erant Lupi."

## Grammar Notes

**se immiscuit gregi**. The reflexive verb **se immiscuit** takes a dative complement.

**aliquam ex eis occidebat**. The pronoun **aliquam** refers to a sheep: **aliquam (ovem)**, "a sheep, one of the sheep."

**quod cum pastor animadvertisset**. The relative pronoun **quod** connects back to the previous sentence (see Fable 4), referring to the general situation described there, i.e., the way the wolf keeps killing the sheep; the subjunctive, introduced by **cum**, gives causal background information as to why the shepherd hanged the wolf (for the placement of **quod** before **cum**, see Fable 37).

**illum suspendit**. The pronoun refers to the wolf: **illum (lupum) suspendit**.

**in altissima arbore**. For this use of the superlative, see Fable 39.

**interrogantibus autem pastoribus**. Ablative absolute construction (see Fable 8), with the postpositive article **autem** in second position (see Fable 16).

**cur ovem suspendisset**. The word **cur** introduces an indirect question with the subjunctive.

**pellis quidem**. The postpositive particle **quidem** puts special emphasis on the word **pellis** (see the *Grammar Overview* for this fable).

**opera autem**. Note the postpositive particle **autem** in second position, parallel to the particle **quidem** in the preceding clause.

Vitula, cum bovem agricolae aculeo agitatum et arantem cerneret, contempsit.

# Fable 24.
# DE VITULA ET BOVE
## (Barlow 52)

## Introduction
### The Heifer and The Ox

This fable is about farm animals, some of whom are working animals, and some of whom are being raised for food. One of the characters you will meet is a heifer, Latin *vitula*, a word that provides the origin of the English word "veal." The other character is an ox, Latin *bos*, which gives us the English word "beef." In this fable, however, the hard-working *bos* manages to avoid being turned into beef, while the *vitula* is not so lucky, as you will see. What are some ways in which this story about animals on a farm could be applied to human society?

For more stories about laziness, see the fable of the ant and the cicada (Fable 16), or the farmer and his plow (Fable 11). For another story about oxen, see the fable of the dog in the manger (Fable 2).

## Grammar Overview
### Cum Plus Indicative

The following fable gives you a good opportunity to compare the use of *cum* with both indicative and subjunctive verbs. The first time you see the word *cum* in this fable, it happens to introduce a subjunctive verb: *vitula, cum bovem arantem cerneret, contempsit*, "the heifer scorned the ox, since she saw he was pulling a plow." The *cum* clause with the subjunctive verb thus explains the reason why the heifer made fun of the ox. In effect, the subjunctive verb puts us into the mind of the heifer, so we can see the reason why she treats the ox as she does. The second *cum* that you will see in the fable introduces an indicative verb: *cum immolationis dies affuit, bos per pascua vagabatur*, "when the day of the sacrifice arrived, the ox was wandering through the fields." This *cum* clause simply provides information about when something occurred. If you are translating into English, you might translate *cum* as "when" for indicative verbs, and translate it as "since" or "because" for subjunctive verbs. The real goal, however, should not be to come up with formulas for English translation, but rather to get a feel for the difference in meaning between the indicative and subjunctive moods in Latin. This is not a distinction we make in English, so it can be difficult to grasp, but getting a feel for the Latin subjunctive is an essential step in learning the language, regardless of what words you use to translate the word *cum* into English. (For more about *cum* clauses in Latin, see the notes to Fable 37.)

# Vocabulary
## Nouns

**aculeus (aculei,** *m.***):** sting, goad
**agricola (agricolae,** *m.***):** farmer
**immolatio (immolationis,** *f.***):** sacrifice, offering of victim
**iugum (iugi,** *n.***):** yoke
**pascuum (pascui,** *n.***):** pasture
**vitula (vitulae,** *f.***):** heifer, young cow

## Adjectives

**lascivus, lasciva, lascivum:** playful, unrestrained
**mollis, molle (mollis):** soft, tender

## Verbs

**agito (agitare), agitavi, agitatus:** drive, guide
**aro (arare):** plow
**cerno (cernere):** see, discern
**conspicor (conspicari):** notice, observe
**contemno (contemnere), contempsi, contemptus:** scorn, disparage
**immolo (immolare):** sacrifice, offer as victim
**laboro (laborare):** work, exert effort
**libero (liberare), liberavi, liberatus:** set free, release
**retineo (retinere), retinui, retentus:** hold back, restrain
**subrideo (subridere):** smile, grin
**vagor (vagari):** roam, wander

## Other

**heus:** hey!
**ideo:** for this reason, therefore

# DE VITULA ET BOVE

## Dramatis Personae

*Vitula*, the heifer, and *Bos*, the ox.

Mollis et lasciva Vitula, cum Bovem agricolae aculeo agitatum et arantem cerneret, contempsit. Sed, cum immolationis dies affuit, Bos, a iugo liberatus, per pascua vagabatur. Vitula vero, ut immolaretur, retenta est. Quod cum Bos conspicatur, subridens ait, "Heus Vitula, ideo non laborabas: ut immolareris!"

## Grammar Notes

**cum bovem cerneret.** The subjunctive, introduced by **cum**, gives causal background information; this is why the heifer felt contempt for the ox (see the *Grammar Overview* for this fable).

**cum immolationis dies affuit.** Note the use of **cum** plus an indicative verb (see the *Grammar Overview* for this fable).

**vitula vero.** For the postpositive particle **vero,** see Fable 60.

**quod cum bos conspicatur.** The relative pronoun **quod** connects back to the previous sentence (see Fable 4), referring to the general situation described there, i.e., the heifer being led away to be sacrificed; note also the use of **cum** plus an indicative verb (see the Grammar Overview for this fable; for the placement of **quod** before **cum**, see Fable 37).

*Bos iugo ducendo natus.*

Grave est fidem fallere.

Simulans amicum
inimicus inimicissimus.

# Fable 25.
# DE AUCUPE ET PERDICE
## (Barlow 90)

## Introduction
### *The Birdcatcher and The Partridge*

Throughout human history, hunters have relied on decoys to help capture their prey. Sometimes the decoys are manufactured (like duck decoys made of wood), but hunters have also been known to use live animals as lures. In this Aesop's fable, you will see what happens when a partridge volunteers to serve as a hunting decoy in order to save her own life. In the seventeenth-century version of this story by Sir Roger L'Estrange, the moral is firmly against the partridge: "Of all scandalous and lewd offices, that of a traitor is certainly the basest, for it undermines the very foundations of society." Based on your assessment of the partridge's behavior, what do you think the moral of this story should be?

For another story about an animal traitor, see the fable about why the bat flies only at night (Fable 8). For stories about the importance of solidarity, see the fable of the farmer and his sons (Fable 71), or the horse who refused to carry part of the load (Fable 36).

## Grammar Overview
### *Future Active Participles*

In this fable, you will see examples of two different verbal phrases constructed with the future active participle. The first example is a future active infinitive, *allecturum esse*, from the verb *allicere*, "to lure, entice." We do not have a future active infinitive in English, but you could roughly paraphrase the Latin *allecturum esse* as "to be ready to entice." The second example is a future active periphrastic, which is formed by a combination of a finite form of the verb "to be" with a future active participle: *proditura es*, "you are ready to betray," from the verb *prodere*, "to betray." A future periphrastic form is a "round-about phrase" (peri-phrastic) for talking about the future. The future active periphrastic conveys not so much the idea that something will happen, but rather the idea that it is ready to happen, right now, as indicated by the present tense form of the verb "to be" (*est*), which is used to create the periphrastic phrase. (For more information about the future periphrastic, see the notes to Fable 31.)

## Vocabulary
### Nouns

**auceps (aucupis,** *m.***):** fowler, birdcatcher
**dubium (dubii,** *n.***):** doubt
**perdix (perdicis,** *f.***):** partridge
**rete (retis,** *n.***):** net, snare
**sodalis (sodalis,** *m.***):** companion, associate
**volucris (volucris,** *f.***):** bird, winged creature

### Adjectives

**plurimus, plurima, plurimum:** most, very many

### Verbs

**allicio (allicere), allexi, allectus:** entice, lure
**capto (captare), captavi, captatus:** grab, grasp
**decipio (decipere):** trick, deceive
**demitto (demittere):** let go, send away
**extendo (extendere), extendi, extensus:** stretch out, spread
**prodo (prodere), prodidi, proditus:** reveal, betray
**promitto (promittere):** promise

### Other

**nequaquam:** no way, by no means
**procul:** far off, far from
**supplicabunde:** pleadingly, humbly

*Semel malus,
semper malus.*

# DE AUCUPE ET PERDICE

## Dramatis Personae

*Auceps*, the birdcatcher, and *Perdix*, the partridge.

Auceps, retibus extensis, captabat Perdicem. Volucris illa captata supplicabunde illum rogabat ut se demitteret, promittens se in retia plurimas Aves allecturam. Cui Auceps: "Nequaquam hoc faciam, nam procul dubio me decipies, quae sodales tuos proditura es."

## Grammar Notes

**retibus extensis.** Ablative absolute construction (see Fable 8).

**se aves allecturam.** Accusative plus infinitive construction in indirect statement (see Fable 7), with **se** as the feminine accusative singular subject of the infinitive, and **aves** as the object: **se aves allecturam (esse).**

**cui auceps.** The referent of the relative pronoun **cui** is **volucris illa**, that is, the partridge, with an implied verb of speaking: **cui (perdici) auceps (inquit).**

**proditura es.** The future active participle used with the verb **es** creates a finite verb phrase referring to the future, also known as a future active periphrastic (see the *Grammar Overview* for this fable).

*Falsum in uno,*
*falsum in toto.*

*Nulli nimium credite.*

*Lupus pilum mutat,
non mentem.*

# Fable 26.
# DE LUPO ET SUE
## (Barlow 13)

## Introduction
### The Wolf and The Sow

This is one of the many Aesop's fables in which a dangerous predator pretends to be a helpful friend—and, as the English saying goes, "with friends like that, who needs enemies?" In this case, the dangerous predator is a wolf, and the sow is in an especially vulnerable position because she is about to give birth to a litter of piglets. Yet, as you will see, the sow manages to do quite a good job of taking care of herself even in this perilous situation. Sir Roger L'Estrange applies this moral to his seventeenth-century version of the fable: "There are no snares so dangerous as those that are laid for us under the name of good offices." What are the words you would choose to express the moral of this story?

For another story about the danger of trusting a wolf, see the fable of the treaty with the wolves (Fable 13), or the fable of the wolf and the crane (Fable 30). For another story about pretend friendship, see the fable of the lion and the horse (Fable 54).

## Grammar Overview
### Fore and Futurum Esse

In this fable, you will meet with the Latin word *fore*, an alternate form of *futurum esse*, the future infinitive form of the verb *esse*, "to be." There are quite a few forms of the verb "to be" that start with the letter *f*, such as the future infinitive *fore*, the future participle *futurus*, as well as the perfect verbs *fui*, *fuisti*, etc. You can even find *forem*, *fores*, *foret*, etc. used as alternatives to the standard subjunctive verbs *essem*, *esses*, *esset*, etc. (see Fable 80 for an example). These verb forms starting with the letter *f* are all derived from an archaic verb *fuo* that has not survived, but that has left traces in the conjugation of the verb *sum*. The process of combining words in a single paradigm from different stems is called "suppletion," and it is something that happens in English, too. The English verb "to be," for example, shows suppletion, with "be" formed from one stem, "is" from another stem, and "was" from yet another stem. Can you think of another common English verb that is built from different stems? (Hint: Look up the word "wend" in the English dictionary and see what you can learn from that.)

## Vocabulary

### Nouns

**absentia (absentiae,** *f.*): absence
**benevolentia (benevolentiae,** *f.*): goodwill, kindness
**custos (custodis,** *m.*): guardian, watcher
**fetus (fetus,** *m.*): offspring, young
**obsequium (obsequii,** *n.*): servility, service
**praesentia (praesentiae,** *f.*): presence
**puerpera (puerperae,** *f.*): female in labor
**sus (suis,** *f.*): sow, swine

### Adjectives

**pius, pia, pium:** dutiful, conscientious

### Verbs

**abeo (abire):** go away, depart
**consto (constare):** consist of, stand upon
**egeo (egere):** need, require
**parturio (parturire):** give birth, be in labor
**polliceor (polliceri):** promise

*Homo homini lupus.*

# DE LUPO ET SUE

## Dramatis Personae

*Sus*, the sow, and *Lupus*, the wolf.

Parturiebat Sus; pollicetur Lupus se custodem fore fetus.
Respondet Puerpera Lupi obsequio se non egere, oratque, si velit
pius haberi, longius abeat; Lupi enim benevolentia constabat non
praesentia, sed absentia.

## Grammar Notes

**se custodem fore.** Accusative plus infinitive construction in indirect statement (see Fable 7); **fore** is the future infinitive of **esse** (see the *Grammar Overview* for this fable), with **se** as the accusative subject, and **custodem** as a predicate noun.

**custodem fetus.** The noun **fetus** is in the genitive case.

**obsequio se non egere.** Accusative plus infinitive construction in indirect statement; the verb **egere** ("be in need of") takes an ablative complement.

**pius haberi.** The passive form of **habere** means "to be held to be, to be thought of, to be considered," with **pius** as the predicate adjective.

**longius abeat.** The subjunctive expresses a wish or command, the result that the sow would like to see happen; **longius** is the comparative form of the adverb.

**lupi enim.** For the postpositive particle **enim,** see Fable 2.

**constabat non praesentia.** The verb **constabat** takes an ablative complement ("consists of").

*Furem fur cognoscit,
et lupum lupus.*

Aegrotus lecto decumbebat milvus, iam ferme moriens.

# Fable 27.
# DE MILVO AEGROTO
## (Barlow 75)

## Introduction
### The Ailing Kite

The kite is a predatory bird, belonging to the hawk family. In this fable, you will see what happens when the kite thinks that he is dying. He decides to beg the gods to spare his life, but his mother has good reason to believe that asking the gods for help will not work. The English version of this story by G. F. Townsend adds this moral to the fable: "We must make friends in prosperity if we would have their help in adversity." What do you think is the main lesson we should learn from the plight of this bird on his deathbed?

For more stories about the predatory kite, see the fable of the mouse and the frog (Fable 44), or the doves and their king (Fable 32). For another story about a fierce predator fallen on hard times, see the fable of the old lion and the donkey (Fable 45).

## Grammar Overview
### The Supine

In this fable, you will meet an example of the Latin supine, which is a verbal noun belonging to the fourth declension. Like the Latin gerund, which looks similar to the future passive participle (see the notes to Fable 14), the Latin supine looks similar to the perfect passive participle—but there is nothing passive about it! The Latin supine is an active verbal noun and can take a direct object in the accusative, as you will see here, when the kite tells his mother "to go beg the gods," *precatum ire deos*. The accusative noun *deos* is the direct object of the supine: *precatum deos*, "beg the gods." When combined with a verb of motion, as here, the supine expresses purpose: *precatum ire*, "to go beg." You can find the supine used in other constructions, often in the ablative case, as in these examples: *difficile dictu est*, "it is difficult to say" or *mirabile visu*, "amazing to see." You will find many supines listed as fourth declension nouns in your Latin dictionary, and most of the time you can safely regard the supine as a noun, without thinking about its verbal nature. But watch out for those situations where the supine takes an object, as it does in the phrase *precatum ire deos*. Like participles, the supine has some traits from the world of nouns (gender, number, case), but it also has some traits from the world of verbs, such as the ability to take a direct object.

## Vocabulary

### Nouns

**ara (arae,** *f.***):** altar
**lectus (lecti,** *m.***):** bed
**ops (opis,** *f.***):** help, means
**rapina (rapinae,** *f.***):** robbery, plunder
**salus (salutis,** *f.***):** health, safety

### Adjectives

**aegrotus, aegrota, aegrotum:** ailing, sick

### Verbs

**decumbo (decumbere):** lie, lie down
**licet (licere):** it is permitted, allowed
**precor (precari), precatus sum:** entreat, pray
**promitto (promittere):** promise
**spero (sperare):** hope
**violo (violare):** dishonor, outrage

### Other

**ferme:** nearly, almost
**toties:** as often, such a number of times

*A deo est omnis medela.*

# DE MILVO AEGROTO

## Dramatis Personae

*Milvus*, the kite, and his mother.

Aegrotus lecto decumbebat Milvus, iam ferme moriens. Matrem orat precatum ire deos, multa promittens, si redire ad salutem liceret. Mater autem respondebat nil opis sperandum a diis, quorum sacra et aras rapinis toties violasset.

## Grammar Notes

**lecto decumbebat.** The verb **decumbebat** takes a dative complement.

**precatum ire deos.** The supine with the verb **ire** expresses purpose (see the *Grammar Overview* for this fable); **deos** is the object of the supine: "to go beg the gods."

**promittens multa.** The participle agrees with the implied subject of the verb, the kite: **(milvus) orat . . . promittens multa.**

**mater autem respondebat.** For the postpositive particle **autem,** see Table 16.

**nil opis.** The noun **opis** is a partitive genitive (see Fable 30): **nil** (nothing) **opis** (of help) = "no help."

**nil opis sperandum.** Accusative plus future passive infinitive construction in indirect statement (see Fable 7), where the phrase **nil opis** is the accusative subject, and **sperandum (esse)** is the infinitive.

**quorum sacra et aras violasset.** The subjunctive, introduced by the relative pronoun **quorum**, provides causal background information; according to the mother, this is why her son has nothing to hope for from the gods.

*Homo proponit, sed deus disponit.*

Canis, ratus virtuti suae tributum hoc decus esse, populares omnes despicit.

Fable 28.

# DE CANE MORDACI
(Barlow 25)

## Introduction
### The Biting Dog

From both archaeological and literary evidence, we know that the ancient Romans would put a warning sign outside their homes, "Beware of dog"—*CAVE CANEM* in Latin. In this story, you will read about a dog owner who ties a bell around his dog's neck to warn everyone that the dog is prone to bite. In the illustration for this fable, you will see another technique that could be used to mark a vicious dog: a wooden "clog" is tied around the dog's neck in order to hobble his movements. At first the badly behaved dog is flattered by this special attention, but another dog soon sets him straight. Based on the dog's original mistake and the lesson that he learns, what would you say is the moral of this story?

For another story about a dangerous dog, see the fable of the dog in the manger (Fable 2). For more stories about being fooled by appearances, see the fable of the dog crossing the stream (Fable 55), or the stag who saw his reflection in the water (Fable 68).

## Grammar Overview
### The Comparative Without Comparison

In Latin, you can find comparative forms both of adjectives and also of adverbs. Most of the time, comparative forms are used in a direct comparison, as in the motto: *Fortior leone iustus*, "The righteous man is stronger than a lion." In this motto, the comparative form of the adjective, *fortior*, expresses an explicit comparison with a lion: the righteous man is more strong than a lion. Yet it is also possible for comparatives to be used without any explicit comparison. In the fable you are about to read, you will learn that this dog does not just bite people often, *saepe*. Instead, this dog bites people *saepius*, "very often" or "rather often." The comparative form of the adverb, *saepius*, is used here without an explicit comparison. If you want, you can consider this be an implied comparison: this dog bites more often than other dogs do. Here is a Latin saying that likewise uses *saepius* without an explicit comparison: *Laesa saepius, repugnat ovis.* What do you think is the meaning of this proverb? (For more information about comparisons in Latin, see the notes to Fable 39.)

## Vocabulary
### Nouns
**auctoritas (auctoritatis,** *f.*): authority, prestige
**decus (decoris,** *n.*): distinction, honor
**dedecus (dedecoris,** *n.*): dishonor, disgrace
**nola (nolae,** *f.*): bell
**popularis (popularis,** *m/f.*): fellow, compatriot
**tributum (tributi,** *n.*): tribute, contribution

### Adjectives
**mordax (mordacis):** biting

### Verbs
**caveo (cavere):** beware, watch out for
**despicio (despicere):** look down on, despise
**erro (errare):** make a mistake, be wrong
**illigo (illigare), illigavi, illigatus:** tie on, fasten
**moneo (monere):** warn, admonish
**mordeo (mordere):** bite
**reor (reri), ratus sum:** think, suppose

### Other
**scilicet:** of course, you know

*Canis mordens non latrat.*

# DE CANE MORDACI

## Dramatis Personae

*Canis mordens*, the dog who bites, and *Canis sapiens*, the dog who is wise.

Cani, saepius homines mordenti, illigavit Dominus nolam, scilicet ut sibi quisque caveret. Canis, ratus virtuti suae tributum hoc decus esse, populares omnes despicit. Accedit tandem ad hunc Canem aliquis, iam aetate et auctoritate gravis, monens eum ne erret. "Nam ista nola (inquit) data est tibi in dedecus, non in decus."

## Grammar Notes

**saepius homines mordenti.** The comparative adverb **saepius** indicates "very often, rather often," without an explicit comparison (see the *Grammar Overview* for this fable).

**tributum hoc decus esse.** Accusative plus infinitive construction in indirect statement (see Fable 7), with **hoc decus** as the accusative subject and **tributum** as the predicate noun.

**aliquis.** The pronoun **aliquis** refers to some other dog: **aliquis (canis).**

*Cave tibi a cane muto et aqua silenti.*

Racemum dependentem frustra conata est vulpecula iteratis saltibus attingere.

# Fable 29.
# DE VULPE ET UVA
## (Barlow 93)

## Introduction
### The Fox and The Grapes

This Aesop's fable about the fox and the grapes is the origin of the famous English phrase, "Sour grapes!" As you will learn from the fable, however, the grapes are not necessarily sour at all, even if the fox says that they are. Many people today know the phrase "sour grapes," but they do not know this fable about the fox and exactly what the phrase implies. So, after reading this fable, you will be one of the few people who know the story! Here is the moral that Joseph Jacobs gives to the fable: "It is easy to despise what you cannot get." How would you express the moral of this story about the fox and the supposedly sour grapes?

For another story about a frustrated fox, see the fable of the fox and the stork (Fable 19). To see a different kind of grudging behavior, look at the fable of the dog in the manger (Fable 2). For another famous phrase that comes from an Aesop's fable, see the story of "the lion's share" (Fable 73).

## Grammar Overview
### Ambiguous Parts of Speech

As you saw in Fable 27, the supine is a verbal noun belonging to the fourth declension. The stem of the supine in turn provides the basis for the perfect passive participle, a verbal adjective. The perfect passive participle is in turn a component of verbs in the perfect, pluperfect and future perfect tenses. So, when you meet a word like *conatus*, you might be dealing with a verbal noun (the supine, *conatus*), a verbal adjective (the participle, *conatus*) or part of a verbal phrase (as in *conatus est, conatus erat,* etc.). In the fable you are about to read, you will see one form of the word *conatus* that is part of a verbal phrase (*conata est*) and another form that is a noun (*conatibus*). So, make sure you pay attention both to the word endings and also to the context in order to identify the part of speech you are dealing with! English, too, is full of ambiguous words, including many words that are spelled the same way, but that are different parts of speech and that are even pronounced differently—something that makes English a quite difficult language to learn. Just to take one example: I could tell you that I live in a "commune" (noun), where I "commune" (verb) with nature. Can you think of any other English word pairs in which different parts of speech are spelled the same way, but pronounced differently? (Hint: What do you write on the front of a letter so that it will reach its destination? And what does the O stand for in the abbreviation, S-V-O, "Subject - Verb - ???")

# Vocabulary
## *Nouns*

**conatus (conatus,** *m.***):** effort, attempt
**humus (humi,** *f.***):** ground, soil
**racemus (racemi,** *m.***):** bunch, cluster
**saltus (saltus,** *m.***):** leap, jump
**uva (uvae,** *f.***):** grape
**vulpecula (vulpeculae,** *f.***):** fox, vixen

## *Adjectives*

**acerbus, acerba, acerbum:** harsh, bitter
**cassus, cassa, cassum:** hollow, fruitless
**immaturus, immatura, immaturum:** unripe, untimely
**indignabundus, indignabunda, indignabundum:** indignant, outraged
**sordidus, sordida, sordidum:** nasty, filthy

## *Verbs*

**attingo (attingere):** touch, reach
**attollo (attollere):** raise up, lift on high
**conor (conari), conatus sum:** try, attempt
**defatigo (defatigare), defatigavi, defatigatus:** tire out, exhaust
**dependeo (dependere):** hang, hang down
**iaceo (iacere):** lie, lie down
**itero (iterare), iteravi, iteratus:** repeat
**offero (offere):** offer, present
**recedo (recedere), recessi, recessus:** go away, depart

## *Other*

**apage:** begone, away with
**frustra:** in vain, unsuccessfully
**gratis:** freely, at no cost
**omnino:** altogether, completely
**sane:** truly, surely

# DE VULPE ET UVA

## Dramatis Persona

*Vulpecula*, the fox.

Racemum dependentem frustra conata est Vulpecula iteratis saltibus attingere. Sed tandem conatibus cassis omnino defatigata, indignabunda recessit, inquiens, "Apage acerbas et immaturas istas uvas, quae sane tam sordidae sunt ut ne quidem humi iacentes attollerem, si mihi gratis offerrentur."

## Grammar Notes

**indignabunda recessit.** The adjective **indignabunda** modifies the subject of the verb, so you might want to translate it as an adverb, rather than an adjective (see Fable 36).

**inquiens.** This is the present active participle of the defective verb **inquam,** used to indicate a direct quotation (see Fable 62).

**ne quidem humi iacentes attollerem.** The use of **ne** with the particle **quidem** expresses the sense of "not even if."

**humi iacentes.** The form **humi** is locative, meaning "on the ground."

**apage uvas.** The interjection **apage** regularly appears with the accusative of exclamation (see Fable 42).

*Edentulus vescentium dentibus invidet.*

Grus os e gutture lupi extrahit.

# Fable 30.
# DE LUPO ET GRUE
## (Barlow 82)

## Introduction
### The Wolf and The Crane

In this fable, the crane relies on her extremely long beak in order to do the wolf a favor. In the end, however, the crane learns that there is not much point in doing favors for wolves! The moral in Sir Roger L'Estrange's seventeenth-century version of the fable makes the comparison between wolves and humans very clear: "One good turn, they say, requires another, but yet he that has to do with wild beasts (as some men are no better) and comes off with a whole skin, let him expect no other reward." G. F. Townsend puts it more simply: "In serving the wicked, expect no reward, and be thankful if you escape injury for your pains." Based on what happens to the crane in this story, what words would you use to express the moral of the fable?

For other stories about misplaced generosity, see the fable of the hedgehogs and the vipers (Fable 76), the trees who helped make an axe (Fable 10), or the peasant who found a snake in the snow (Fable 35).

## Grammar Overview
### The Partitive Genitive

One of the most common uses of the genitive in Latin is the so-called partitive genitive, when the genitive is used to indicate a portion or a part of something. For example, in this fable you will see that the wolf thinks the crane has received "enough (of a) reward," *satis pretii*. In English, we sometimes use the word "of" with "enough," as in the statement, "I've had enough of that!" Yet we also use the word "enough" without the word "of" in expressions like "enough time" or "enough money." The presence or absence of the word "of" in English is purely idiomatic, and is not a good predictor of when you can expect to find the genitive in Latin. For example, the Latin word *satis* always takes a complement in the genitive case, so you would render the English phrase "enough money" as *satis pecuniae* in Latin, "enough (of) money." There is a famous saying in Latin that uses the word *nihil*, nothing, with a partitive genitive: *Nihil novi sub sole*, "There is nothing (of) new under the sun." Do you happen to know where the phrase comes from? (Hint: It is from a book in the Bible.)

## Vocabulary

### Nouns

**dens (dentis,** *m.***):** tooth, fang
**guttur (gutturis,** *n.***):** throat, gullet
**iactura (iacturae,** *f.***):** loss, damage
**os (ossis,** *n.***):** bone
**pretium (pretii,** *n.***):** reward, prize

### Verbs

**acuo (acuere):** sharpen
**crucio (cruciare):** torment, torture
**educo (educere), eduxi, eductus:** draw out, take out
**extraho (extrahere), extraxi, extractus:** pull out, extract
**offero (offere), obtuli, oblatus:** offer, present
**postulo (postulare):** demand, require
**promitto (promittere):** promise
**retineo (retinere), retinui, retentus:** hold back, trap
**subrideo (subridere):** smile, grin

### Other

**multum:** much, greatly, a lot

*Bonis nocet qui malis parcit.*

# DE LUPO ET GRUE

## Dramatis Personae

*Lupus*, the wolf, and *Grus*, the crane.

Lupus, osse in gutture retento, cum multum cruciaretur, Grui pretium obtulit, si illud e gutture extraheret. Grus autem, cum os e gutture Lupi extraxerat, pretium sibi promissum postulat. Cui Lupus, subridens simulque dentes acuens, dixit, "Satis pretii tibi esse debet quod ex meo ore caput sine capitis iactura eduxeris."

## Grammar Notes

**osse retento.** Ablative absolute construction (see Fable 8).

**cum multum cruciaretur.** The subjunctive, introduced by **cum**, gives causal background information; this is why the wolf needed the crane's help.

**si illud extraheret.** The pronoun refers to the bone: **illud (os)**.

**grus autem.** For the postpositive particle **autem**, see Fable 16.

**grus cum os extraxerat.** Note the use of **cum** plus an indicative verb (see Fable 22).

**cui lupus dixit.** The referent of the relative pronoun **cui** is **grus** in the previous sentence (see Fable 4): **cui (grui) lupus dixit.**

**satis pretii.** The noun **pretii** is a partitive genitive (see the *Grammar Overview* for this fable): **satis** (enough) **pretii** (of a reward) = "enough reward."

**satis pretii tibi esse debet quod.** The implied subject of the verb **debet** provides the referent of the relative pronoun **quod**: "(It) should be reward enough for you that . . ."

**quod caput eduxeris.** The subjunctive, introduced by the relative pronoun **quod**, gives causal background information; according to the wolf, this is the reason why the crane has received enough of a reward already.

*Hodie mihi, cras tibi.*

*Ex amico fit inimicus,*
*hostis ex socio.*

# Fable 31.
# DE VULPE ET AQUILA
## (Barlow 10)

## Introduction
### The Fox and The Eagle

There are many different versions of this fable about what happens when an eagle kidnaps the offspring of a fox. In some versions of the story, the fox is able to rescue her pups from the eagle, unharmed. In other versions of the story, the eagle feeds the baby foxes to her chicks, whereupon the fox sets fire to the eagle's nest and then devours the eagle's chicks one by one as they fall from the burning nest. So, be prepared: the story you are about to read could go either way. After you see how things turn out at the end of this version of the story, what would you say is the moral of the fable?

For some more stories about eagles, see the fable of the eagle and the tortoise (Fable 39), or the battle between the birds and the beasts (Fable 8). For another story about the fox and her litter, see the debate between the lioness and the fox (Fable 1).

## Grammar Overview
### The Future Active Periphrastic, Subjunctive

In Fable 25, you saw an example of the future active participle used with an indicative form of the verb "to be" in order to create the future active periphrastic, a round-about way of referring to the future. In this fable, you will see the future active participle combined with *esset*, a subjunctive form of the verb "to be." The fox grabs up a torch, *quasi nidum incendio absumptura esset*, "as if she were about to destroy the nest with fire." Normally, Latin does not have subjunctive forms for the future tense, but this periphrastic form allows you to combine a sense of futurity (in the future active participle *absumptura*) with a hypothetical mood (in the subjunctive verb *esset*). You can tell that the subjunctive here has a hypothetical quality from the use of the word *quasi*, which is really a compound of two words: *qua* (as) + *si* (if), meaning "as if." Like the word *si*, the word *quasi* can introduce a hypothetical statement in Latin. Do you recognize that the word "quasi" is an English word, too? Look up the word "quasi" in an English dictionary if you are not sure about its meaning in English: can you see how the meaning of the English "quasi" derives from the Latin *quasi*? (For more about future periphrastic constructions, see the notes to Fable 69.)

# Vocabulary

## Nouns

**fax (facis,** *f.***):** torch, firebrand
**incendium (incendii,** *n.***):** fire, conflagration
**liberi (liberorum,** *m.***):** children
**nidus (nidi,** *m.***):** nest
**proles (prolis,** *f.***):** offspring, young
**pullus (pulli,** *m.***):** chick, young bird

## Adjectives

**captivus, captiva, captivum:** imprisoned, caught
**parvus, parva, parvum:** small, little

## Verbs

**absumo (absumere), absumpsi, absumptus:** consume, destroy
**accurro (accurrere):** run to, run up
**comprehendo (comprehendere), comprehendi, comprehensus:** grasp, seize
**corripio (corripere), corripui, correptus:** seize, carry off
**dimitto (dimittere):** let go, send away
**excurro (excurrere):** run out, sally forth
**imploro (implorare):** beg for, call for
**insequor (insequi):** pursue, chase after
**nanciscor (nancisci), nactus sum:** find, stumble on
**parco (parcere):** be sparing, show consideration
**subvolo (subvolare):** fly up
**trepido (trepidare):** tremble, fear

## Other

**foris:** outside, out of doors
**quidquid:** whatever, everything

# DE VULPE ET AQUILA

## Dramatis Personae

*Vulpes*, the fox, and *Aquila*, the eagle.

Dum Vulpis proles foris excurrebant, ab Aquila comprehensae Matris fidem implorabant. Accurrit Vulpes Aquilamque rogat ut captivam prolem dimittat. Aquila, nacta praedam, ad pullos subvolat. Vulpes, correpta face, quasi nidum incendio absumptura esset, insequitur. Trepidans Aquila: "Parce (inquit) mihi parvisque liberis, et tuum quidquid habeo reddidero."

## Grammar Notes

**nacta praedam.** The deponent participle **nacta** is transitive and takes a direct object in the accusative (see Fable 9).

**correpta face.** Ablative absolute construction (see Fable 8).

**quasi absumptura esset.** The future active participle with verb **esset** creates a future active periphrastic construction (see the *Grammar Overview* for this fable); the mood is subjunctive, introduced by **quasi.**

**parce mihi parvisque liberis.** The verb **parce** takes a dative complement.

**tuum quidquid habeo reddidero.** The idea is that "whatever I have (which is) yours," with the entire phrase being the object of the verb **reddidero.**

*Ut tibi, sic alteri.*

*Estote simplices sicut columbae.*

*Sub nomine pacis bellum latet.*

# Fable 32.
# DE COLUMBIS ET ACCIPITRE
## (Barlow 16)

## Introduction
### The Doves and The Hawk

Even today, we use the dove as a symbol of peace, while the hawk is a symbol of war. So, not surprisingly, things do not go well for the doves in this fable when they choose the hawk to be their king. G. F. Townsend applies this moral to the fable: "Avoid a remedy that is worse than the disease." The poet Christopher Smart expressed the moral in a rhyming couplet: "He that would have the wicked reign / instead of help will find his bane." Can you invent a rhyming moral for this story, either in English or in Latin?

For more stories about the hawk, see the fable of the hawk and the nightingale (Fable 6), or the hawk caught in a farmhouse (Fable 18). For another story about foolishly submitting to the rule of a king, see the fable of Jupiter and the frogs (Fable 77).

## Grammar Overview
### The Postpositive Particle, Igitur

In this fable, you will find another one of the postpositive particles: *igitur*. Like the explanatory *enim* (Fable 2), the adversative *autem* (Fable 16), and the emphatic *quidem* (Fable 23), the particle *igitur* helps you to see the connection between the current sentence and what has come before. Although *igitur* can indicate a variety of different types of connections, you most commonly see it used to express a logical relationship, alerting you that the current sentence expresses a necessary outcome of the previous sentence. This sense of a logical result or consequence can be expressed in English with the words "therefore" or "so." You may be familiar with the famous example of postpositive *igitur* in the popular Latin drinking song: *Gaudeamus igitur*, "So let us rejoice!" The doves in this fable, alas, are in just the opposite situation, regretting instead of rejoicing: *Paenitebat igitur Columbas incepti*, "the doves, as a result, regretted what they had started." (For another particle that expresses the idea of a logical consequence, see the use of *ergo* in Fable 66.)

## Vocabulary

### Nouns

**inceptum (incepti, *n.*):** undertaking, beginning
**tyrannis (tyrannidis, *f.*):** tyranny, regime

### Adjectives

**incruentus, incruenta, incruentum:** bloodless, without casualties

### Verbs

**deligo (deligere), delegi, delectus:** pick, select
**expugno (expugnare):** assault, conquer
**lanio (laniare):** mangle, tear to pieces
**paeniteo (paenitere):** regret, feel remorse
**patior (pati), passus sum:** suffer, undergo
**rapio (rapere):** grab, snatch
**subeo (subire):** go under, undergo

### Other

**haud:** not
**olim:** formerly, once upon a time
**penitus:** thoroughly, completely
**segniter:** slowly, lazily

*Novus rex, nova lex.*

# DE COLUMBIS ET ACCIPITRE

## Dramatis Personae

*Columbae*, the doves, *Milvus*, the kite, and *Accipiter*, the hawk.

Columbae olim cum Milvo haud incruentum gerebant bellum et, ut Milvum penitus expugnarent, delegerunt sibi regem Accipitrem. Qui rex factus, hostem agit, non regem. Nam, non segnius ac Milvus, Columbas rapit laniatque. Paenitebat igitur Columbas incepti, satius fuisse putantes bella pati Milvi quam Accipitris subire tyrannidem.

## Grammar Notes

**haud incruentum gerebant bellum.** The phrase **haud incruentum bellum** wraps around the verb (see Fable 6).

**delegerunt regem accipitrem.** The nouns **regem** and **accipitrem** are a double predicate (see Fable 71): "the doves chose the hawk (as) their king."

**qui rex factus.** The referent of the relative pronoun **qui** is **accipitrem** in the previous sentence (see Fable 4): **qui (accipiter) rex factus.**

**hostem agit, non regem.** The word **agere** here means "to play the role of, act as."

**segnius.** This is comparative form of the adverb, **segniter.**

**paenitebat igitur.** For the postpositive particle **igitur** in second position, see the *Grammar Overview* for this fable.

**paenitebat columbas incepti.** The impersonal verb **paenitebat** takes an accusative complement for the ones feeling regret, **columbas,** and a genitive complement for the cause of the feeling, **incepti.**

**satius fuisse putantes.** The infinitive **fuisse** is part of an indirect statement (see Fable 7) with the participle **putantes**: "thinking (that) it would have been more satisfactory. . ."

**satius bella pati quam subire tyrannidem.** The word **quam** coordinates a comparison, introduced by **satius**, with the infinitive phrases as the things being compared.

**bella pati.** The deponent infinitive **pati** is transitive and takes a direct object in the accusative (see Fable 9).

Invocata advenit Mors, percontata senex quid secum velit.

# Fable 33.
# DE SENE ET MORTE
## (Barlow 101)

## Introduction
### *The Old Man and Death*

You could consider this fable to be an example of the English saying, "Be careful what you ask for, because you just might get it." The story is about a man who summons Death to come to him—and much to the man's surprise, Death shows up! In some versions of the story, the man is an "old man," and in other versions he is a "poor man," and in some versions, like the one here, the man is suffering from both hardships; he is a *senex misellus*. As you will see, however, the man still has wits about him. What do you think is the lesson we can learn from the actions of the old man in this story?

For more stories about the dangers of getting what you ask for, see the fable of the mouse who married a lion (Fable 37), or the lion who fell in love with a woman (Fable 20). Meanwhile, for the story of an animal on its deathbed, see the fable of the kite and his mother (Fable 27).

## Grammar Overview
### *Intensified Adjectives*

Just as you can add prefixes to verbs in Latin in order to modify their meaning, it is also possible to add prefixes to Latin adjectives. There are two prefixes, *prae-* and *per-*, which can be added to adjectives to intensify their meaning. So, for example, something that is *clarus* in Latin is "clear, bright," while something that is *praeclarus* is "very clear, very bright, splendid." Similarly, if something is *magnus* in Latin, it is "big, large," but if it is *permagnus*, it is "very big, very large, important." In the fable you are about to read, the poor old man is not just *gravatus*, "weighed down," by his burden; he is *praegravatus*, "extremely weighed down." As a result of all his troubles, he is not just disgusted, *taesus*, with his lot in life; he is *pertaesus*, "thoroughly disgusted." Based on your understanding of these prefixes, see if you can identify the meaning of these Latin adjectives: *perbonus - praedulcis - pergrandis - praegravis*. (For more about variations on the standard form of adjectives, see the notes about diminutive adjectives in Fable 67.)

## Vocabulary

### Nouns

**adventus (adventus,** *m.***):** arrival, coming
**auxilium (auxilii,** *n.***):** help
**fascis (fascis,** *m.***):** bundle, packet
**sors (sortis,** *f.***):** fate, lot in life
**umerus (umeri,** *m.***):** shoulder, upper arm

### Adjectives

**aerumnosus, aerumnosa, aerumnosum:** troubled, full of difficulty
**misellus, misella, misellum:** poor, unfortunate
**pertaesus, pertaesa, pertaesum:** tired, disgusted
**praegravatus, praegravata, praegravatum:** weighed down, burdened

### Verbs

**advenio (advenire):** come to, arrive
**collabor (collabi):** fall down, slip down
**defigo (defigere):** fix, pin down
**impono (imponere):** put on, set
**invoco (invocare):** call upon, pray for
**percontor (percontari), percontatus sum:** inquire, ask
**terreo (terrere), terrui, territus:** scare, frighten

### Other

**rursus:** again, in turn

*Timor mortis morte peior.*

# DE SENE ET MORTE

## Dramatis Personae

*Senex*, the old man, and *Mors*, Death.

Fasce praegravatus Senex, et misellae suae pertaesus sortis,
Mortem invocabat, ut finem aerumnosae vitae tandem defigeret.
Invocata advenit Mors, percontata Senex quid secum velit; ad cuius
adventum territus, nil respondit sed "Ut auxilio mihi sis, et fascem
collapsum rursus umeris imponas!"

## Grammar Notes

**misellae suae pertaesus sortis.** The adjective **pertaesus** takes a genitive complement ("be thoroughly tired of"), with the phrase **misellae suae sortis** wrapping around the adjective (see Fable 6).

**senex quid velit.** The word **quid** introduces an indirect question with the subjunctive verb, **velit**, whose subject is **senex**.

**secum.** The reflexive pronoun **se** (**secum** = **cum se**) refers back to **Mors**, the subject of the main verb: "Death asked what an old man wanted with him" (i.e., with Death).

**ad cuius adventum.** The referent of the relative pronoun **cuius** is Death: **ad cuius (Mortis) adventum**.

**ut auxilio mihi sis.** The predicate dative expresses the purpose that Death should serve; the man wants Death to be "helpful" to him (see Fable 61).

*Nemo est tam senex
qui se annum non putet
posse vivere.*

*Absente domino, res male geritur.*

*Stercus optimum vestigium domini.*

# Fable 34.
# DE CERVO IN BOVIUM STABULO
## (Barlow 107)

## Introduction
### The Stag in the Oxen's Stable

You could consider this fable about the stag in the stable to illustrate the old English saying, "One eye of the master sees more than four of the servants." In his seventeenth-century version of this fable, Sir Roger L'Estrange concludes: "He that would be sure to have his business well done, must do it himself." Joseph Jacobs says simply, "Nothing escapes the master's eye." If the poor stag were able to gasp out the moral of the story as he is being attacked at the end by the master and his neighbors, what do you think he might say?

For more stories about the hunted stag, see the fable of the stag gazing at his reflection (Fable 68), or the deer who was caught by an old dog (Fable 61). For another story about the master taking care of business himself, see the fable of the lark in the field (Fable 49).

## Grammar Overview
### Huc et Illuc

In Latin, there is an elegant system of adverbs used to express position in a place, as well as movement from a place or to a place. To express position in a place, you can say *hic* (here) or *illic* (there). To express movement from a place, you can say *hinc* (from here) or *illinc* (from there). To express movement towards a place, you can say *huc* (to here) or *illuc* (to there). English likewise once had a system of adverbs of motion: hither - thither - whither (to here - to there - to where) and hence - thence - whence (from here - from there - from where). When translating from Latin into English, some people like to use old-fashioned English words like "hither" and "thither" in order to make the translation sound a bit lofty or archaic, whereas other people prefer a plain and simple English style. So, if you want to translate this fable about the stag in the stable, you will need to decide if the servant looks "here and there" or "hither and thither" when he comes to the stable to make his inspection! (For a similar dilemma in English language style, see the comments about "neither" and "nor" in Fable 18.)

## Vocabulary
### Nouns
**cornu (cornus,** *n.***):** horn
**fustis (fustis,** *m.***):** club, stick
**servus (servi,** *m.***):** servant, groom
**stabulum (stabuli,** *n.***):** stall, stable
**vicinus (vicini,** *m.***):** neighbor

### Adjectives
**laetabundus, laetabunda, laetabundum:** rejoicing, cheerful
**tutus, tuta, tutum:** safe, secure

### Verbs
**abscondo (abscondere):** hide, conceal
**adeo (adire):** go to, approach
**adorior (adoriri):** assail, attack
**applaudo (applaudere), applausi, applausus:** clap, applaud
**autumo (autumare):** assert, reckon
**circumfero (circumferre):** cast about, move in circles
**confugio (confugere):** flee, take refuge
**decedo (decedere), decessi, decessus:** depart, withdraw
**detego (detegere), detexi, detectus:** uncover, lay bare
**ingredior (ingredi):** enter, go into
**perlustro (perlustrare), perlustravi, perlustratus:** scan, scrutinize
**persequor (persequi), persecutus sum:** chase, overtake

### Other
**curiose:** carefully, diligently
**huc:** here, to this place
**illuc:** to that place, there
**negligenter:** carelessly, indifferently
**nimis:** too much, very much
**oscitanter:** lazily, listlessly
**praeterquam:** except, besides
**statim:** immediately, at once

# DE CERVO IN BOVIUM STABULO

## Dramatis Personae

*Cervus*, the stag, *Servus*, the servant, and *Herus*, the master.

Persecutus a canibus, Cervus ad stabulum bovium confugiebat
et ibi totum corpus, praeterquam cornua, abscondebat. Adibat
stabulum Servus et ille, oscitanter et negligenter huc et illuc
oculos circumferens, mox decessit. Fortunae suae nimis applausit
laetabundus Cervus et sese tutissimum autumabat. Sed statim,
ipso Hero ingrediente locum, et rebus curiosius perlustratis,
cornua Cervi detexit et fustibus cum vicinis adoriebatur.

## Grammar Notes

**persecutus a canibus.** This deponent participle, normally active in meaning, is used passively here, with an ablative of agent, "chased by dogs."

**ille decessit.** The pronoun refers to the servant: **ille (servus) decessit.**

**fortunae suae applausit.** The verb **applausit** takes a dative complement.

**applausit laetabundus cervus.** The adjective **laetabundus** modifies the subject of the verb, so you might want to translate it as an adverb, rather than an adjective (see Fable 36).

**sese tutissimum.** Accusative plus infinitive construction in indirect statement (see Fable 7), with **sese** (alternate form of **se**) as the accusative subject and **tutissimum** as the predicate adjective: **sese (esse) tutissimum** (for this use of the superlative, see Fable 39; for the implied infinitive, see Fable 13).

**hero ingrediente . . . rebus perlustratis.** Ablative absolute constructions (see Fable 8).

**curiosius.** The comparative form of the adverb expresses the idea of "very carefully, quite carefully," without an explicit comparison (see Fable 28).

**adoriebatur.** The deponent verb **adoriebatur** is transitive and takes an implied direct object, **cervum** (see Fable 9).

*Serpens eiiciendus
e domo.*

*Nihil homine ingrato
peius.*

# Fable 35.
# DE RUSTICO ET COLUBRO
## (Barlow 50)

## Introduction
### The Peasant and The Snake

This little story about the peasant and the snake is a perfect example of the English saying, "No good deed goes unpunished." The peasant does a good deed for a snake that he finds frozen in the snow, but things go very wrong once that snake thaws out. The man in this Latin version of the story should consider himself lucky; in other versions of this fable, the snake actually bites the man and kills him! What moral would you give to the story if you wanted to rebuke the snake for its lack of gratitude? What if you wanted instead to criticize the man for having brought the snake home in the first place?

For more stories about misguided good deeds, see the fable of the crane who helped the wolf (Fable 7), or the trees who gave wood for an axe handle (Fable 10). For another story about a dangerous snake, see the fable of the unfortunate birdcatcher (Fable 15).

## Grammar Overview
### The Interrogative Particle, Num

The Latin word *num* is an interrogative particle that is used to introduce a question, anticipating the answer "no." This particle serves much the same function as a question mark in English, but it does more than that, because it also anticipates the answer to the question. There is no easy way to render Latin *num* with a single English word, but the tone of a *num* question in Latin sounds something like "Surely you don't mean that, do you?" or "That isn't really possible, is it?" These kinds of questions, which already posit an answer, are sometimes called rhetorical questions. Rhetorical questions do not solicit information, as a question normally does. Instead, a rhetorical question is posed in order to make a statement of some kind. In this fable, the man uses a rhetorical question beginning with *num* in order to criticize the snake for its behavior, speaking about the snake in the third person and not even addressing it directly: *Num haec est quam retulit gratia?* See if you can find a way to translate the man's question into English in a way that conveys the rhetorical tone of the Latin *num*.

# Vocabulary
## Nouns
**coluber (colubri,** *m.***):** snake, serpent
**flamma (flammae,** *f.***):** flame, blaze
**focus (foci,** *m.***):** hearth, fireplace
**frigus (frigoris,** *n.***):** cold, frost
**iniuria (iniuriae,** *f.***):** injury, injustice
**nix (nivis,** *f.***):** snow
**sudis (sudis,** *f.***):** stake, log
**tugurium (tugurii,** *n.***):** cottage, hut
**verber (verberis,** *n.***):** lash, whipping
**virus (viri,** *n.***):** venom, poison

## Verbs
**accurro (accurrere):** run to, run up
**adiicio (adiicere), adieci, adiectus:** throw to, toss towards
**corripio (corripere), corripui, correptus:** seize, carry off
**eneco (enecare), enecui, enectus:** kill, exhaust
**eripio (eripere):** snatch away, take from
**expostulo (expostulare), expostulavi, expostulatus:** complain, remonstrate
**inficio (inficere), infeci, infectus:** corrupt, poison
**recipio (recipere):** regain, recover
**reperio (reperire), repperi, repertus:** find, discover
**sibilo (sibilare):** hiss, whistle

## Other
**amplius:** more, any more
**num:** introduces question expecting negative answer
**prope:** near, nearly

# DE RUSTICO ET COLUBRO

## Dramatis Personae

*Rusticus*, the peasant, and *Coluber*, the snake.

Rusticus repertum in altiori nive Colubrum, frigore prope enectum, domum tulit et ad focum adiecit. Coluber ab igni vires virusque recipiens et non amplius flammam ferens, totum tugurium sibilando infecit. Accurrit Rusticus et, correpta sude, verbis verberibusque cum eo iniuriam expostulat: "Num haec est quam retulit gratia, eripiendo vitam illi cui vitam debuit?"

## Grammar Notes

**repertum colubrum domum tulit.** You might translate the passive participle with an active verb (see Fable 5): the peasant found the snake (**repertum**) and then carried it home (**tulit**).

**in altiori nive.** The comparative is used here to indicate "very deep, rather deep," without an explicit comparison (see Fable 28).

**domum.** This use of **domum** in the accusative means "to the house, homeward."

**correpta sude.** Ablative absolute construction (see Fable 8).

**haec est quam retulit gratia.** The referent of the relative pronoun **quam** is the noun **gratia** in the main clause: **num haec est gratia?**

**eripiendo vitam illi.** The gerund here takes an accusative object (see Fable 14), along with a dative complement, "snatching away (something) from (somebody)."

*In sinu colubrum habet.*

Asinus oneri totus succubuit et halitum clausit supremum.

# Fable 36.
# DE EQUO ET ASELLO ONUSTO
## (Barlow 100)

## Introduction
### *The Horse and The Laden Donkey*

This fable is one that has been acted out by various casts of characters over the centuries. In an ancient Greek version mentioned by the philosopher Plutarch, the story is about an ox carrying a heavy load who asks a camel for help. In a medieval Latin version of the story, a laboring ox asks a donkey for help. In the version you are about to read here, it is an exhausted donkey who begs a horse to help him. No matter what animals are involved, however, the moral of the story is still the same: the creature who refuses to help another may end up bearing an even bigger burden as a result. If you were going to create your own version of the story, what two animals would you use as the main characters?

For more stories about the need for mutual support and solidarity, see the fable of the lion and the bulls (Fable 66), the farmer and his quarrelsome sons (Fable 71), or the two friends who ran into a bear (Fable 65).

## Grammar Overview
### *Adjectives and Adverbs*

In Latin, the system of nouns and adjectives is very strong and flexible, but the adverb system is much less fully developed. As a result, there are often instances where Latin will use an adjective while in English we might tend to use an adverb instead. This is especially true when Latin uses an adjective to modify the subject of the verb. Consider this example from the fable you are about to read: *asinus oneri totus succubuit*. The adjective *totus* modifies *asinus*, the subject of the verb. So, translated literally, the sentence would read: "The whole donkey collapsed under the weight." That is what the Latin says, but it sounds quite odd in English! If you use an adverb in your English translation, instead of an adjective, the result will sound much more idiomatic: "The donkey collapsed completely under the weight." So, whenever you see an adjective being used to modify the subject of a verb in Latin, it is worth thinking about whether that adjective really belongs with the noun, or whether it is perhaps better rendered in English with an adverb instead. (Similarly, if you are translating from English into Latin or composing in Latin, think twice before you use an adverb: there are many situations where we might use an adverb in English, while Latin would prefer to use an adjective instead.)

## Vocabulary
### *Nouns*
**asellus (aselli,** *m.***):** donkey, little donkey
**coriarius (coriarii,** *m.***):** tanner, leather-worker
**halitus (halitus,** *m.***):** breath, exhalation
**onus (oneris,** *n.***):** burden, load
**pellis (pellis,** *f.***):** skin, hide
**portiuncula (portiunculae,** *f.***):** small part, tiny portion
**sarcina (sarcinae,** *f.***):** pack, bundle
**socius (socii,** *m.***):** ally, partner

### *Adjectives*
**misellus, misella, misellum:** poor, unfortunate
**onustus, onusta, onustum:** laden, burdened
**supremus, suprema, supremum:** highest, last

### *Verbs*
**agito (agitare):** drive, guide
**claudo (claudere), clausi, clausus:** conclude, finish
**cogo (cogere):** compel, drive
**detraho (detrahere), detraxi, detractus:** drag down, take off
**excorio (excoriare), excoriavi, excoriatus:** flay, strip
**fatisco (fatiscere):** give way, wear out
**impono (imponere), imposui, impositus:** put on, set
**ingemo (ingemere), ingemui, ingemitus:** groan, moan
**recuso (recusare):** refuse, decline
**sentio (sentire), sensi, sensus:** perceive, feel
**succumbo (succumbere), succubui:** collapse, lie down
**succurro (succurrere):** run to help, assist
**superaddo (superaddere), superaddidi, superadditus:** add on to, heap on top
**tolero (tolerare):** bear, endure

### *Other*
**una:** together

# DE EQUO ET ASELLO ONUSTO

## Dramatis Personae

*Coriarius*, the tanner, *Equus*, the horse, and *Asinus*, the donkey.

Agitabat Coriarius quidam una Equum et Asinum onustum.
Sed in via fatiscens, Asinus rogabat Equum ut sibi succurreret et
velit portiunculam oneris tanti tolerare. Recusabat Equus et mox
Asinus oneri totus succubuit et halitum clausit supremum. Herus
accedens mortuo Asino sarcinam detraxit et, pelle superaddita
excoriata, omnia Equo imposuit. Quod cum sensisset Equus,
ingemuit, inquiens, "Quam misellus ego, qui, cum portiunculam
oneris socii ferre recusaverim, iam totam sarcinam cogar tolerare."

## Grammar Notes

**oneri totus succubuit.** The verb **succubuit** takes a dative complement, **oneri,** while the adjective **totus** modifies the subject of the verb, so you might want to translate it as an adverb, rather than an adjective (see the *Grammar Overview* for this fable).

**halitum clausit supremum.** The phrase **halitum supremum** wraps around the verb (see Fable 6).

**asino sarcinam detraxit.** The verb **detraxit** takes a direct object, **sarcinam**, as well as a dative complement, **asino**: "take (something) off (somebody)."

**pelle superaddita excoriata.** An ablative absolute construction (see Fable 8), consisting of the ablative participle **superaddita** and the ablative noun phrase **pelle excoriata** (the hide that the man has stripped from the donkey).

**quod cum sensisset equus.** The relative pronoun **quod** connects back to the previous sentence (see Fable 4), referring to the general situation described there, i.e., the horse having to bear all the extra weight; the subjunctive, introduced by **cum**, gives causal background information as to why the horse groaned (for the placement of **quod** before **cum,** see Fable 37).

**inquiens.** This is the present active participle of the defective verb **inquam,** used to indicate a direct quotation (see Fable 62).

**quam misellus ego.** The verb sum is implied: **quam misellus ego (sum),** "how miserable am I!"

**cum portiunculam ferre recusaverim.** The subjunctive, introduced by **cum**, gives causal background information; this is why the horse now has to carry the whole load.

Nova nupta, ad virum veniens, casu illum pede pressit et contrivit.

# Fable 37.
# DE LEONE ET MURE
## (Barlow 24)

## Introduction
### *The Lion and The Mouse*

In this Renaissance fable by the Latin author Abstemius, there are two stories combined into one. The first story is a famous fable that goes back to ancient Rome: the story of the mouse who rescued a lion from a trap (see Fable 67). The second story, invented by Abstemius, is about what happened next: the story of how the mouse married the lion's daughter. Unfortunately for the mouse, this marriage does not turn out at all as he had hoped. If the mouse could manage to squeak a few words at the end of this fable, what do you think he would say is the lesson he has learned, at the cost of his life?

For another story of mismatched love, see what happened when a man fell in love with a cat (Fable 75). For more stories by Abstemius, see the fable of the bear and the bees (Fable 41), or the vipers and the hedgehogs (Fable 76).

## Grammar Overview
### *Relative Pronouns and Cum Clauses*

It is usually easy to recognize a *cum* clause in Latin because, at least in prose, the word *cum* likes to come first in the clause. Yet sometimes the word *cum* can be displaced by another word, and does not appear first in its clause. For example, when you are dealing with a relative pronoun, the relative pronoun has an even greater tendency to come first (this makes sense, of course, because a relative pronoun is almost always making a direct connection to something stated previously). So, don't be surprised when you see a combination of a relative clause and a *cum* clause in which the relative pronoun comes before the *cum*, as in this sentence from the fable you are about to read: *Quod cum Mus fecisset . . .* , "Which thing when the mouse had done. . ." (in other words, "When the mouse had done this thing. . ."). Even though the word *cum* does not come first, this entire phrase—*quod cum Mus fecisset*—is still a *cum* clause. If you follow the advice given in the notes to Fable 19, you might choose to replace the *quod* with *hoc*, and rearrange the clause with *cum* in first position: *Cum Mus hoc fecisset.* Such a variation breaks the direct connection with the preceding sentence that is indicated by the relative pronoun *quod*, but it does make it more clear that what you are dealing with here is, in fact, a *cum* clause.

## Vocabulary
### *Nouns*
**benefactor** (**benefactoris,** *m.*): benefactor
**beneficium** (**beneficii,** *n.*): kindness, favor
**casus** (**casus,** *m.*): chance, accident
**filia** (**filiae,** *f.*): daughter
**laqueus** (**laquei,** *m.*): snare, trap
**nupta** (**nuptae,** *f.*): bride
**uxor** (**uxoris,** *f.*): wife

### *Adjectives*
**gratus, grata, gratum:** agreeable, acceptable
**immemor** (**immemoris**): unmindful, forgetful

### *Verbs*
**abnuo** (**abnuere**), **abnui:** refuse, decline
**abrodo** (**abrodere**), **abrosi, abrosus:** gnaw away, chew off
**contero** (**conterere**), **contrivi, contritus:** crush, grind into bits
**explico** (**explicare**): unfold, untangle
**irretio** (**irretire**), **irretivi, irretitus:** entangle, catch in a net
**libero** (**liberare**): set free, release
**premo** (**premere**), **pressi, pressus:** press, press upon
**promitto** (**promittere**): promise
**trado** (**tradere**): hand over, bestow

### *Other*
**prompte:** willingly, readily

# DE LEONE ET MURE

## Dramatis Personae

*Leo*, the lion, and *Mus*, the mouse.

Leo, laqueo captus, cum ita se irretitum videret ut nullis viribus sese explicare posset, Murem rogavit, ut, abroso laqueo, eum liberaret, promittens tanti beneficii se non futurum immemorem. Quod cum Mus prompte fecisset, Leonem rogavit ut filiam eius sibi traderet in uxorem. Nec abnuit Leo ut benefactori suo rem gratam faceret. Nova autem nupta, ad virum veniens, cum eum non videret, casu illum pede pressit et contrivit.

## Grammar Notes

**cum videret.** The subjunctive, introduced by **cum**, gives causal background information; this is why the lion had to ask the mouse for help.

**se irretitum.** Accusative plus infinitive construction in indirect statement (see Fable 7): **se irretitum (esse).**

**abroso laqueo.** Ablative absolute construction (see Fable 8).

**beneficii immemorem.** The adjective **immemorem** takes a genitive complement.

**se non futurum immemorem.** Accusative plus infinitive construction in indirect statement, with **se** as the accusative subject and **immemorem** as the predicate adjective: **se non futurum (esse) immemorem.**

**quod cum mus prompte fecisset.** The relative pronoun **quod** connects back to the previous sentence (see Fable 4), referring to the general situation described there, i.e., setting the lion free; the subjunctive, introduced by **cum**, gives causal background information as to why the mouse was able to ask the lion for a favor (see the *Grammar Overview* for this fable).

**traderet in uxorem.** This idiom is roughly like the English phrase, "bestow in marriage."

**nec abnuit leo.** You can replace the word nec with the words **et non** (see Fable 18): **et non abnuit leo,** "and the lion did not refuse."

**nova autem nupta.** For the postpositive particle **autem,** see Fable 16.

**cum eum non videret.** The subjunctive, introduced by **cum**, gives causal background information; this is why the lioness stepped on the mouse.

*Neminem pecunia
divitem fecit.*

*Gallus in sterquilinio suo
plurimum potest.*

# Fable 38.
# DE GALLO GALLINACEO
## (Barlow 1)

## Introduction
### The Barnyard Rooster

There are two very different versions of this fable. In one version, the rooster is a negative exemplum, a foolish creature who does not recognize something of real value. He can only understand the simple things that are familiar to him (like barley), and he cannot understand something truly exquisite and rare (a gemstone). In the other way of telling this story, the rooster is a positive exemplum, a creature who wisely prefers some plain, simple food (like barley), to something that is beautiful but useless (a gemstone). So, after you read this story, you need to decide which version you are dealing with here. Is this particular Latin rooster a wise bird, or a foolish one?

For more stories about the choice between a simple life and luxury, see the fable of the city mouse and the country mouse (Fable 4), the wolf and the dog (Fable 80), or the donkey and the horse (Fable 21).

## Grammar Overview
### Hypothetical Statements

In this fable, you will meet with two different hypothetical statements. The first hypothetical statement is introduced by *si* ("if"), a word you are used to seeing with the subjunctive: *si gemmarius invenisset* . . . If a jeweler had found the jewel, as the rooster explains, things would have turned out differently—but a jeweler did not find the jewel; the rooster did. As the rooster ponders the irony of the situation, he uses a different word, *quamvis* ("although, even if"), to introduce another hypothetical statement: *quamvis micent,* "even if the jewels do gleam." So, be prepared to find words other than *si* in Latin that introduce hypothetical statements using subjunctive verbs. One of the most common functions of the subjunctive in Latin is to express a hypothetical sense of possibility or potential, and there are many Latin words and phrases—not just *si* and *nisi*—which are used to introduce these subjunctive statements. (For an example of *licet* with the subjunctive, see Fable 40.)

# Vocabulary

## Nouns

**gemma (gemmae,** *f.*): jewel, gem
**gemmarius (gemmarii,** *m.*): jeweller
**granum (grani,** *n.*): grain, seed
**hordeum (hordei,** *n.*): barley, barley-corn
**invidia (invidiae,** *f.*): envy, grudge
**opprobrium (opprobrii,** *n.*): reproach, shame
**pretium (pretii,** *n.*): prize, price
**sterquilinium (sterquilinii,** *n.*): dung heap
**usus (usus,** *m.*): use, enjoyment

## Adjectives

**armatus, armata, armatum:** armor-clad, spurred
**fulgurans (fulgurantis):** glittering, flashing
**gallinaceus, gallinacea, gallinaceum:** poultry, barnyard
**laetabundus, laetabunda, laetabundum:** rejoicing, cheerful
**pretiosus, pretiosa, pretiosum:** valuable, precious

## Verbs

**aestimo (aestimare):** assess, consider
**disiicio (disiicere):** toss aside, break up
**dissipo (dissipare):** scatter, disperse
**exulto (exultare):** jump about, rejoice
**mico (micare):** sparkle, gleam
**reperio (reperire):** find, discover

## Other

**etenim:** as a matter of fact, because
**quamvis:** although, even if
**quid:** why, for what reason
**quippe:** obviously, as you see

# DE GALLO GALLINACEO

## Dramatis Persona

*Gallus gallinaceus*, the rooster.

Gallus gallinaceus, dum armato pede sterquilinium dissipando disiicit, invenit gemmam: "Quid (inquiens) rem tam fulgurantem reperio? Si gemmarius invenisset, laetabundus exultaret, quippe qui scivit pretium. Mihi quidem nulli est usui, nec magni aestimo. Unum etenim hordei granum est mihi longe pretiosius quam omnes gemmae, quamvis ad invidiam micent diei opprobriumque solis."

## Grammar Notes

**sterquilinium dissipando disiicit.** The gerund is used here in the ablative case (see Fable 48).

**quid (inquiens) rem reperio?** The interrogative **quid** here means "why? for what reason?" (see Fable 21), with the present participle **inquiens** indicating a direct quotation (see Fable 62).

**quippe qui scivit pretium.** The particle **quippe** is often used with the relative pronoun to mean "inasmuch as (he is) someone who . . ."

**mihi quidem.** For the postpositive particle **quidem,** see Fable 23.

**mihi nulli est usui.** The predicate dative expresses the purpose the jewel serves for the rooster; it is **nulli usui,** "no use" to him (see Fable 61).

**nec magni aestimo.** You can replace the word **nec** with the words **et non** (see Fable 18), with the predicate genitive expressing a quantity of value: **et non magni aestimo,** "and I do not consider it to be of great value."

**pretiosius quam.** The word **quam** coordinates a comparison introduced by the comparative adjective, **pretiosius** (neuter singular, agreeing with **granum**).

**quamvis ad invidiam micent diei.** The phrase **ad invidiam diei** wraps around the verb (see Fable 6); the subjunctive, introduced by **quamvis,** states a hypothetical possibility (see the *Grammar Overview* for this fable): "even if (the jewels) gleam to (the point that they are) the envy of the daylight."

**opprobrium solis.** This construction parallels **ad invidiam diei**, with the preposition **ad** omitted: **(quamvis micent ad) opprobrium solis**, "and even if they gleam to the point that they are the sun's shame (i.e., a source of shame for the sun)."

*Iam testudo volat.*

*Aquilam testudo vincit.*

# Fable 39.
# DE AQUILA ET TESTUDINE
## (Barlow 110)

## Introduction
### The Eagle and The Tortoise

You are probably familiar with the famous fable about the race between the tortoise and the hare (see Fable 57). In the fable you are about to read here, the tortoise is going to race against another swift opponent: the eagle. Of course, you won't be surprised to discover that the tortoise manages to win this race, too. This story about the eagle and the tortoise is not found in the ancient collections of Aesop's fables, but it is included as one of the proverbs in the *Adagia* of Erasmus: *Aquilam testudo vincit*, "The tortoise defeats an eagle." What moral would you give to this story if you wanted to praise the tortoise for her victory? What moral would you use if you wanted instead to rebuke the eagle for her defeat?

For another story about the eagle's defeat by a weaker creature, see the fable of the fox and the eagle (Fable 31). For other boastful animals, see the fable of the frog and the ox (Fable 14), or the peacock debating with the crane (Fable 7).

## Grammar Overview
### The Superlative without Comparison

Just as the Latin comparative can be used in the absence of a specific comparison (see Fable 28), the superlative form can also be used without any specific comparison being made. Used in this way, the superlative form simply expresses the supreme, absolute degree of an adjective. In this fable, for example, you will see that the eagle is described as *velocissima*, "supremely fast, incredibly fast." You can also consider this use of the superlative to express an implied comparison, "the fastest of all." The same is true for the superlative form of the adverb, as when the eagle thinks she will reach the finish line *brevissime*, "incredibly quickly" or "the most quickly of all." This independent use of the superlative in Latin is quite common, as you can see, for example, in this proverb about friendship: *Firmissima inter pares amicitia*. How would you translate the superlative *firmissima* as it is used in this saying?

# Vocabulary
## *Nouns*
**ala (alae,** *f.***)**: wing
**calculus (calculi,** *m.***)**: reckoning, calculation
**certamen (certaminis,** *n.***)**: contest, competition
**impetus (impetus,** *m.***)**: attack, charge
**sollertia (sollertiae,** *f.***)**: skill, cleverness
**spatium (spatii,** *n.***)**: space, time
**victor (victoris,** *m.***)**: winner, victor

## *Adjectives*
**indefatigabilis, indefatigabile (indefatigabilis)**: untiring, tireless
**intentus, intenta, intentum:** attentive, eager
**negligens (negligentis)**: careless, indifferent
**reptilis, reptile (reptilis)**: creeping, crawling
**tardigradus, tardigrada, tardigradum:** slow-paced, limping
**velox (velocis)**: rapid, swift

## *Verbs*
**arrepo (arrepere), arrepsi, arreptus:** creep up to
**autumo (autumare)**: think, reckon
**avolo (avolare)**: fly away, fly off
**contemno (contemnere), contempsi, contemptus:** scorn, disparage
**designo (designare), designavi, designatus:** select, appoint
**evado (evadere), evasi, evasus:** get out, turn out to be
**ineo (inire)**: go in, enter into
**propono (proponere), proposui, propositus:** put forward, propose
**saluto (salutare)**: greet, hail
**secedo (secedere), secessi, secessus:** withdraw, secede

## *Other*
**breviter:** shortly, briefly
**infra:** below, beneath
**prius:** before, earlier

# DE AQUILA ET TESTUDINE

## Dramatis Personae

*Testudo*, the turtle, and *Aquila*, the eagle.

Certamen inire voluit Testudo reptilis cum Aquila velocissima. Locus designatus est et, qui spatio trium dierum ad propositum locum prius venerat, victor salutaretur. Aquila tardigradam contempsit Testudinem, autumans se alarum impetu posse brevissime ad locum avolare. Negligens igitur secessit, aliis intenta, sed Testudo indefatigabili labore et sollertia infra tempus et ante Aquilam arrepsit ad locum et omnium calculis victor evasit.

## Grammar Notes

**victor salutaretur.** The subjunctive expresses the hypothetical result of what happens to the one who reaches the finish line first within the allotted time: "he would be hailed (as) the winner" (for **victor** as a predicate noun, see Fable 71).

**tardigradam contempsit testudinem.** The phrase **tardigradam testudinem** wraps around the verb (see Fable 6).

**se posse.** Accusative plus infinitive construction in indirect statement (see Fable 7).

**brevissime.** This is the superlative form of the adverb, **breviter** (see the *Grammar Overview* for this fable).

**negligens igitur.** For the postpositive particle **igitur,** see Fable 32.

**infra tempus.** The phrase means "within (under) the time limit."

**victor evasit.** The noun **victor** is part of the predicate: "turned out to be the winner, " "emerged (as) the winner."

Herus, qui vagum fallacemque asinum perdiderat, occurrit.

# Fable 40.
# DE ASINO LEONIS PELLE INDUTO
## (Barlow 72)

## Introduction
### The Donkey Dressed in a Lion's Skin

The donkey is an animal who doesn't get a lot of respect, so in this fable he decides to disguise himself as a lion. The disguise seems to work at first, but in the end the donkey's true identity is revealed. In some versions of this fable, the donkey gives himself away by starting to bray loudly, and everybody can tell that a donkey's bray is different from a lion's roar. In other versions of the story, the people see the would-be lion's feet, and they recognize the hooves of a donkey. As you read this Latin version of the story, pay attention to just what it is that betrays the donkey's identity. If the donkey were to bray a few words at the end of the fable, what do you think he might say about the lesson he has learned?

For more stories about donkeys, see the fable about the donkey who chased a lion (Fable 60), or the humble donkey and the horse (Fable 21). For another animal in disguise, see the fable of the wolf in sheep's clothing (Fable 23).

## Grammar Overview
### The Emphatic Use of Personal Pronouns

Latin finite verbs express both person and number much more clearly than English verbs do. In Latin, if you say *clamo*, it is clear that the subject of the verb is *ego*, first person singular: "I shout." As a result of the information about person and number already conveyed by the verb itself, the nominative forms of the first person and second person pronouns—*ego, tu, nos, vos*—do not need to accompany the verb as they do in English. Yet sometimes these nominative pronouns are used in Latin for emphasis. The verb already tells you the subject, and by adding in the pronoun as well, you can throw even more emphasis on the identity of that subject. For example, in this fable, when the master says to the donkey: *ego te novi*, "I know you," the pronoun *ego* provides a parallel to the accusative pronoun, *ego - te*, while also emphasizing the contrast between the master, who knows the donkey, and other people, who don't. So, whenever you see the nominative forms *ego, tu, nos* or *vos*, they are there for a reason—a stylistic reason, not a grammatical one. Consider, for example, this famous saying attributed to Diocletian, who was the emperor of Rome during the late third century CE: *Ego apros occido, sed alter fruitur pulpamento.* What does this saying mean, and how does the inclusion of the word *ego* contribute to that meaning? (To get the full sense of the saying in its historical context, take a look at the *Historia Augusta: Life of Carus, Numerian and Carinus.*)

# Vocabulary

## *Nouns*

**armentum (armenti,** *n.*): herd, cattle
**auricula (auriculae,** *f.*): ear, little ear
**exuviae (exuviarum,** *f.*): skin, something that is shed
**grex (gregis,** *m.*): flock, herd
**pascuum (pascui,** *n.*): pasture
**pellis (pellis,** *f.*): skin, hide
**rugitus (rugitus,** *m.*): roar, bellow

## *Adjectives*

**fallax (fallacis)**: deceitful, misleading
**vagus, vaga, vagum:** wandering, unreliable

## *Verbs*

**exto (extare)**: stand out, protrude
**fallo (fallere)**: deceive, beguile
**fugo (fugare)**: chase away, put to flight
**induo (induere), indui, indutus:** put on, dress in
**occurro (occurrere)**: run into, meet
**offendo (offendere)**: bump into, stumble upon
**perdo (perdere), perdidi, perditus:** lose, destroy
**prehendo (prehendere), prehendi, prehensus:** grab, take in hand
**territo (territare)**: frighten, intimidate

## *Other*

**licet:** even if, although
**obviam:** in the way of, running into
**probe:** rightly, thoroughly

# DE ASINO LEONIS PELLE INDUTO

## Dramatis Personae

*Asinus*, the donkey, and *Herus*, the master.

Asinus, in silvam veniens, exuvias leonis offendit. Quibus
indutus, in pascua redit, greges et armenta territans fugansque.
Herus autem, qui vagum fallacemque Asinum perdiderat,
occurrit. Asinus, viso Hero, cum rugitu obviam fecit. At Herus,
prehensis quae extabant auriculis, "Alios licet (inquit) fallas; ego
te probe novi."

## Grammar Notes

**quibus indutus.** The referent of this relative pronoun **quibus** is **exuvias** in the previous
   sentence (see Fable 4): **quibus (exuviis) indutus**.

**herus autem.** For the postpositive particle **autem,** see Fable 16.

**viso hero.** Ablative absolute construction (see Fable 8).

**obviam fecit.** The phrase **obviam facere** means "to meet, run towards."

**prehensis auriculis.** Ablative absolute construction using the diminutive **auriculis**—an
   ironic diminutive, of course, since the donkey's ears are hardly little! (For the various uses
   of diminutives, see Fable 41.).

**quae extabant.** The referent of the relative pronoun **quae** is the noun **auriculis**.

**alios licet fallas.** The hypothetical subjunctive is introduced by **licet,** meaning "even if,
   although" (see Fable 38).

**ego te probe novi.** Note the emphatic use of the personal pronoun (see the *Grammar Overview* for this fable).

*In propria pelle quiesce.*

Apes omnes, velut agmine facto, in faciem ursi involabant.

# Fable 41.
# DE URSO ET ALVEARI
## (Barlow 86)

## Introduction
### The Bear and The Beehive

This is a fable invented by the Renaissance Latin author, Abstemius. It has all the features of a traditional Aesop's fable: the bear makes a foolish mistake, and there is a lesson to be learned as a result. What gets this bear into trouble is his love of honey. Bears are notorious for their love of honey, of course, but as a Latin saying warns, *Ubi mel, ibi apes,* "Where there is honey, there are bees." The bear in this fable gets into trouble with one bee in particular, and ends up with the whole hive chasing after him. If the bees were given the task of pronouncing the moral at the end of the story, what do you think they would say?

For other stories about bears, see the fable of the bear and the two travelers (Fable 65), or the fable of the bear and the lion (Fable 48). For another story about unexpected consequences, see the fable of the goose who laid the golden egg (Fable 56).

## Grammar Overview
### Diminutives

In this fable, the bee is called *apis*, the standard form for "bee," and also *apicula*, a diminutive form. Latin is a language very rich in diminutive forms, and you can find diminutive forms for many animal names, such as *avicula* from *avis*, *bestiola* from *bestia*, and *ursulus* from *ursus*, etc. Often diminutives refer to physical smallness, but sometimes they have other connotations. Diminutive forms can be endearing, in the sense that something small is dear or sweet or charming. Yet diminutives can also be disparaging or insulting, in the sense that something small is pathetic or diminished. So, each time you meet a diminutive form in Latin, you need to ask whether it simply refers to smallness in size, or whether it has other connotations, positive or negative. Take this Latin proverb for example, which uses the diminutive adjective *vetulus* (from *vetus*): *Vetulus bos lugetur a nemine,* "The old ox is lamented by no one." The diminutive is applied here to a very large animal, the ox—so that means it cannot be referring to the physical smallness of the animal. What then is the meaning conveyed by this diminutive form? (For more examples of diminutives in Latin, see the notes to Fable 43.)

# Vocabulary

## *Nouns*

**aculeus (aculei, *m*.):** sting, goad
**agmen (agminis, *n*.):** army, marching column
**alveare (alvearis, *n*.):** beehive
**apicula (apiculae, *f*.):** bee, little bee
**apis (apis, *f*.):** bee
**concussio (concussionis, *f*.):** shaking, rough blow
**examen (examinis, *n*.):** swarm
**facies (faciei, *f*.):** face, appearance

## *Adjectives*

**indignabundus, indignabunda, indignabundum:** indignant, outraged
**violentus, violenta, violentum:** violent, impetuous

## *Verbs*

**crucio (cruciare), cruciavi, cruciatus:** torment, torture
**ico (icere), ici, ictus:** strike, stab
**involo (involare):** fly into, rush at
**irrito (irritare), irritavi, irritatus:** annoy, irritate
**irruo (irruere):** rush in, rush into

## *Other*

**acriter:** sharply, pointedly
**leviter:** lightly, slightly
**patienter:** patiently, tolerantly
**temere:** rashly, impetuously
**velut:** just as, as if

# DE URSO ET ALVEARI

## Dramatis Personae

*Apes*, the bees, and *Ursus*, the bear.

Ab Apiculis irritatus et leviter ictus, Ursus indignabundus
in totum alveare totis viribus irruebat. Ad quam violentam
concussionem, Apes omnes, velut agmine facto, in faciem Ursi
involabant. Quarum acriter cruciatus aculeis Ursus: "Quanto
(inquit) satius mihi fuisset unius Apiculae tulisse patienter
aculeum, quam tam temere totum examen irritasse!"

## Grammar Notes

**ursus indignabundus irruebat.** The adjective **indignabundus** modifies the subject of the
verb, so you might want to translate it as an adverb, rather than an adjective (see Fable 36).

**ad quam concussionem.** The relative pronoun **quam** connects this sentence and the previous sentence (see Fable 4), with **quam concussionem** referring back to the blow struck by
the bear when he rushed at the hive.

**velut agmine facto.** Ablative absolute construction (see Fable 8), used as a simile: the bees
attacked like an army arrayed in columns (for the compound **vel + ut**, see the comments
about **ut** in Fable 55).

**quarum cruciatus aculeis.** The referent of the relative pronoun **quarum** is **apes,** the bees,
in the previous sentence, with the phrase **quarum (apium) aculeis** wrapping around the
participle (see Fable 6).

**quanto satius fuisset.** The ablative expresses the degree of difference with **satius**, the comparative form of **satis**, while the subjunctive expresses a hypothetical possibility, something that might have been, if only the bear had kept his temper.

**unius apiculae tulisse aculeum.** The phrase **unius apiculae aculeum** wraps around the
infinitive.

**satius . . . quam totum examen irritasse.** The word **quam** coordinates a comparison introduced by the comparative **satius**; the infinitives **tulisse** and **irritasse** are the things being
compared.

O infelicem augurem et tui et mei infortunii!

# Fable 42.
# DE IUVENE ET HIRUNDINE
## (Barlow 95)

## Introduction
### The Young Man and The Swallow

The swallow is often called a harbinger of spring and warm weather, yet there is also a proverb that warns: "One swallow does not make a spring," *Hirundo una ver non facit.* In this fable, you will see what happens to a reckless young man who apparently does not know this proverb! When he sees a single swallow, he decides that warm weather is on its way—but winter returns in full force, with disaster in store for both the young man and the bird. After you see how the story ends, what do you think is the most important lesson we can learn here?

For another story about the swallow, see the fable of the birds and the flax seed (Fable 59). For travelers who find themselves out in the cold, see the fable of the sun and the wind (Fable 79), or the man rescued by the satyr (Fable 64).

## Grammar Overview
### Interjections and Exclamations

In Fable 15, you saw an example of the accusative of exclamation—*Me miserum!*—meaning something like the English expression "Unlucky me!" It is also possible to use the accusative of exclamation with various interjections in Latin such as *o* and *eheu*, among others. In this fable, for example, you will see the interjection *o* used with the accusative. The interjection *o* can also be found with the vocative, and you need to recognize what it means to choose one case or the other. The use of *o* with the vocative is literally a calling out to someone, an exclamation addressed directly to them, invoking them as the partner in a conversation. For example, in Fable 61, the dog cries out to his master, *O dure magister*, "O harsh master!" The vocative signals that the dog expects the master to be present and hear his words. With the accusative case, however, the *o* is simply an exclamation, an interjection of surprise, horror, or dismay. In this fable, the young man exclaims *o* when he finds the dead swallow. He knows that there is no point in addressing the swallow directly, now that the swallow is dead. Instead, as you will see, the young man uses the interjection *o* and the accusative of exclamation to express his despair at the sight of that ominous dead bird. (For another example of an exclamatory form in Latin, see the notes to Fable 80.)

# Vocabulary

## Nouns

**aestas (aestatis, *f.*)**: summer, summer heat

**augur (auguris, *m.*)**: prophet, seer

**augurium (augurii, *n.*)**: omen, sign

**avicula (aviculae, *f.*)**: bird, little bird

**bruma (brumae, *f.*)**: winter weather, cold

**frigus (frigoris, *n.*)**: cold, frost

**hirundo (hirundinis, *f.*)**: swallow, martin

**infortunium (infortunii, *n.*)**: misfortune, bad luck

**patrimonium (patrimonii, *n.*)**: inheritance

**pecunia (pecuniae, *f.*)**: money

**popina (popinae, *f.*)**: cookshop, bistro

**reliquia (reliquiae, *f.*)**: remains, vestiges

**venum (veni, *n.*)**: something for sale

**vestimentum (vestimenti, *n.*)**: garment, clothing

**vestitus (vestitus, *m.*)**: clothing, clothes

## Adjectives

**dissolutus, dissoluta, dissolutum**: careless, loose

**infelix (infelicis)**: unhappy, unlucky

**integer, integra, integrum**: entire, complete

**seminudus, seminuda, seminudum**: half-naked

**temulentus, temulenta, temulentum**: drunken, tipsy

## Verbs

**appropinquo (appropinquare), appropinquavi, appropinquatus**: approach, draw near

**circumvagor (circumvagari)**: wander around, roam

**circumvolo (circumvolare)**: fly around, flit

**conicio (conicere)**: put together, conjecture

**decoquo (decoquere), decoxi, decoctus**: melt down, consume

**delitesco (delitescere), delitui**: lurk in, seek shelter in

**eneco (enecare)**: kill, kill off

**exuo (exuere), exui, exutus**: take off, strip

**offendo (offendere)**: bump into, stumble upon

**saevio (saevire)**: rage, rave

## Other

**illico**: immediately, on the spot

# DE IUVENE ET HIRUNDINE

## Dramatis Personae

*Iuvenis*, the young man, and *Hirundo*, the swallow.

Temulentus et dissolutus quidem Iuvenis, qui patrimonium
integrum decoxerat, ipsa etiam vestimenta solebat pro pecuniis
venum dare. Ad hoc, ex augurio circumvolantis Hirundinis
coniciens iam aestatem appropinquasse, illico vestitus exuit
et seminudus in popinas delituit. Sed, cum brumae reliquiae
redeuntes maiori frigore saeviebant et Hirundinem enecassent,
Iuvenis tandem circumvagabatur et Aviculam mortuam offendens
inquit, "O infelicem augurem et tui et mei infortunii!"

## Grammar Notes

**dissolutus quidem.** The postpositive particle **quidem** adds emphasis to the word before it
(see Fable 23).

**ipsa etiam vestimenta.** The phrase **ipsa vestimenta** wraps around the adverb (see Fable 6).

**venum dare.** The phrase means "to put up for sale."

**ad hoc.** The phrase means "in addition; on top of that."

**aestatem appropinquasse.** Accusative plus infinitive construction in indirect statement
(see Fable 7); **appropinquasse** is an alternate form of **appropinquavisse.**

**vestitus exuit.** The word **vestitus** is accusative plural (for more about this type of verbal
noun, called the supine, see Fable 27).

**enecassent.** The subjunctive **enecassent** is an alternate form of **enecavissent**. Note that
**cum** here takes both an indicative verb—**cum brumae reliquiae saeviebant**—which
explains when the event took place, along with a subjunctive verb—**cum hirundinem
enecassent**—which provides specific causal background information as to why the young
man cried out.

**o infelicem augurem.** An exclamation using the accusative, with the interjection **o** (see the
*Grammar Overview* for this fable).

**et tui et mei infortunii.** Note the double use of **et,** meaning "both . . . and" (see Fable 65).

Formica tibiale aucupi gravissime mordebat.

# Fable 43.
# DE FORMICA ET COLUMBA
## (Barlow 108)

## Introduction
### The Ant and The Dove

This fable provides an illustration of the English saying, "One good turn deserves another." Although you would not think that a dove and an ant could be heroic creatures, this dove is able to save the life of the ant, and the ant, in turn, is able to save the dove. The actions of the animals provide a positive model for humans to imitate, as the ancient Greek version of this fable reminds us: "The story shows that even dumb beasts experience fellow feeling and come to one another's aid." Imagine the words of the dove as she flies off to safety: what do you think she would say is the moral of the story?

For stories about animals who are selfish rather than generous, see the fable of the ant and the cicada (Fable 16), or the horse who would not carry part of the load (Fable 36). For another story about a birdcatcher, see the fable of the birdcatcher and the snake (Fable 15).

## Grammar Overview
### Diminutive Word Pairs

In Fable 41, you learned about Latin diminutives. In this fable about the deeds of two tiny heroes, you will meet quite a few diminutive nouns, such as *fonticulus* (from *fons*) and *ramusculus* (from *ramus*). There is also the word *adminiculum*, which originally meant a support for the hand, *ad-manus*, a small prop or handy little thing to lean on. More specifically, the *adminiculum* was a garden stake that plants or vines could lean on as they grew. Later, the word *adminiculum* came to mean any kind of support or assistance. It ceased to be a diminutive word used as an alternative to a standard form; instead, it simply became a word in its own right, not the diminutive part of a word pair. Many Latin words are the result of this same process. The word *puella*, for example, was originally a diminutive of *puera*, an old Latin word for "girl." Over time, however, the word *puella* replaced the word *puera* completely. As a result, *puer* is the standard Latin word for "boy" while *puella* (originally a diminutive) is the standard Latin word for "girl." So, as you work on your Latin vocabulary, it's important to recognize diminutive forms, and you also need to be aware of whether the diminutive is used as part of a word pair, or if instead the diminutive has become a word in its own right, like *adminiculum* and *puella*. (For more about diminutives in Latin, see the notes to Fable 67.)

# Vocabulary
## *Nouns*
**adminiculum (adminiculi,** *n.***):** prop, support
**auceps (aucupis,** *m.***):** fowler, birdcatcher
**fonticulus (fonticuli,** *m.***):** little spring, fountain
**insidiae (insidiarum,** *f.***):** ambush, snare
**lympha (lymphae,** *f.***):** water
**ramusculus (ramusculi,** *m.***):** twig, tiny branch
**sitis (sitis,** *f.***):** thirst
**tibiale (tibialis,** *n.***):** leg, shin

## *Adjectives*
**contiguus, contigua, contiguum:** near, touching

## *Verbs*
**absorbeo (absorbere), absorbui, absorptus:** swallow up, engulf
**admoneo (admonere):** suggest, prompt
**avolo (avolare), avolavi, avolatus:** fly away, fly off
**deiicio (deiicere), deieci, deiectus:** throw down, drop
**diripio (diripere), diripui, direptus:** seize, tear off
**elabor (elabi), elapsus sum:** slip, slide
**evado (evadere), evasi, evasus:** escape, get out
**frico (fricare):** rub, scratch
**insideo (insidere):** sit on, settle upon
**mordeo (mordere):** bite
**percipio (percipere), percepi, perceptus:** perceive, notice
**sedo (sedare):** allay, calm
**servo (servare), servavi, servatus:** preserve, save
**tendo (tendere), tetendi, tensus:** stretch, extend

## *Other*
**graviter:** heavily, seriously
**impune:** unpunished, without harm
**interea:** meanwhile
**paene:** almost, mostly

# DE FORMICA ET COLUMBA

## Dramatis Personae

*Formica*, the ant, *Columba*, the dove, and *Auceps*, the birdcatcher.

Formica, ut sitim sedaret, fonticulum accessit, sed in fonticulum
elapsa et paene lymphis absorpta est. Columba, arborem insidens
fonticulo contiguam, ramusculum ore direptum in fonticulum
deiecit, cuius adminiculo servata Formica evasit. Sed interea affuit
Auceps, Columbae insidias tensurus. Formica tibiale gravissime
mordebat. Cui cum fricandi gratiam admonebat, percepit id
Columba et impune avolavit.

## Grammar Notes

**ramusculum direptum deiecit.** You might translate the passive participle with an active
verb (see Fable 5): the dove seized the little branch (**direptum**) and then threw it (**deiecit**).

**gravissime.** This is the superlative form of the adverb, **graviter** (see Fable 39).

**cui cum admonebat fricandi gratiam.** The referent of the relative pronoun **cui** is **auceps**,
whose shin was bitten: **cui (aucupi) admonebat**, "when (the bite on the shin) suggested to
the birdcatcher the pleasantness of scratching. . ." (for the gerund in the genitive case, see
Fable 78).

**percepit id columba.** The pronoun **id** refers to the scratching motion prompted by the bite.

*Gratia gratiam parit.*

Post longe exercita odia, mus et rana in bellum ruebant.

# Fable 44.
# DE MURE ET RANA
## (Barlow 35)

## Introduction
### The Mouse and The Frog

In the ancient Greek versions of this fable, the frog pretends to help the mouse across a river, but once they reach mid-stream, he decides to drown the mouse, who cannot swim. Meanwhile, a passing hawk sees them splashing in the water, swoops down, and carries them both off. In the version of the fable that you will read here, however, the story begins quite differently: the mouse and the frog are at war with one another, engaged in single combat, fighting one another with lances as if they were knights on horseback! This notion of the frog and the mouse at war was probably inspired by the ancient mock-epic poem called *Batrachomyomachia*, "The Battle of the Frogs and the Mice." If the mouse or the frog were to pronounce the moral at the end of this story, what do you think they would say?

For other stories about animal battles, see the fable of the bear and the lion fighting one another (Fable 48), or the war between the birds and the beasts (Fable 8). For another story about the predatory kite, see the fable of the kite and his mother (Fable 27).

## Grammar Overview
### The Compound Word, Uter + Que

One of the more elegant features of Latin is the enclitic *-que*, which attaches to the end of a word and means the same thing as if there were an *et* before the word. You can see a good example in this Latin proverb: *Stultus puerque vera dicunt*, "A fool and a child speak the truth." In addition to being used as an alternative to *et*, the suffix *-que* can also be used to create compound words. In this fable, you will see an example of one such compound: *uterque*, meaning "each of two, both." When you decline the word, you can clearly see that it is a compound of two parts: *uter* declines (*utrius* for the genitive, *utri* for the dative, and so on), but the *-que* does not change, so you get forms like these: *utriusque* (genitive), *utrique* (dative), and so on. Can you think of any other Latin words that are formed as a compound with *-que*? (Hint: Take a look at the notes to Fable 18.) What about another Latin compound in which the first part declines, but the second part does not? (Hint: Take a look at the notes to Fable 3.)

# Vocabulary

## Nouns

**bellator (bellatoris,** *m.*): warrior, combatant

**certamen (certaminis,** *n.*): contest, competition

**hasta (hastae,** *f.*): spear, javelin

**herba (herbae,** *f.*): herb, grass

**imperium (imperii,** *n.*): rule, supreme
power

**insidiae (insidiarum,** *f.*): ambush, snare

**insultus (insultus,** *m.*): jumping, insulting

**Mars (Martis,** *m.*): god of war, battle

**nodus (nodi,** *m.*): knot, node

**odium (odii,** *n.*): hatred

**palus (paludis,** *f.*): swamp, marsh

**pugna (pugnae,** *f.*): fight, battle

## Adjectives

**ambo, ambae, ambo (ambos,** *acc. plural*):
both, two together

**anceps (ancipitis):** two-headed, doubtful

**formosus, formosa, formosum:** shapely,
handsome

**improvisus, improvisa, improvisum:**
unexpected, unforeseen

**iunceus, iuncea, iunceum:** made of rushes

**neuter, neutra, neutrum (neutrius):**
neither, not either

**par (paris):** equal, like

## Verbs

**adorior (adoriri):** assail, attack

**adpropero (adproperare):** hasten, hurry
towards

**aggredior (aggredi):** approach, attack

**attollo (attollere):** raise up, lift on high

**caveo (cavere):** beware, watch out for

**exerceo (exercere), exercui, exercitus:**
conduct, carry out

**lanio (laniare):** mangle, tear to pieces

**pugno (pugnare):** fight, do battle

**ruo (ruere):** rush, rush into

**struo (struere):** build, construct

## Other

**egregie:** exceptionally, admirably well

**prae:** in view of, because of

**procul:** far off, at a distance

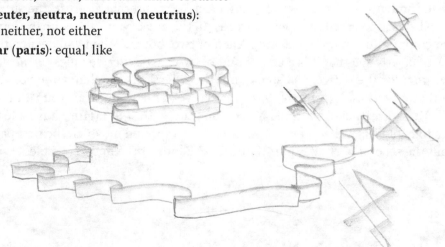

the kite carried away both of the warriors who were
battling so exceptionally with itself and butchered them

# DE MURE ET RANA

## Dramatis Personae

*Mus*, the mouse, *Rana*, the frog, and *Milvus*, the kite.

Post longe exercita odia, Mus et Rana in bellum ruebant. Causa
certaminis erat de paludis imperio. Anceps pugna fuit. Mus
insidias sub herbis struebat et improviso Marte Ranam adoritur.
Rana, viribus melior et pectore, insultuque valens, hostem
aggreditur. Hasta utrique erat iuncea et paribus formosa nodis.
Sed, certamine procul viso, Milvus adproperat, dumque prae
pugnae studio neuter sibi cavebat, bellatores ambos egregie
pugnantes Milvus secum attollit laniatque.

*(interlinear glosses, handwritten: carry out, hatred, mouse, frog, war, rush; contest, swamp, power, doubtful, fight, mouse; ambush, under herb, building, unexpected, god of war, attack; frog, string, more, bad, jumping, host; approach, spear, made of, rushed, equal, shapley, knot; But, contest, far off, see, kite, hasten; fight, neither, beware, warrior, both, exceptionally; battle, kite, raise up, mangle)*

*(handwritten translation below:)* After the hatred has been curried out for a long time, the frog and the mouse were rushing into battle.

## Grammar Notes

**improviso Marte.** Mars was the Roman god of war and the name of the god also stands for warfare itself and for battle, so this phrase means "a surprise Mars, a surprise attack."

**ranam adoritur.** The deponent verb **adoritur** is transitive and takes a direct object in the accusative (see Fable 9).

**viribus melior et pectore.** The phrase **viribus et pectore** wraps around the adjective (see Fable 6); the word **pectus** refers physically to the chest, but metaphorically to "heart, spirit, the fighting spirit," etc., so while the mouse may have the advantage of surprise, the frog has more strength and fighting spirit.

**insultu valens.** The ablative **insultu** explains in what way the frog was strong.

**hostem aggreditur.** The deponent verb **aggreditur** is transitive and takes a direct object in the accusative.

**hasta utrique erat.** The dative indicates possession, something that each combatant had at their disposal: each one had a spear (see Fable 64).

**paribus formosa nodis.** The phrase **paribus nodis** wraps around the adjective (see Fable 6), the number of knots in the reed referring to the overall length: "with an equal number of knots," meaning the reeds were equal in length.

**certamine viso.** Ablative absolute construction (see Fable 8).

**secum.** This is a compound word, with inverted order: se + cum = cum se.

*(handwritten translation below:)* The cause of the battle was about ruling the swamp. The fight was doubtful. The mouse was constricting traps under the herbs and attacked the frog by means of battle. The frog, better in strength and spirit, and strong in jumping, he attacked the enemy. There was a spear for both made of rushes are formed with equal knots. But with the contest being seen far away, the kite hurried, while on account of their eagerness, neither was watching out for themselves

Asinus leoni imbelli calce minitatus est.

# Fable 45.
# DE LEONE SENE
## (Barlow 99)

## Introduction
### The Old Lion

In the version of this fable by the Roman poet Phaedrus, the old lion is attacked first by a boar and then by a bull, two creatures whom the lion considers to be worthy opponents. Then, the old lion is attacked by a donkey, which is far worse, according to the lion, as the donkey is not a worthy opponent at all. In the version of the fable you will read here, the story focuses on just the donkey and the lion. As you read the story, see what you think about the character of the lion. Do you feel sorry for him? It seems that Joseph Jacobs does, as you can see from the moral he applies to this story: "Only cowards insult dying majesty." Based on how you assess the relative merits of the lion and the donkey in this fable, what do you think should be the moral of the story?

For another story about a feeble lion, see the fable of the lion in the cave (Fable 46), or the lion in love (Fable 20). For a story where a donkey foolishly confronts a more vigorous lion, see the fable of the rooster, the lion and the donkey (Fable 60).

## Grammar Overview
### Substantive Adjectives

One of the stock figures in Roman comedy is the *senex*, "the old man." The adjective *senex* is used so often in Latin substantively, referring to an old man, that you might forget that the word is actually an adjective. In this fable, though, you will see that the *senex* is not an old man, but a *leo senex,* an old lion. Since adjectives can so easily function as nouns in Latin, it is worth thinking about the ways in which Latin nouns and adjectives differ from one another. Latin nouns, for example, have five possible declensions. Adjectives, on the other hand, have only three declensions; there are no fourth- and fifth-declension adjectives. Adjectives, however, can take on degrees, with distinctive comparative and superlative forms, while nouns do not have different degrees. So, since *senex* is an adjective, that means it has a comparative degree. In fact, the comparative degree of *senex* is a word you are very familiar with even in English; do you know what it is? (Hint: Think about your last year of high school or college.)

# Vocabulary
## Nouns

**animans (animantis, *n.*):** animal, living being
**calx (calcis, *f.*):** heel, hoof
**contemptus (contemptus, *m.*):** scorn, disdain
**fera (ferae, *f.*):** wild beast, animal
**iniuria (iniuriae, *f.*):** injury, injustice
**metus (metus, *m.*):** fear, dread
**numerus (numeri, *m.*):** number
**odium (odii, *n.*):** hatred
**senectus (senectutis, *f.*):** old age
**vitium (vitii, *n.*):** fault, defect

## Adjectives

**imbellis, imbelle (imbellis):** unwarlike, defenseless
**iustus, iusta, iustum:** fair, right
**longaevus, longaeva, longaevum:** aged, long in years
**vilis, vile (vilis):** cheap, worthless

## Verbs

**appareo (apparere):** appear, show up
**deprivo (deprivare), deprivavi, deprivatus:** deprive of
**infero (inferre), intuli, inlatus:** bring in, inflict
**laboro (laborare):** work, exert effort
**minitor (minitari), minitatus sum:** threaten, menace
**suspiro (suspirare):** sigh, utter with a sigh
**ulciscor (ulcisci):** avenge, punish

## Other

**olim:** formerly, once upon a time

# DE LEONE SENE

## Dramatis Personae

*Leo*, the lion, and *Asinus*, the donkey.

Leo, longaevae senectutis laborans vitio et viribus deprivatus, odio et contemptui fuit omnium ferarum. In quarum numero Asinus (omnium animantium vilissimus) apparebat, et Leoni imbelli calce minitatus est. Quod cum vidisset Leo, suspirans inquit iustum fuisse ut tandem iniurias suas ferae ulciscerentur, et ut iam odio haberetur, qui olim omnibus metum intulisset.

## Grammar Notes

**longaevae senectutis laborans vitio.** The phrase **longaevae senectutis vitio** wraps around the participle (see Fable 6).

**viribus deprivatus.** The participle **deprivatus** takes an ablative complement ("deprived of").

**odio et contemptui fuit.** The predicate datives express the lion's function; he has become the object of all the animals' hatred and contempt (see Fable 61).

**in quarum numero.** The referent of the relative pronoun **quarum** is **ferarum** in the previous sentence: **in quarum (ferarum) numero** (see Fable 10 for the preposition standing first in the relative clause).

**leoni imbelli minitatus est.** The verb **minitatus est** takes a dative complement.

**quod cum vidisset leo.** The relative pronoun **quod** connects back to the previous sentence (see Fable 4), referring to the general situation described there, i.e., the donkey making threats; the subjunctive, introduced by **cum**, gives causal background information as to why the lion sighed (for the placement of **quod** before **cum,** see Fable 37).

**iustum fuisse.** Accusative plus infinitive construction in indirect statement (see Fable 7); the subject is impersonal (you can consider the following **ut** clauses to be the subject if you want), and **iustum** supplies the predicate: "it was right."

**iniurias suas ulciscerentur.** The deponent verb **ulciscerentur** is transitive and takes a direct object in the accusative (see Fable 9); **suas** refers back to the animals, i.e., the animals are avenging the wrongs they suffered in the past.

**haberetur.** The passive form of **habere** means "to be held to be, to be thought of."

**qui intulisset.** The referent of the relative pronoun **qui** is the lion and the subjunctive, introduced by the relative pronoun, provides causal background information; according to the lion, this is the cause of his present condition.

*Leo fortissimus bestiarum.*

*Leonina societas periculorum plena.*

# Fable 46.
# DE LEONE ET VULPE
## (Barlow 27)

## Introduction
### *The Lion and The Fox*

The story you are about to read is another fable that can be found in the works of the Roman poet Horace. Writing in one of his verse epistles, Horace invokes "what the cautious fox said once upon a time to the ailing lion," *olim quod vulpes aegroto cauta leoni respondit.* Of course, you already know that the fox is a trickster, so it is no surprise to learn that she is also on her guard against the tricks of others—*cauta*, as Horace calls her. Although the lion tries to trick the fox, she nevertheless manages to outfox him, so to speak. What do you think is the lesson we can learn from the wise fox in this fable?

For more stories about the fox, see the fable of the fox who lost her tail (Fable 51), or the fable of the fox and the rooster (Fable 47). For another story about the treacherous lion, see the fable of the lion's share (Fable 73).

## Grammar Overview
### *The Compound Word, Solum + Modo*

In this fable, you will meet the Latin adverb *solummodo.* This word is a compound of *solum + modo*, with *solum* meaning "single, one," and *modo* emphasizing the sense of "just, only." Put the two parts together and you get *solummodo*, "just one, only" (the similarly formed word *tantummodo* has much the same meaning). So, in the fable you are about to read, you will see that it is only the fox who puts off her duty of going to visit the ailing lion: *vulpes solummodo distulit officium*. There are some other compound Latin words formed with *-modo*, which adds the sense of a measure to something, a limit or a way in which something is defined (from the noun *modus*, meaning a measure, a defining limit or rule). The word *omnimodo*, for example, means "in every way, entirely." Can you think of any other Latin compounds formed with *-modo*? (Hint: How do you ask "how?" in Latin?)

## Vocabulary

### Nouns

**legatus (legati,** *m.***):** envoy, deputy
**officium (officii,** *n.***):** duty, obligation
**praesentia (praesentiae,** *f.***):** presence
**vestigium (vestigii,** *n.***):** track, trace

### Adjectives

**aegrotus, aegrota, aegrotum:** ailing, sick
**gratus, grata, gratum:** agreeable, acceptable

### Verbs

**aegroto (aegrotare):** be ill, sick
**convalesco (convalescere):** get well, grow strong
**differo (differre), distuli, dilatus:** put off, delay
**exeo (exire), exii, exitus:** go out, come out
**indico (indicare):** point out, show
**introeo (introire), introii, introitus:** go into, enter
**opto (optare):** choose, wish for
**terreo (terrere):** scare, frighten
**viso (visere):** visit, go see

### Other

**ceterum:** moreover, as for the rest
**minime:** not at all, least of all
**solummodo:** only, just one

*Alienis malis discimus.*

# DE LEONE ET VULPE

## Dramatis Personae

*Leo*, the lion, and *Vulpes*, the fox.

Leonem aegrotantem visebant animalia. Vulpes solummodo distulit officium. Ad hanc Leo legatum mittit, indicans gratissimam rem aegroto fore eius unius praesentiam. Respondet Vulpes optare se ut Leo convalescat; ceterum se minime visuram, terreri enim vestigiis quae indicabant multum quidem animalium introisse, sed exiisse nullum.

## Grammar Notes

**gratissimam rem fore eius praesentiam.** Accusative plus infinitive construction in indirect statement, with **praesentiam** as the accusative subject, **gratissimam rem** as the predicate, and **fore** as the future infinitive of **esse** (see Fable 26); for this use of the superlative, see Fable 39.

**eius unius praesentiam.** The pronoun **eius** (feminine singular genitive) refers to the fox, with the adjective **unius** in agreement: **eius (vulpis) unius praesentiam.**

**optare se . . . se visuram, terreri.** Accusative plus infinitive construction in indirect statement (see Fable 7), with **se** as the subject of all three infinitives: **optare, visuram (esse),** and **terreri.**

**multum quidem animalium introisse.** Accusative plus infinitive construction in indirect statement; **animalium** is a partitive genitive (see Fable 30) with the accusative subject of the infinitive, **multum** ("a great many animals").

**exiisse nullum.** The accusative plus infinitive construction parallels the previous construction: **exiisse nullum (animalium).**

*Felix quem faciunt aliena pericula cautum.*

*Dolo eluditur dolus.*

*Oportet vulpinari
cum vulpibus.*

# Fable 47.
# DE VULPE, CANE ET GALLO
## (Barlow 7)

## Introduction
### The Fox, The Dog, and The Rooster

Here you see the fox in her usual role as a trickster. In order to capture the rooster, who is so famous for his singing, the fox offers to teach the rooster a new song, a new ode, as the fox herself says, making the offer seem more glamorous by using this fancy Greek word. Of course, you should always be careful when the fox offers to do you some kind of favor, and the rooster in this fable is no fool. What moral would you give to the story if you wanted to emphasize the fox's mistake? What if you wanted instead to praise the rooster for his wisdom?

For more stories about the rooster, see the rooster who found a precious gem (Fable 38), or the rooster who crowed at dawn (Fable 74). For another story where the fox goes down to defeat, see the fable of the fox and the cat (Fable 72).

## Grammar Overview
### Gerunds with Prepositions

As you already saw in Fable 14, the Latin gerund is a verbal noun. Like other nouns, the gerund can be declined and thus it can serve as the complement of a preposition. For example, the Latin gerund can be used with the preposition *inter* to express the idea of "while something is going on, while something is happening." In this fable, you will see that the fox is pleading with the rooster *inter salutandum*, "while greeting" him. Another preposition you will often see with the gerund is *ad*, which expresses the idea of purpose or readiness, as in the phrase *promptus ad audiendum*, "ready for listening, ready to listen," or in the saying, *Ne sis velox ad irascendum*, "Do not be quick to get angry"—a motto that would have been good advice for the bear in Fable 41! (For more information about the use of *ad* with the gerund to express purpose, see Fable 54.)

# Vocabulary

## Nouns

**auris (auris,** *f.*): ear
**comes (comitis,** *m.*): companion, parter
**ode** (*acc.* oden, *f.*): ode, song [Greek]
**rus (ruris,** *n.*): countryside, farm

## Adjectives

**avidus, avida, avidum:** eager, insatiable
**canorus, canora, canorum:** melodious, resonant
**intempestus, intempesta, intempestum:** unseasonable, untimely
**optimus, optima, optimum:** best
**securus, secura, securum:** safe, untroubled

## Verbs

**accurro (accurrere):** run to, run up
**apprehendo (apprehendere):** grab hold of, seize
**appropinquo (appropinquare):** approach, draw near
**ascendo (ascendere):** climb up, go up
**descendo (descendere):** go down, come down
**dormio (dormire):** sleep
**edo (edere), edidi, editus:** bring forth, put out
**expergiscor (expergisci):** wake up, awake
**irruo (irruere):** rush in, rush into
**lanio (laniare):** mangle, tear to pieces
**obambulo (obambulare):** traverse, walk about
**praetereo (praeterire):** go by, pass by
**promitto (promittere), promisi, promissus:** promise
**saluto (salutare):** greet, hail

## Other

**infra:** below, beneath
**quod:** because, that
**saltem:** at least, except
**subito:** suddenly, quickly

# DE VULPE, CANE ET GALLO

## Dramatis Personae

*Canis*, the dog, *Gallus*, the rooster, and *Vulpes*, the fox.

Canis et Gallus rus obambulabant. Nocte appropinquante, Gallus altam ascendebat arborem, Canis autem ad pedem arboris securus dormiebat. Intempesta nocte, Gallus canoram vocem edidit. Vulpes praeteriens audit accurritque et inter salutandum promisit quod optimam doceret novamque oden, si ab arbore descenderet. "Descendam subito," respondebat Gallus. "Saltem a te peto ut Comitem expergiscaris meum, qui infra in utramque aurem dormit." Vulpes, novae praedae avida, Canem expergiscitur. Canis subito in eam irruens apprehendit laniatque.

## Grammar Notes

**nocte appropinquante.** Ablative absolute construction (see Fable 8).

**altam ascendebat arborem.** The phrase **altam arborem** wraps around the verb (see Fable 6).

**canis autem.** For the postpositive particle **autem,** see Fable 16.

**securus dormiebat.** The adjective **securus** modifies the subject of the verb, so you might want to translate it as an adverb, rather than an adjective (see Fable 36).

**intempesta nocte.** The phrase means "in the dead of night."

**inter salutandum.** The use of the gerund with the preposition **inter** indicates "while" something is happening (see the *Grammar Overview* for this fable): "while greeting (the rooster)."

**promisit quod.** For the use of **quod** to introduce a subordinate clause, see Fable 49.

**optimam doceret novamque oden.** The phrase **optimam novamque oden** wraps around the verb; **oden** is a Greek noun in the accusative case with a Greek accusative ending.

**comitem expergiscaris meum.** The phrase **comitem meum** wraps around the verb; the deponent verb is being used here with a transitive meaning and takes a direct object in the accusative (see Fable 9).

**in utramque aurem dormit.** The phrase **dormire in utramque aurem** means "to sleep soundly."

**novae praedae avida.** The adjective **avida** takes a genitive complement.

Eheu nos miseros, quia vulpi laboravimus.

# Fable 48.
# DE LEONE ET URSO
## (Barlow 38)

## Introduction
### The Lion and The Bear

This fable is an illustration of the English saying, "Divide and conquer." Normally, a fox would be no match for a lion and a bear united against her, but when the bear and the lion are busy fighting each other, the fox is easily able to triumph over them both. Imagine that the fox were to shout some final words at the lion and the bear as she runs off carrying the prize: what words do you think that sly creature would use in order to express the moral of the story?

For another story about a third party intervening during a contest, see the fable of the frog and the mouse (Fable 44). For more stories on the theme of "divide and conquer," see the fable of the lion and the bulls (Fable 66), or the fable of the farmer and his sons (Fable 71).

## Grammar Overview
### Gerunds in the Ablative Case

The Latin gerund, as a verbal noun, can be declined as other nouns are. In this fable, you will see how the gerund can be used in the ablative case in order to explain just how something is done or the way in which something happens. The fox in this story is able to snatch the prize *circumcirca eundo*, "by going around in a circle," and then *per utrosque percurrendo*, "by running in-between the both of them," that is, between the two contending predators, the lion and the bear. As always with the gerund, remember that while it may resemble the future passive participle in form, there is nothing passive about the gerund—it is an active verbal noun, as you can see by watching the very active fox in this fable. (For more about the use of gerunds in Latin, see the notes to Fable 78.)

# Vocabulary

## Nouns

**hinnulus (hinnuli,** *m.*): deer, fawn
**medium (medii,** *n.*): middle, center
**pugna (pugnae,** *f.*): fight, battle
**vertigo (vertiginis,** *f.*): dizziness

## Adjectives

**furax (furacis)**: thieving

## Verbs

**abeo (abire), abivi, abitus:** go away, depart
**adipiscor (adipisci), adeptus sum:** get, win
**afficio (afficere), affeci, affectus:** afflict, weaken
**concerto (concertare)**: fight over, argue over
**corripio (corripere)**: seize, carry off
**defatigo (defatigare), defatigavi, defatigatus:** tire out, exhaust
**iaceo (iacere)**: lie, lie down
**laboro (laborare), laboravi, laboratus:** work, exert effort
**percurro (percurrere)**: run through
**prosterno (prosternere), prostravi, prostratus:** stretch out, lay low
**rapio (rapere)**: grab, snatch
**surgo (surgere)**: rise up, get up

## Other

**circumcirca:** round about, all around
**eheu:** alas, woe
**graviter:** heavily, seriously
**interea:** meanwhile

# DE LEONE ET URSO

## Dramatis Personae

*Leo*, the lion, *Ursus*, the bear, and *Vulpes*, the fox.

Leo et Ursus, simul magnum adepti hinnulum, de eo concertabant. Graviter autem a se ipsis affecti, ut ex multa pugna etiam vertigine corriperentur, defatigati iacebant. Vulpes interea, circumcirca eundo ubi prostratos eos vidit et hinnulum in medio iacentem, hunc, per utrosque percurrendo, rapuit fugiensque abivit. At illi videbant quidem furacem Vulpem sed, quia non potuerunt surgere, "Eheu nos miseros," dicebant, "quia Vulpi laboravimus."

## Grammar Notes

**magnum adepti hinnulum.** The phrase **magnum hinnulum** wraps around the participle (see Fable 6); the deponent participle is transitive and takes a direct object in the accusative (see Fable 9).

**graviter autem.** For the postpositive particle **autem,** see Fable 16.

**se ipsis.** The reflexive pronoun phrase is ablative plural, referring to the compound subject of the verb: **leo et ursus.**

**circumcirca eundo.** Gerund in the ablative case (see the *Grammar Overview* for this fable).

**hunc rapuit.** The pronoun refers to the fawn: **hunc (hinnulum) rapuit.**

**per utrosque percurrendo.** The pronoun **utrosque** refers to the lion and the bear; the gerund is in the ablative case.

**videbant quidem.** The postpositive particle **quidem** adds a special emphasis to the preceding word (see Fable 23): the lion and bear were able to see the fox, it's true, but all they could do was watch—they could not chase after her.

**eheu nos miseros.** An exclamation using the accusative, with the interjection **eheu** (see Fable 42).

*Cavendo tutus eris.*

*Est sapientis providere.*

# Fable 49.
# DE ALAUDA ET PULLIS EIUS
## (Barlow 6)

## Introduction
### The Lark and Her Chicks

In this fable about the lark and her chicks, you will see how the wise bird uses her knowledge of human nature in order to keep her chicks safe. The problem the lark faces is that she builds her nest on the ground, hidden in a field, so she needs to make sure she and her chicks fly away before the humans come to mow the field for the harvest. There was a version of this fable recorded in the writings of the archaic Roman poet, Ennius, dating back to around the year 200 BCE. That makes it one of the oldest fables in the Roman literary tradition! Ennius applied this moral to the fable: *Ne quid exspectes amicos quod tute agere possis*, "Don't expect your friends (to do) anything that you yourself are able to take care of." In his English version of the story, G. F. Townsend says simply: "Self-help is the best help." What words would you use to express the moral of this story?

   For another wise bird, see the thirsty crow and the water jar (Fable 5). For another story about asking others for help, see the fable of the fox in the well (Fable 22), or the fable of Hercules and the plow (Fable 11).

## Grammar Overview
### Quod

This fable provides an example of how the Latin word *quod* can be used to introduce indirect statement, much as the word "that" is used to introduce indirect statement in English. In classical Latin, indirect statement was regularly expressed using the accusative plus infinitive construction (see Fable 7). Over time, however, the use of *quod* to introduce indirect statements and other subordinate clauses grew increasingly common, and ultimately became the standard way to introduce those clauses in the Romance languages. Thus, while Spanish, French, and Italian are derived from Latin, they do not use the accusative plus infinitive construction for indirect speech. Instead, they use "that" (Spanish *que*, French *que*, Italian *che*, etc.) to introduce indirect statement. So, in the fable you are about to read, you will find this statement made by the lark: *scio quod illi res cordi est*, "I know that this is something important to him." Using the accusative plus infinitive construction, the lark could have said instead: *scio illi rem cordi esse*, "I know this to be important to him." The meaning is basically the same in both statements but the style is markedly different, with the use of *quod* representing the more informal, less refined style that is characteristic of many later Latin texts.

# Vocabulary

## Nouns

ager (agri, *m*.): field

alauda (alaudae, *f*.): crested lark

cor (cordis, *m*.): heart, mind

falx (falcis, *f*.): sickle, scythe

messis (messis, *f*.): harvest, crop

opera (operae, *f*.): work, effort

pastus (pastus, *m*.): pasture, feeding ground

pullus (pulli, *m*.): chick, young bird

seges (segetis, *f*.): field of grain, crop

sermo (sermonis, *m*.): speech, talk

vicinus (vicini, *m*.): neighbor

## Adjectives

anxius, anxia, anxium: uneasy, worried

securus, secura, securum: safe, untroubled

tertius, tertia, tertium: third

trepidus, trepida, trepidum: fearful, anxious

## Verbs

absum (abesse): be away, be absent

attendo (attendere): pay attention to

intro (intrare): enter, enter into

mando (mandare), mandavi, mandatus: entrust, commit

meto (metere): reap, harvest

moneo (monere): warn, admonish

narro (narrare): tell, relate

praetereo (praeterire): go by, pass by

statuo (statuere), statui, statutus: establish, decide

## Other

diligenter: carefully, diligently

item: likewise

iterum: again, a second time

mane: in the morning

postremo: at last, finally

probe: rightly, thoroughly

quod: that, as for the fact that

*Sapiens a se ipso pendet.*

# DE ALAUDA ET PULLIS EIUS

## Dramatis Personae

*Alauda*, the lark, *Pulli*, the chicks, and *Dominus*, the master.

Alauda positos in segete Pullos monet ut, dum ipsa abest, diligenter attendant praetereuntium sermones de messe. Redit a pastu Mater. Pulli anxii narrant Dominum agri operam illam mandasse vicinis. Respondet nihil esse periculi. Item, alio die, trepidi aiunt rogatos ad metendum esse amicos. Iubet iterum illa ut sint securi. Tertio, ut audivit ipsum Dominum cum filio statuisse postremo mane cum falce messem intrare, "Iam (inquit) est tempus ut fugiamus. Dominum enim agri timeo, quia probe scio quod illi res cordi est."

## Grammar Notes

**anxii narrant.** The adjective **anxii** modifies the subject of the verb, so you might want to translate it as an adverb, rather than an adjective (see Fable 36).

**dominum mandasse operam vicinis.** Accusative plus infinitive construction in indirect statement (see Fable 7); **mandasse** is an alternative form of **mandavisse**, with **dominum** as the accusative subject, and **operam** as the object.

**nihil esse periculi.** Accusative plus infinitive construction in indirect statement, with the partitive genitive phrase (see Fable 30) wrapped around the infinitive: **nihil** (nothing) **periculi** (of danger) = "there is no danger."

**rogatos ad metendum esse amicos.** Accusative plus infinitive construction in indirect statement, with the infinitive wrapped around the gerund phrase, **ad metendum**; for the use of the gerund with the preposition **ad** to express purpose, see Fable 47.

**ut audivit.** This is a temporal use of **ut**, meaning "as, as soon as" (for the use of **ut** with the indicative, see Fable 55).

**dominum statuisse messem intrare.** Accusative plus infinitive construction in indirect statement, with **dominum** as the accusative subject and **statuisse** as the infinitive, which in turn takes the complementary infinitive, **intrare**, whose object is **messem**.

**dominum enim timeo.** For the postpositive particle **enim**, see Fable 2.

**quia probe scio quod.** The word **quod** is used here to introduce an indirect statement, "Because I know full well that . . ." (see the *Grammar Overview* for this fable).

**illi res cordi est.** The pronoun refers to the master: **illi** (domino) **res cordi est** (for this use of the predicate dative, see Fable 61).

*Si satis est, multum est.*

*Vivis piscibus aqua,
mortuis vinum.*

# Fable 50.
# DE PISCATORE ET PISCICULO
## (Barlow 78)

## Introduction
### *The Fisherman and The Little Fish*

This Latin fable about the fisherman and the little fish might make you think about the famous English saying, "A bird in the hand is worth two in the bush." There is a medieval Latin version of that same saying: *Est avis in dextra melior quam quattuor extra*, "A bird in the hand is better than four on the loose." Like so many medieval Latin sayings, this one rhymes: *dextra-extra*. Although classical Latin poetry was not based on rhyme, rhyme was widely used in medieval Latin poetry and proverbs. Can you think of a way to put the moral of this fable about the fisherman and the fish into rhyming form?

    For another story about a little fish, see the fable about the dolphin beached in the sand (Fable 62). For more stories about animals begging for their lives, see the fable of the stork caught in the snare (Fable 17), the hawk and the nightingale (Fable 6), or the lamb and the wolf (Fable 53).

## Grammar Overview
### *Donec*

In this fable, you will meet the Latin conjunction, *donec,* which means "while, so long as" or "until." As with so many Latin expressions that can involve future time, you will find the word *donec* used either with an indicative verb, expressing a definite sense of the future, or with a subjunctive verb, expressing a more hypothetical sense of possibility in the future. In this fable, the fish asks the fisherman to let him go *donec grandesceret,* until such time as he might (subjunctive) grow large enough to feed the fisherman and all his guests. Of course, the fisherman is not really interested in subjunctive possibilities; as you will see, he prefers the indicative, the actual fish he has in his hand right now, no matter how small! (For another Latin word that can take either indicative or subjunctive verbs, see the notes to Fable 52.)

# Vocabulary
## Nouns
**commodum (commodi,** *n.***):** convenience, advantage
**faux (faucis,** *f.***):** gullet, throat
**hospes (hospitis,** *m.***):** host, guest, visitor
**piscator (piscatoris,** *m.***):** fisherman
**pisciculus (pisciculi,** *m.***):** little fish
**prex (precis,** *f.***):** prayer, request
**promissum (promissi,** *n.***):** promise
**smaris (smaridis,** *m.***):** picarel (tiny sea-fish)

## Adjectives
**futilis, futile (futilis):** worthless, useless
**importunus, importuna, importunum:** inconvenient, annoying
**incertus, incerta, incertum:** uncertain, unsure
**insulsus, insulsa, insulsum:** stupid, tedious
**lubricus, lubrica, lubricum:** slippery, tricky

## Verbs
**adhibeo (adhibere):** apply, extend to
**capto (captare):** grab, grasp
**commuto (commutare):** change, exchange
**demitto (demittere):** let go, send away
**expleo (explere):** satisfy, fulfill
**fatigo (fatigare), fatigavi, fatigatus:** exhaust, tire
**grandesco (grandescere):** grow, increase

## Other
**donec:** until
**laute:** lavishly, sumptuously
**luculente:** splendidly, excellently
**sane:** truly, surely

# DE PISCATORE ET PISCICUL

## Dramatis Personae

*Pisciculus*, the fish, and *Piscator*, the fisherman.

Smaridem Pisciculum captabat Piscator, quem, ut se tunc
demitteret donec grandesceret unde luculentius et lautius
hospitum fauces expleret, importunis precibus fatigavit.
Cui Piscator: "Me sane insulsum crederes, si tam futilibus
et lubricis promissis fidem adhiberem et certum commodum
pro spe incerta commutarem."

*(Handwritten interlinear glosses: tiny seafish fish — grasp fisherman; send to until grow under excellently lavishly; throat satisfy annoying prayer exhaust; fisherman me stupid if worthless; slippery send apply convenience; unsure change)*

## Grammar Notes

**donec grandesceret et expleret.** The subjunctives are introduced by **donec,** stating a hypothetical possibility about the future (see the *Grammar Overview* for this fable).

**quem fatigavit.** The referent of the relative pronoun **quem** is the fisherman and the implied subject is the little picarel: **quem (piscatorem) fatigavit (smaris pisciculus).**

**luculentius et lautius.** These comparative adverbs express an implied comparison: the fish would more splendidly and lavishly feed the guests in the future (implied: more so than if the man were to cook and eat the fish now).

**hospitum fauces.** The genitive plural **hospitum** refers to the banquet guests whose gullets would be filled by the full-grown fish.

**cui piscator.** The referent of this relative pronoun **cui** is **pisciculum** in the previous sentence (see Fable 4), with an implied verb of speaking: **cui (pisciculo) piscator (inquit).**

**me insulsum crederes.** The pronoun **me** is the accusative subject of an implied infinitive in indirect statement, with **insulsum** as the predicate adjective: **me (esse) insulsum crederes** (for the omission of the verb "to be," see Fable 13).

Mos iamiam novellus est, ut omnes ferae detruncent caudas.

# Fable 51.
# DE VULPE SINE CAUDA
## (Barlow 66)

## Introduction
### The Fox Without Her Tail

You could consider this fable about the fox who lost her tail to be an example of the English saying "Misery loves company." In Joseph Jacobs's version of the fable, he applies a different moral: "Distrust interested advice." In some versions of the fable, in fact, the other foxes wisely reject the interested advice of the fox who lost her tail. "If you had not yourself lost your tail, my friend," the foxes say, "you would not thus counsel us." Unfortunately, the foxes in the version of the fable you are about to read are not so wise, as you will see! What do you think is the lesson we could learn from the foolish foxes in this Latin version of the story?

For another story about how misery loves company, see the fable of the dolphin and the little fish (Fable 62). For more stories about the fox and physical appearances, see the fox and the leopard (Fable 9), or the fox and the frog (Fable 78).

## Grammar Overview
### The Gender of Animal Names

In this fable, you will see an interesting problem regarding the grammatical gender of an animal's name, and what you might call the "cultural gender" of that animal. The Latin name for the fox, *vulpes*, is feminine, as you can see from the way the diminutive is formed: *vulpecula*. Yet for the author of this particular fable, the fox "felt" like a masculine animal; he imagined this story to be about male foxes, not females, and he has the fox address the other foxes as *fraterculi*, a diminutive form of "brothers." As you might guess, different cultures imagine the gender of animal names differently. Just to take one example of a difference between Latin and Greek, the Latin frog, *rana*, is feminine, while the frog in Greek is masculine, βάτραχος (*batrachos*). When you imagine a frog in English, do you think of the frog more as a "he" or as a "she"—or is the frog just an "it"? What about a cat? a mouse? a wolf? What do you think are the different factors involved in how different cultures imagine and define the gender of animals? (For more information about gender in Latin, see the notes for Fable 58.)

# Vocabulary

## Nouns

**basilica (basilicae,** *f.***):** great hall, court
**cauda (caudae,** *f.***):** tail
**fera (ferae,** *f.***):** wild beast, animal
**fovea (foveae,** *f.***):** pit, snare
**fraterculus (fraterculi,** *m.***):** little brother
**pudor (pudoris,** *m.***):** shame, embarrassment
**socius (socii,** *m.***):** ally, partner
**vulpecula (vulpeculae,** *f.***):** fox, vixen

## Adjectives

**novellus, novella, novellum:** fresh, new

## Verbs

**consolor (consolari):** cheer, comfort
**conspicio (conspicere), conspexi, conspectus:** observe, witness
**creo (creare), creavi, creatus:** create, make
**detrunco (detruncare), detruncavi, detruncatus:** cut off, lop off
**incido (incidere):** fall into, meet with
**irrideo (irridere), irrisi, irrisus:** mock, scoff at
**occurro (occurrere):** run into, meet
**vado (vadere):** go

## Other

**iamiam:** already, now
**illico:** immediately, on the spot
**indignabunde:** indignantly, angrily
**nuper:** recently, just now
**profecto:** certainly, as a matter of fact
**quo:** to where, whither
**saltem:** at least, except

# DE VULPE SINE CAUDA

## Dramatis Personae

*Vulpes* (*Vulpeculae*), the foxes.

In foveam incidit Vulpecula; inde, cauda detruncata, occurrit multis Vulpeculis. Quas cum indignabunde conspexerat, inquit, "Fraterculi, quo vaditis?" "Ad leonis basilicam eundum est nobis," respondebant. "Ad leonis basilicam?" inquit Vulpes. "Profecto ego ab ea nuperrime redii et mos iamiam novellus est, ut omnes ferae detruncent caudas." Quibus auditis, illico detruncabant illae suas caudas. Quas cum vidit Vulpes, irrisit et consolabatur se socios, si non periculi, saltem pudoris, creavisse.

## Grammar Notes

**cauda detruncata.** Ablative absolute construction (see Fable 8).

**occurrit multis vulpeculis.** The verb **occurrit** takes a dative complement.

**quas cum conspexerat.** The referent of the relative pronoun **quas** is **vulpeculis** in the previous sentence: **quas (vulpeculas) cum conspexerat**; for the placement of **quas** before **cum,** see Fable 37, and for the use of **cum** plus an indicative verb, see Fable 22.

**fraterculi.** The grammatical gender of the fox is feminine (see the *Grammar Overview* for this fable), but the fox addresses "his" fellow foxes as **fraterculi,** "little brothers" (for the diminutive, see Fable 41).

**eundum est nobis.** The dative **nobis** is used to express agency with the future passive periphrastic, **eundum est** (see Fable 69).

**ab ea.** The pronoun refers to the lion's palace, **ab ea (basilica).**

**nuperrime.** This is the superlative form of the adverb, **nuper** (see Fable 39).

**quibus auditis.** The relative pronoun **quibus** connects back to the previous sentence (see Fable 4), referring to the things that the fox has just said.

**se socios creavisse.** Accusative plus infinitive construction in indirect statement (see Fable 7), with **se** as the accusative subject of the infinitive, and **socios** as the object.

**socios si non periculi, saltem pudoris.** The genitives **periculi** and **pudoris** are parallel: **socios** (partners) **periculi** (of danger) = "partners in danger," and **socios pudoris,** "partners in shame."

*Fortuna belli fluxa.*

*Malo ad campanam quam ad tubae surgere clangorem.*

# Fable 52.
# DE TUBICINE CAPTIVO
## (Barlow 88)

## Introduction
### The Trumpeter Taken Captive

Throughout history, there have been musicians—trumpeters, drummers, and so on—who have been involved in military action, even if they were not armed combatants. In this Aesop's fable, you will find out what happens when one of these musicians is captured by the enemy. The trumpeter begs for mercy because he did not actually injure any of the enemy soldiers. What do you think: is the trumpeter as innocent as he claims to be?

For another story of a prisoner protesting his innocence, see the fable of the stork in the snare (Fable 17), or the wolf and the lamb (Fable 53). For another story about a musician held captive, see the fable of the hawk and the nightingale (Fable 6).

## Grammar Overview
### The Compound Word, Quando + Quidem

In this fable you will meet the compound word, *quandoquidem*. Like the words *cum* (see Fable 24) and *donec* (see Fable 50), *quandoquidem* can introduce both indicative and subjunctive verbs. The first part of *quandoquidem* is the word *quando*, which means "when" (temporal) or "since, because" (causal), and the second part is the intensifying adverb *quidem*, which adds an affirmative emphasis, "in fact, indeed" (for more about *quidem*, see Fable 23). The result when you put the two parts together is that *quandoquidem* can introduce an indicative verb to make a temporal statement ("when indeed") or it can introduce a subjunctive verb to provide a causal explanation ("since in fact"). In this fable, you will see *quandoquidem* used with a subjunctive verb, as the trumpeter pleads for his life to be spared "since in fact he was totally harmless," *quandoquidem totum inermis esset.* That, at least, is what the trumpeter claims—and you will see that the enemy soldiers do not share his opinion! As often in Latin, the subjunctive is used here as a way to put you in the mind of one of the characters, giving you access to that individual's point of view, which may or may not be shared by other characters in the story.

# Vocabulary
## Nouns
**cantus (cantus,** *m.***):** song, tune
**inimicus (inimici,** *m.***):** enemy, foe
**pugna (pugnae,** *f.***):** fight, battle
**tuba (tubae,** *f.***):** trumpet
**tubicen (tubicinis,** *m.***):** trumpeter

## Adjectives
**captivus, captiva, captivum:** imprisoned, caught
**excors (excordis):** brainless, lacking understanding
**inermis, inerme (inermis):** unarmed, harmless
**supplicabundus, supplicabunda, supplicabundum:** pleading, entreating

## Verbs
**concito (concitare), concitavi, concitatus:** urge, spur
**detineo (detinere):** hold back, detain
**interficio (interficere):** kill, do away with
**pugno (pugnare):** fight, do battle
**vulnero (vulnerare), vulneravi, vulneratus:** wound, hurt

## Other
**ideo:** for this reason, therefore
**quandoquidem:** since, when in fact
**totum:** completely, wholly

# DE TUBICINE CAPTIVO

## Dramatis Personae

*Tubicen*, the trumpeter, and *Hostes*, the enemy soldiers.

Tubicen quidam in bello captivus detinebatur. Qui Hostes supplicabundus orabat ut non se interficerent, quandoquidem totum inermis esset et nullum eorum vulnerasset. Cui sic Hostes: "Quia tu sis inermis et pugnandi excors, ideo moriere, qui tubae cantu inimicos nostros ad pugnam concitaveris."

## Grammar Notes

**qui supplicabundus orabat.** The referent of the relative pronoun **qui** is **tubicen** in the previous sentence (see Fable 4): **qui (tubicen) orabat;** the adjective modifies the subject, so you might want to translate it as an adverb, rather than an adjective (see Fable 36).

**ut non se interficerent.** In classical Latin, you would expect a **ne** in this negative purpose clause, but the use of **ut non** is commonly used for negative purpose clauses in later Latin.

**quandoquidem inermis esset et nullum vulnerasset.** The subjunctives, introduced by **quandoquidem**, give causal background information (see the *Grammar Overview* for this fable); according to the trumpeter, this is why his life should be spared.

**nullum eorum.** The pronoun **eorum** is a partitive genitive (see Fable 30).

**cui hostes.** The referent of the relative pronoun **cui** is **tubicen,** the implied subject of **orabat** in the previous sentence, with an implied verb of speaking: **cui (tubicini) hostes (inquiunt).**

**quia tu sis.** The subjunctive, introduced by **quia** ("because"), gives causal background information; according to the enemy soldiers, this is why the trumpeter deserves to die (for the emphatic use of the personal pronoun, see Fable 40).

**pugnandi excors.** The word **excors** means "without the brains for something, without the heart for something," taking a genitive complement, the gerund **pugnandi.**

**ideo moriere.** The future active indicative **moriere,** "you will die," is an alternate form of **morieris.**

**qui concitaveris.** The subjunctive, introduced by the relative pronoun **qui,** gives further causal background information; according to the enemy soldiers, this is why the trumpeter must die.

Agnos lupi vorant.

Regnant qualibet
urbe lupi.

# Fable 53.
# DE LUPO ET AGNO
## (Barlow 2)

## Introduction
### The Wolf and The Lamb

You have probably heard the English phrase "a dog-eat-dog world." Well, as you will see from this story about the wolf and the lamb, the world of Aesop's fables is a "wolf-eat-lamb world." Even though the lamb protests his innocence, there is nothing he can do or say to put a stop to the wolf. As G. F. Townsend explains the moral of the story, "The tyrant will always find a pretext for his tyranny." Sir Roger L'Estrange uses this English proverb to express the moral: "'Tis an easy Matter to find a Staff to beat a Dog." After you read the dialogue between the wolf and the lamb in this Latin version of the story, what moral would you give to the fable? What are the different ways in which this animal story could be applied to human society?

For another story about a creature pleading for its life, see the fable of the man and the stork (Fable 17), the fish and the fisherman (Fable 50), or the nightingale and the hawk (Fable 6). For a story where the wolf gets his just deserts, see what happened to the wolf disguised in sheep's clothing (Fable 23).

## Grammar Overview
### Ne . . . Quidem

In Fable 23, you saw how the postpositive particle *quidem* can be used to emphasize the word that precedes it (as likewise in the compound word *quandoquidem*, which you just read about in Fable 52). In this fable, you will see how *quidem* can be combined with *ne* to create a negative emphasis, "not even . . ." as we might say in English. In this negative construction, the word *quidem* is still functioning as a postpositive particle, meaning that it must come after the word it emphasizes. As a result, the form of the construction is *ne . . . quidem*, with the specific word or phrase being negated inserted between the *ne* and the *quidem*. This can be a difficult construction to recognize, since you might at first mistake the *ne* for the negative particle that introduces a subjunctive verb. Just keep an eye out for the *quidem* nearby, and that way you will be able to recognize the *ne . . . quidem* construction. Consider this famous Latin saying: *Cum necessitate ne di quidem pugnant*, "Not even the gods (*ne di quidem*) put up a fight against necessity." Here is another example: *Ne Iupiter quidem omnibus placet*. What do you think the meaning of this saying could be? (For yet another use of *ne* in Latin, see the notes to Fable 80.)

# Vocabulary

## Nouns

**agnus (agni,** *m.***)**: lamb
**flumen (fluminis,** *n.***)**: stream, river
**fons (fontis,** *m.***)**: spring, source of water
**mora (morae,** *f.***)**: delay, pause
**poena (poenae,** *f.***)**: penalty, punishment
**potus (potus,** *m.***)**: drink, beverage
**sitis (sitis,** *f.***)**: thirst
**umor (umoris,** *m.***)**: liquid, fluid

## Adjectives

**fremebundus, fremebunda, fremebun-
dum:** roaring, murmuring
**innocens (innocentis):** harmless, innocent
**invisus, invisa, invisum:** hated, despised
**sitibundus, sitibunda, sitibundum:**
thirsty
**trepidus, trepida, trepidum:** fearful,
anxious
**vanus, vana, vanum:** meaningless, useless
**vitreus, vitrea, vitreum:** glass, glassy

## Verbs

**accurro (accurrere):** run up, run to
**adversor (adversari):** oppose, be against
**bibo (bibere):** drink
**haurio (haurire):** drain, drink
**increpo (increpare):** rebuke, chide
**innecto (innectere):** weave, devise
**intono (intonare):** thunder, boom
**levo (levare):** lighten, alleviate
**saevio (saevire):** rage, rave
**supplico (supplicare), supplicavi, suppli-
catus:** plead, beg
**turbo (turbare), turbavi, turbatus:** agitate, muddy

## Other

**contra:** opposite, in opposition to
**hodie:** today, this day
**infra:** below, downstream
**ne . . . quidem:** not . . . even
**nedum:** still less, much less
**procul:** far off, at a distance
**quid:** why, for what reason
**quod:** because, that
**sacrilege:** impiously, outrageously
**sedulo:** carefully, attentively

# DE LUPO ET AGNO

## Dramatis Personae

*Lupus*, the wolf, and *Agnus*, the lamb.

Sitibundus Lupus, dum ad caput fontis accedit ut sitim levaret,
videt innocentem Agnum, procul fluminis umorem haurientem.
Accurrit igitur; Agnum increpat quod vitreum turbavit fontem.
Trepidus ad haec supplicavit Agnus in innocentem ne saeviret;
se quidem, cum tam longe infra biberet, potum Lupi ne potuisse
quidem turbare, nedum voluisse. Lupus contra fremebundus
intonat, "Quid vanas sacrilege innectis moras? Pater, Mater, et
omne tuum invisum genus sedulo mihi et semper adversantur.
Tu autem hodie mihi poenas dabis!"

## Grammar Notes

**fluminis umorem haurientem.** The accusative participle agrees with **agnum** and takes **fluminis umorem** as its direct object.

**accurrit igitur.** For the postpositive particle **igitur,** see Fable 32.

**vitreum turbavit fontem.** The phrase **vitreum fontem** wraps around the verb (see Fable 6).

**ad haec.** The neuter plural pronoun refers to the "things" that are happening here, both the words of the wolf and his actions.

**se quidem.** For the postpositive particle **quidem,** see Fable 23.

**cum tam longe infra biberet.** The subjunctive, introduced by **cum,** gives causal background information; this is why the lamb could not have disturbed the wolf's drinking water.

**ne potuisse quidem.** The phrase **ne . . . quidem** (see the *Grammar Overview* for this fable) puts a strong emphasis on the word **potuisse,** an infinitive in indirect statement, with an implied verb of speaking: **(dicens) se ne potuisse quidem.**

**nedum voluisse.** This infinitive continues the accusative plus infinitive statement, with **se** as the implied accusative subject: **nedum (se) voluisse**.

**potum lupi turbare.** This infinitive phrase is a complement to both **potuisse** and **voluisse**.

**quid vanas innectis moras?** The interrogative **quid** here means "why? for what reason?" (see Fable 21), while the phrase **vanas moras** wraps around the verb.

**sedulo mihi et semper.** The adverbial phrase **sedulo et semper** wraps around the pronoun.

**tu autem.** For the postpositive particle **autem,** see Fable 16; for the emphatic use of the personal pronoun, see Fable 40.

Equus multa vi calcem leoni impingit.

# Fable 54.
# DE EQUO ET LEONE
## (Barlow 55)

## Introduction
### The Horse and The Lion

This is another fable about "the trickster tricked." The story starts with the lion playing a trick, but his intended victim, a horse, manages to fool the lion and escape. In some versions of the story, the predatory animal is a wolf instead of a lion, but in either case, the result is the same: because the predator acts against his own nature, pretending to be friendly, he fails to get his prey. What moral would you give to the story if you wanted to rebuke the lion for his failure to capture the horse? What if you wanted instead to praise the horse for his success in escaping from the lion?

For another story about an animal playing doctor, see the fable of the frog and the fox (Fable 78). For a story about an animal who really is sick, see the fable of the sick kite and his mother (Fable 27), or the wolf who choked on a bone (Fable 30). For another hypocritical offer of help, see the fable of the wolf and the sow (Fable 26).

## Grammar Overview
### Gerundives

As you have already learned, the gerund is a Latin verbal noun (see the notes to Fable 14). The gerundive is the corresponding verbal adjective, also known as the future passive participle. In this fable, you will see an example of the Latin gerundive used with the preposition *ad* to express purpose. The gerund can also be used with *ad* to express purpose (see the notes to Fable 47), but if the verb needs to take an object, the gerundive is usually used instead of the gerund, as you will see in the first sentence of this fable: *venit ad equum comedendum*, "(the lion) came to eat the horse." The gerundive, like any other adjective, agrees with its noun in gender, number, and case. So, in this sentence the gerundive *comedendum* is masculine singular accusative, agreeing with *equum*. If the lion had come to eat roses instead of a horse, the Latin would read: *venit ad rosas comedendas*, "he came in order to eat the roses," with the gerundive *comedendas* agreeing with *rosas*. (For more information about the various uses of the Latin gerundive, see the notes about the future passive periphrastic in Fable 69.)

# Vocabulary
## Nouns
**ambages (ambagis,** *f.*): long story, convoluted words

**calx (calcis,** *f.*): heel, hoof

**dolus (doli,** *m.*): trick, treachery

**ictus (ictus,** *m.*): hit, blow

**medicus (medici,** *m.*): medical doctor, physician

**pretium (pretii,** *n.*): prize, price

**senecta (senectae,** *f.*): old age

**sentis (sentis,** *m.*): thorn, briar

**stultitia (stultitiae,** *f.*): foolishness, stupidity

## Adjectives
**exanimatus, exanimata, exanimatum:** deprived of air, deprived of life

**spinosus, spinosa, spinosum:** thorny, prickly

## Verbs
**careo (carere):** lack

**comedo (comedere):** eat, consume

**conicio (conicere):** hurl, make go

**educo (educere):** draw out, take out

**effugio (effugere), effugi:** escape, flee

**fingo (fingere):** contrive, pretend

**impingo (impingere):** thrust, strike against

**inspicio (inspicere):** look at, look into

**meditor (meditari):** ponder, plan

**moror (morari):** delay, entertain

**oppono (opponere):** oppose, counter

**pareo (parere):** obey, comply

**profiteor (profiteri):** claim, declare

**pungo (pungere), pupugi, punctus:** prick, puncture

**ulciscor (ulcisci), ultus sum:** avenge, punish

## Other
**continuo:** immediately, at once

**dudum:** a while ago

**iure:** justly, deservedly

**ob:** on account of

**prae:** in view of, because of

**prope:** near, nearly

**vix:** scarcely, hardly

# DE EQUO ET LEONE

## Dramatis Personae

*Leo*, the lion, and *Equus*, the horse.

Venit ad Equum comedendum Leo. Carens autem prae senecta viribus, meditari coepit artem, medicumque se esse profitetur verborumque ambagibus Equum moratur. Equus dolo dolum, artem opponit arti; fingit se dudum in loco spinoso pupugisse pedem oratque ut inspiciens sentem medicus educat. Paret Leo, at Equus multa vi calcem Leoni impingit, et se continuo conicit in pedes. Leo, vix tandem ad se rediens, ictu enim prope exanimatus fuerat: "Pretium (inquit) fero ob stultitiam, et is iure effugit. Dolum enim dolo ultus est."

## Grammar Notes

**ad equum comedendum.** The gerundive with the preposition **ad** expresses purpose (see the *Grammar Overview* for this fable).

**carens autem viribus.** For the postpositive particle **autem,** see Fable 16; the participle **carens** ("lacking in") takes an ablative complement.

**meditari artem.** The deponent infinitive **meditari** is transitive and takes a direct object in the accusative (see Fable 9).

**medicum se esse.** Accusative plus infinitive construction in indirect statement (see Fable 7), with **se** as the accusative subject and **medicum** as a predicate noun.

**equum moratur.** The deponent verb **moratur** is transitive and takes a direct object in the accusative.

**se pupugisse pedem.** Accusative plus infinitive construction, with **se** as the accusative subject and **pedem** as the object.

**calcem leoni impingit.** The verb takes a direct object in the accusative ("the horse banged his hoof, struck with his hoof") along with an indirect object in the dative ("at the lion").

**ictu enim.** For the postpositive particle **enim,** see Fable 2.

**is iure effugit.** The pronoun refers to the horse: **is (equus) iure effugit.**

**dolum ultus est.** The deponent verb **ultus est** is transitive and takes a direct object in the accusative; the implied subject is the horse: **dolum ultus est (equus).**

Dives est qui nihil cupit.

Avarus ipse miseriae
causa est suae.

# Fable 55.
# DE CANE ET UMBRA
## (Barlow 80)

## Introduction
### *The Dog and His Shadow*

In this famous fable, a greedy dog is fooled by a reflection that he sees in the water. In his fifteenth-century version of the story, Caxton applies this moral: "He that desyreth to haue other mens goodes oft he loseth his owne good," in other words, "He that desires to have other men's goods often loses his own." Joseph Jacobs emphasizes the contrast between shadow and substance in his moral for the story: "Beware lest you lose the substance by grasping at the shadow." Based on what you see happen to the dog in this story, what do you think is the lesson that the fable teaches? What are the different ways in which this story about a dog can stand for the choices that people face in their own lives?

For another dog who is fooled by appearances, see the fable of the dog wearing a bell (Fable 28). For more stories about greed, see the fable of the dog in the manger (Fable 2), or the goose who laid the golden egg (Fable 56).

## Grammar Overview
### *Ut Plus Indicative*

The little word *ut* has quite a wide range of meanings and functions in Latin. You are probably most familiar with the use of *ut* ("so, so as to") to introduce a subjunctive clause expressing purpose or result in Latin. You also need to recognize that *ut* ("as") is sometimes used with indicative verbs. There is a good example in the fable you are about to read, which contains this phrase: *ut plerumque fit,* "as often happens." The word *ut* is also commonly used in Latin to introduce a metaphor or simile, as in this saying: *Ut piscis extra aquam,* "Like a fish out of water." There is also a compound word, *sicut* (*sic + ut*), which is used to introduce similes, as in this famous Bible saying, which has a nice resonance with the fable you are about to read: *Sicut umbra sunt dies nostri super terram,* "Our days upon this earth are like a shadow." Here's another famous saying that contains the words *ut* and *sic* used in tandem: *Ut tibi, sic alteri.* Can you figure out what it means? (Hint: Take a look at the comments about the Golden Rule in Fable 18).

# Vocabulary
## *Nouns*
**caro (carnis,** *f.***):** flesh, meat
**cupiditas (cupiditatis,** *f.***):** desire, greed
**faux (faucis,** *f.***):** gullet, throat
**fluvius (fluvii,** *m.***):** river, stream
**fundus (fundi,** *m.***):** bottom, base
**infortunium (infortunii,** *n.***):** misfortune, bad luck
**ocellus (ocelli,** *m.***):** eye, little eye
**rictus (rictus,** *m.***):** jaws, open mouth
**umbra (umbrae,** *f.***):** shadow, reflection

## *Adjectives*
**vagus, vaga, vagum:** wandering, unreliable
**vorabundus, vorabunda, vorabundum:** voracious, gulping

## *Verbs*
**capto (captare):** grab, grasp
**circumfero (circumferre), circumtuli, circumlatus:** cast about, move in circles
**desipio (desipere), desipui:** act foolishly
**desum (deesse):** lack, have not
**elatro (elatrare), elatravi, elatratus:** bark, bark out
**luceo (lucere):** shine, be apparent
**percello (percellere), perculi, perculsus:** strike down, dismay
**perdo (perdere), perdidi, perditus:** lose, destroy
**pereo (perire), perii, peritus:** be lost, perish
**recipio (recipere):** regain, recover
**splendeo (splendere):** shine, be radiant
**trano (tranare):** swim across
**veho (vehere):** carry, convey

## *Other*
**avide:** eagerly, insatiably
**huc:** here, to this place
**illuc:** to that place, there
**ni:** if not, unless
**plerumque:** often, for the most part

# DE CANE ET UMBRA

## Dramatis Persona

*Canis*, the dog.

Canis quidam, tranans fluvium, vorabunda fauce vehebat carnem, splendente sole, et (ut plerumque fit) umbra carnis lucebat in aquis. Quam avide captans, quod in rictu oris erat perdiderat. Quo infortunio perculsus, huc illuc vagos circumtulit ocellos et, tandem animum recipiens, sic elatravit: "Miserae deerat cupiditati modus! Satis superque esset ni desipuissem. Iam tota spes et res in fundo perierunt."

## Grammar Notes

**splendente sole.** Ablative absolute construction (see Fable 8).

**ut plerumque fit.** For the use of **ut** with the indicative, see the *Grammar Overview* for this fable.

**quam captans.** The referent of the relative pronoun **quam** is **umbra** in the previous sentence (see Fable 4): **quam (umbram) captans**.

**quod in rictu oris erat perdiderat.** The object of **perdiderat** is the implied referent of the relative pronoun: **(hoc), quod in rictu oris erat, perdiderat**.

**quo infortunio.** The relative phrase refers back to the events of the previous sentence, when the dog unluckily dropped the meat in the water.

**vagos circumtulit ocellos.** The phrase **vagos ocellos** wraps around the verb (see Fable 6).

**animum recipiens.** The phrase **animum recipere** means "to recover your wits, return to your senses."

**miserae deerat cupiditati.** The dative phrase **miserae cupiditati** wraps around the verb.

**deerat cupiditati modus.** The noun **modus** is the subject of the verb: "a limit was lacking to my greed" (i.e., "there was no limit to my greed").

**satis superque esset ni desipuissem.** The subjunctive verbs express hypothetical statements, introduced by **ni**, which is equivalent here to **nisi**, "if not."

**in fundo.** The phrase refers to the bottom of the stream: **in fundo (fluvii)**.

*Cupiditati nihil satis est.*

*Avarus aurum deum habet.*

# Fable 56.
# DE ANU ET ANSERE
## (Barlow 96)

## Introduction
### The Old Woman and The Goose

You probably have heard the story of *The Goose Who Laid The Golden Eggs,* although perhaps you did not know that it was an Aesop's fable! In some versions of the fable, the owner of the goose is a man, and in other versions, the owner is a woman, but in either case the result is the same: the owners of the goose are not content with one golden egg a day, and their greed for more gold brings about a total loss. The fifteenth-century English version by Caxton states, "By cause that he supposeth to wynne al he leseth al that he hath," in other words, "Because he thinks to win all, he loses all that he has." Jacobs expresses the moral of the fable with these words: "Greed oft o'er reaches itself." What words would you use to express the lesson that this fable teaches?

For another story about unexpected results, see the fable of the maids and the rooster (Fable 74), or the mountains in labor (Fable 3). For another story about greed, see the fable of the lion's share (Fable 73).

## Grammar Overview
### Tantus

This story gives you a good opportunity to compare the different uses of the Latin adjective, *tantus.* Very often, this adjective refers to something that is "so big, so great, so much," as in this phrase from the fable: *tantae crudelitatis conscia,* "conscious of her so great cruelty" (*tantae crudelitatis*). Yet *tantus* can also refer to the other end of the scale, meaning "so little, so small." From this sense of *tantus* at the small end of the scale comes the adverb *tantum,* meaning "scarcely, barely, only," as you can also see in this fable: *unicum tantum ovum,* "a single egg only" (this is the same use of *tantum* in the compound *tantummodo*). So, be careful with all forms of the word *tantus,* remembering that it can be found at either end of the quantity scale, from extra small to extra large! (For the use of *tantum* in the correlative pair, *tantum-quantum,* see Fable 63.)

# Vocabulary

## Nouns

**anser (anseris,** *m.***):** goose
**anus (anus,** *f.***):** old woman
**crudelitas (crudelitatis,** *f.***):** roughness, cruelty
**cupiditas (cupiditatis,** *f.***):** desire, greed
**fodina (fodinae,** *f.***):** pit, mine
**lucrum (lucri,** *n.***):** gain, profit
**ovum (ovi,** *n.***):** egg
**viscera (viscerum,** *n.***):** entrails, vitals

## Adjectives

**aureus, aurea, aureum:** gold, golden
**avarus, avara, avarum:** greedy, grasping
**conscius, conscia, conscium:** aware of, accomplice in
**contentus, contenta, contentum:** satisfied, content
**inanis, inane (inanis):** empty, foolish
**infelix (infelicis):** unhappy, unlucky
**modicus, modica, modicum:** modest, small
**unicus, unica, unicum:** single, only

## Verbs

**alo (alere):** nourish, raise
**commoveo (commovere), commovi, commotus:** provoke, disturb
**deprehendo (deprehendere), deprehendi, deprehensus:** seize, pounce on
**exclamo (exclamare):** shout, cry out
**excludo (excludere):** thrust out, hatch
**existimo (existimare):** value, estimate
**interficio (interficere), interfeci, interfectus:** kill, do away with
**perdo (perdere), perdidi, perditus:** lose, destroy
**perscrutor (perscrutari):** search through, investigate
**sublacto (sublactare), sublactavi, sublactatus:** entice, dupe

## Other

**confestim:** immediately, at once
**quotidie:** daily, each day
**tantum:** only

# DE ANU ET ANSERE

## Dramatis Personae

*Anus*, the old woman, and *Anser*, the goose.

Anus quaedam Anserem alebat, qui illi quotidie ovum aureum
excludebat. Anus avarissima, existimans Anserem habuisse
in visceribus fodinam auream, cupiditate commota, Anserem
confestim interfecit et, cum viscera perscrutabatur et unicum
tantum ovum deprehenderat, spe sublactata inani, exclamabat,
"O me infelicem, tantae crudelitatis consciam, quae, non modico
contenta lucro, iam omnia perdiderim."

## Grammar Notes

**qui illi ovum excludebat.** The dative pronoun refers to the old woman for whom the goose
laid the egg each day: **qui (anser) illi (anui) ovum excludebat.**

**anus avarissima.** For this use of the superlative, see Fable 39.

**anserem habuisse fodinam auream.** Accusative plus infinitive construction in indirect
statement (see Fable 7), with **anserem** as the accusative subject and **fodinam auream** as
the object.

**cum viscera perscrutabatur.** The deponent verb **perscrutabatur** is transitive and takes a
direct object in the accusative (see Fable 9; for **cum** plus an indicative verb, see Fable 22).

**unicum tantum ovum**. For this adverbial use of **tantum**, see the *Grammar Overview* for
this fable.

**spe sublactata inani.** The phrase **spe inani** wraps around the participle (see Fable 6).

**o me infelicem.** An exclamation using the accusative, with the interjection **o** (see Fable 42);
the adjective agrees with the pronoun **me.**

**tantae crudelitatis consciam.** The adjective **consciam** ("aware of, accomplice in") takes a
genitive complement; like **infelicem**, this adjective also agrees with the pronoun **me.**

**modico contenta lucro.** The phrase **modico lucro** wraps around the adjective, which takes
an ablative complement.

**quae perdiderim.** The subjunctive, introduced by the relative pronoun **quae,** provides
causal background information; according to the woman, this is the reason why she is an
accomplice in her own misfortune.

Si periculum in cursu feceris, quis sit velocior liquido cognosces.

# Fable 57.
# DE LEPORE ET TESTUDINE
## (Barlow 70)

## Introduction
### The Hare and The Tortoise

The story of the tortoise and the hare is one of the most famous of Aesop's fables. In his English version of the fable, G. F. Townsend adds the familiar moral: "Slow but steady wins the race." An ancient Greek version of the fable puts the emphasis not on the persistence of the tortoise, but on the foolishness of the hare: "The story shows that many people have good natural abilities that are ruined by idleness." What moral would you give to the story if you wanted to praise the tortoise for her victory? What if you wanted instead to criticize the hare for his failure?

For more animal contests, see the fable of the tortoise and the eagle (Fable 39), or the battle between the frog and the mouse (Fable 44). For a story about another fleet-footed animal, see the fable of the stag and his horns (Fable 68).

## Grammar Overview
### Haud

In this fable, you will meet the Latin word *haud*, which is an emphatic negative adverb meaning "not at all" or "by no means." It is basically a stronger version of the more familiar Latin word *non*. The word *haud* is most often found with adverbs and adjectives, but it can also be used to negate verbs, as you will see in this fable where the tortoise "did not rest at all," *haud quievit*. You can also meet with *haud* in compounds such as *haudquaquam*, "by no means whatsoever"—in other words, "no way!" Because *haud* is typical of archaic and popular Latin (as opposed to the more refined classical style), you will find it used in proverbs and other popular expressions, such as *Sine pennis volare haud facile est*. What do you think is the metaphorical meaning of this saying? (For another example of negation in Latin, see the comments about *ne ... quidem* in the notes to Fable 53.)

# Vocabulary
## *Nouns*

**cursus (cursus,** *m.***):** running, race
**lepus (leporis,** *m.***):** hare, rabbit
**segnities (segnitiei,** *f.***):** sluggishness, inertia
**somnus (somni,** *m.***):** sleep
**terminus (termini,** *m.***):** end, boundary

## *Adjectives*

**ambo, ambae, ambo (ambobus,** *dat. plural***):** both, two together
**velox (velocis):** rapid, swift

## *Verbs*

**arripio (arripere):** assail, jump at
**cognosco (cognoscere):** learn, find out
**constituo (constituere):** establish, put in position
**curro (currere), cucurri, cursus:** run, race
**derideo (deridere):** laugh at, make fun of
**eligo (eligere), elegi, electus:** choose, select
**excito (excitare), excitavi, excitatus:** stir up, arouse from
**fateor (fateri):** admit, confess
**fido (fidere):** put trust in, believe in
**pervenio (pervenire), perveni, perventus:** reach, arrive at
**quiesco (quiescere), quievi, quietus:** rest, be inactive
**removeo (removere), removi, remotus:** put away, put aside
**reperio (reperire):** find, discover
**subrideo (subridere):** smile, grin
**supero (superare), superavi, superatus:** overcome, outdo

## *Other*

**donec:** until
**haud:** not
**liquido:** clearly, plainly
**paululum:** a small amount, a short while
**postquam:** after, since

# DE LEPORE ET TESTUDINE

## Dramatis Personae

*Testudo*, the tortoise, *Lepus*, the hare, and *Vulpes*, the fox.

Testudo, cum pedes eius Lepus deridebat, subridens dixit, "Si periculum in cursu feceris, quis sit velocior liquido cognosces." Elegerunt igitur Vulpem, quae ambobus et locum et terminum cursus constitueret. Testudo, omni segnitie remota, iter arripiens, haud quievit donec ad terminum pervenerat. Lepus vero, pedibus fidens, postquam paululum quievit, somno excitatus, quantum pedes valuerunt ad terminum cucurrit ubi, cum Testudinem quiescentem reperit, se fatetur a Testudine superatum.

## Grammar Notes

**cum pedes eius lepus deridebat.** Note the use of **cum** plus an indicative verb (see Fable 22); the pronoun **eius** refers to the tortoise, **pedes eius (testudinis).**

**quis sit velocior.** The word **quis** introduces an indirect question with the subjunctive.

**elegerunt igitur vulpem, quae constitueret.** The subjunctive, introduced by the relative pronoun **quae,** explains the purpose for which the fox was elected (for the postpositive **igitur,** see Fable 32).

**et locum et terminum cursus.** The word **cursus** is genitive singular (see Fable 27); the double **et** means "both . . . and" (see Fable 65).

**segnitie remota.** Ablative absolute construction (see Fable 8).

**donec ad terminum pervenerat.** For the use of **donec** with an indicative verb, see Fable 50.

**lepus vero.** For the postpositive particle **vero,** see Fable 60.

**somno excitatus.** The participle **excitatus** ("aroused from") takes an ablative complement.

**quantum pedes valuerunt cucurrit.** The main verb is **cucurrit,** and **quantum pedes valuerunt** is an adverbial clause explaining just how fast the rabbit ran.

**se superatum.** Accusative plus infinitive construction in indirect statement (see Fable 7): **se superatum (esse).**

*Flecti, non frangi.*

*Nec invideamus altius stantibus.*

# Fable 58.
# DE QUERCU ET ARUNDINE
## (Barlow 33)

## Introduction
### The Oak and The Reed

Although Aesop's fables are usually about animals, the actions of those animals serve as a kind of code for the human world. The same is true for the trees in this fable, where the qualities of the oak and of the reed provide a lesson about flexibility that holds true both for trees and for people. In an ancient Greek version of the story, the moral of the fable is "Those who adapt to the times will emerge unscathed." The fifteenth-century English version by Caxton has this moral: "The prowde shall be allwey humbled and the meke and humble shalle be enhaunced," in other words, "The proud shall always be humbled, and the meek and the humble shall be exalted." If you put the oak and the reed at opposite ends of the flexibility scale, how would you rate yourself: are you more like the oak tree, or more like the reed?

For another story about trees, see the fable of the man and the axe (Fable 10). For another story about wind and weather, see the fable of the contest between the sun and the wind (Fable 79), or the young man and the swallow (Fable 42).

## Grammar Overview
### The Gender of Trees and Fruit

Gender in Latin is, for the most part, a grammatical category, not a natural one. So, each time you learn a new noun in Latin, you have to memorize the gender. There is, however, an odd little rule regarding the names of trees in Latin: almost every tree name in Latin is feminine, including tree names that end in *-us*. This applies to tree names in the second declension, such as *pinus* (pine tree) and *cedrus* (cedar tree), and it also applies to tree names in the fourth declension, such as *cupressus* (cypress tree) and *quercus* (oak tree), as you will see in this fable. The trees are feminine in gender and, if the tree produces fruit, the name of the fruit is usually a neuter noun, such as the pear, *pirum* (neuter), from the pear tree, *pirus* (feminine), or the apple, *malum* (neuter), from the apple tree, *malus* (feminine). There is a famous saying in Latin about *mala*, apples: *Ab ovo usque ad mala*. What do you think this saying refers to? (Hint: It is sometimes rendered in English with the analogous phrase, "from soup to nuts").

# Vocabulary
## *Nouns*
**amnis (amnis,** *m.***):** river, stream
**arundo (arundinis,** *f.***):** reed
**Boreas** (*acc.* **Boream,** *m.***):** North wind [Greek]
**Eurus (Euri,** *m.***):** East wind [Greek]
**flatus (flatus,** *m.***):** blowing, breeze
**Notus (Noti,** *m.***):** South wind [Greek]
**quercus (quercus,** *f.***):** oak, oak tree
**ramus (rami,** *m.***):** branch, bough
**turbo (turbinis,** *m.***):** whirlwind, tornado
**ventus (venti,** *m.***):** wind

## *Adjectives*
**incolumis, incolume (incolumis):** unharmed, safe
**mirus, mira, mirum:** wondrous, strange
**tutus, tuta, tutum:** safe, secure
**validus, valida, validum:** strong, powerful

## *Verbs*
**cedo (cedere):** yield, give way
**declino (declinare):** swerve, bend
**effringo (effringere), effregi, effractus:** break open, smash
**excido (excidere), excidi:** perish, disappear
**figo (figere), fixi, fixus:** fasten, fix
**fluito (fluitare):** flow, float
**haereo (haerere):** stick, cling
**inclino (inclinare):** bend, lower
**miror (mirari):** be amazed, marvel at
**molior (moliri), molitus sum:** struggle, strive
**praecipito (praecipitare), praecipitavi, praecipitatus:** throw headlong, cast down
**resisto (resistere):** oppose, make a stand

## *Other*
**denique:** finally, in the end
**etenim:** as a matter of fact, because
**forte:** by chance, accidentally
**huc:** here, to this place
**illuc:** to that place, there

# DE QUERCU ET ARUNDINE

## Dramatis Personae

*Quercus*, the oak, and *Arundo*, the reed.

Validiore vento effracta Quercus huc illuc in amnem praecipitata fluitat et, ramis suis in Arundine forte fixis, haeret miraturque Arundinem in tanto turbine stare incolumem. Arundo respondet cedendo et declinando se esse tutam; inclinare se etenim ad Boream, ad Notum, ad Eurum, denique ad omnem flatum; nec mirum esse si Quercus exciderit, quae non cedere, sed resistere molita est.

## Grammar Notes

**validiore vento.** The comparative is used here to indicate "very strong, quite strong," without an explicit comparison (see Fable 28).

**ramis fixis.** Ablative absolute construction (see Fable 8).

**arundinem stare incolumem.** Accusative plus infinitive construction in indirect statement (see Fable 7), with **arundinem** as the accusative subject and **incolumem** as a predicate adjective.

**cedendo et declinando.** The gerunds are in the ablative case (see Fable 48).

**se esse tutam.** Accusative plus infinitive construction in indirect statement, with **se** as the accusative subject and **tutam** as the predicate adjective.

**inclinare se.** Accusative plus infinitive construction in indirect statement.

**nec mirum esse.** Accusative plus infinitive construction in the continuing indirect statement; you can replace the word **nec** with the words **et non** (see Fable 18): **et non mirum esse,** "and it is not strange."

Sciens cavebo.

Sero in periculis est
consilium quaerere.

# Fable 59.
# DE HIRUNDINE ET ALIIS AVICULIS
## (Barlow 18)

## Introduction
### The Swallow and The Other Little Birds

Like the story of the bat who flies only at night (Fable 8), this story provides an explanation of an animal behavior, why it is that the swallow makes her nest in the eaves of human houses, instead of living out in the woods with the other wild birds. Meanwhile, in addition to explaining why the swallow nests in human houses, the fable also teaches a lesson. In Jacobs's version of the story, the moral advises: "Destroy the seed of evil, or it will grow up to your ruin." If one of the wild birds caught in a snare at the end of the fable were to pronounce the moral of the story, what do you think she would say?

For another story about the swallow, see the fable of the young man in winter (Fable 42). For other stories about wise birds, see the fable of the lark and her chicks (Fable 49), or the fable of the crow and the pot (Fable 5).

## Grammar Overview
### Frequentative Verbs

In addition to the prefixes that can be attached to the beginning of verbs in order to form new meanings (*ex-clamo*, *in-venio*, etc.), suffixes can be attached to the end of a verbal stem to create new meanings. Two such suffixes are *-tare* and *-itare*, which are used to create frequentative forms of the verb, indicating repeated or intense action. So, for example, *captare*, "to grasp," is derived from *capere*, "to get hold of," and *clamitare*, "to shout repeatedly," is derived from *clamare*, "to shout." In this fable, you will meet with the verb *dictitare*, "to say repeatedly," which is derived from *dicere*, "to say," and also the verb *cohabitare*, "to live together," which is derived from *habere*, "to have." In English, we also have frequentative verb forms, created with the *-le* suffix. For example, you can "sniff" something once in English or "sniffle" repeatedly, just as something can "spark" once, or it can "sparkle" repeatedly. Can you think of another frequentative verb form in English? (Hint: Listen to the sound of Rice Krispies˚ cereal.)

# Vocabulary

## *Nouns*

**avicula (aviculae,** *f.***):** bird, little bird
**foedus (foederis,** *n.***):** treaty, agreement
**hirundo (hirundinis,** *f.***):** swallow, martin
**insidiae (insidiarum,** *f.***):** ambush, snare
**laqueus (laquei,** *m.***):** snare, trap
**linum (lini,** *n.***):** flax, flax seed
**rete (retis,** *n.***):** net, snare
**seges (segetis,** *f.***):** field of grain, crop
**sementis (sementis,** *f.***):** sowing, seeding

## *Adjectives*

**garrulus, garrula, garrulum:** talkative, chattering

## *Verbs*

**cohabito (cohabitare):** live together
**consulo (consulere):** advise, offer advice
**dictito (dictitare):** say, repeat
**evello (evellere):** pluck, tear out
**hortor (hortari):** encourage, urge
**impedio (impedire):** hinder, obstruct
**ineo (inire):** go in, enter into
**irrideo (irridere):** mock, scoff at
**maturesco (maturescere):** mature, ripen
**moneo (monere):** warn, admonish
**populor (populari):** lay waste, strip
**sero (serere), sevi, satus:** sow, plant
**suadeo (suadere):** urge, exhort
**surgo (surgere):** rise up, get up

## *Other*

**iterum:** again, a second time
**ne . . . quidem:** not . . . even
**rursum:** on the contrary, again

# DE HIRUNDINE ET ALIIS AVICULIS

## Dramatis Personae

*Hirundo*, the swallow, and *Aviculae*, the birds.

Hirundo, cum linum coeptum esset seri, suadebat aliis Aviculis impedire sementem, dictitans omnibus fieri insidias. Irridebant illae garrulamque vocabant. Surgente lino, rursum monebat evellere sata; irridebant iterum. Maturescente lino, hortabatur populari segetem et, cum ne tunc quidem consulentem audirent, Hirundo cum homine foedus init cohabitatque cum eo. Ceteris Avibus e lino retia fiunt et laquei.

## Grammar Notes

**cum linum coeptum esset seri.** The subjunctive, introduced by **cum**, gives causal background information; this is why the swallow tried to warn the other birds.

**omnibus fieri insidias.** Accusative plus infinitive construction in indirect statement (see Fable 7), and **insidias** as the predicate noun: **omnibus fieri insidias**, "it would be made into snares for them all."

**garrulam vocabant.** The adjective **garrulam** is being used predicatively: **vocabant eam garrulam**, "they called her a chatter-box."

**surgente lino.** Ablative absolute construction (see Fable 8).

**evellere sata.** The participle **sata** is used substantively, meaning "crops, things sown."

**maturescente lino.** Ablative absolute construction; **maturescente** is an inchoative verb (see Fable 70).

**populari segetem.** The deponent verb is transitive and takes a direct object in the accusative (see Fable 9).

**cum ne tunc quidem audirent.** The phrase **ne . . . quidem** phrase puts a strong emphasis on the word **tunc,** "not even then" (see Fable 53); the subjunctive, introduced by **cum**, gives causal background information as to why the swallow went to live with people, rather than with the other birds.

**e lino retia fiunt et laquei.** The compound subject **retia et laquei** wraps around the verb (see Fable 6).

Gallus aliquando cum asino pascebatur; leo autem asinum aggressus est.

# Fable 60.
# DE LEONE, ASINO ET GALLO
## (Barlow 46)

## Introduction
### The Lion, the Donkey, and The Rooster

This fable is based on a rather odd belief: according to ancient Greek and Roman legends, lions were terrified by the sound of a rooster crowing! So, in this fable you will see that the lion runs away when he hears the sound of the rooster. The poor donkey doesn't quite understand what is going on, and this leads to a fatal mistake on his part. Sir Roger L'Estrange applied this moral to the fable: "The Fool that is Wise and Brave only in his Own Conceit runs on without Fear or Wit." In the version of the fable you are about to read, the donkey pronounces the moral of the story just before he dies. If instead the lion were assigned the task of expressing the moral of the story, what do you think he would say?

For other stories about donkeys and lions, see the old lion and the donkey (Fable 45), or the donkey dressed in the lion skin (Fable 40). For another story about the rooster crowing, see the fable of the old woman and her maids (Fable 74).

## Grammar Overview
### The Postpositive Particle, Vero

As you have seen already, postpositive particles are commonly used in Latin in order to build meaningful relationships between one sentence and the next. In this fable, you will see another example of a postpositive particle: *vero*. Although *vero* can be used as an adverb anywhere in a sentence, it has a special meaning when it is used as a postpositive particle. Like *quidem* (see Fable 23), *vero* strongly affirms the statement, but at the same time, like the postpositive particle *autem* (see Fable 16), *vero* also emphasizes a contrast with the previous statement. If you had to try to express those two functions in a single phrase in English you could say "but indeed" or "but as a matter of fact." So, pay attention to the use of *vero* in the fable you are about to read, and see how it carries out both these affirmative and adversative functions as it connects the two sentences. (For more postpositive particles in Latin, see the notes to Fable 66.)

# Vocabulary
## Nouns
**acies (aciei,** *f.*): sharp edge, battle line
**gallicinium (gallicinii,** *n.*): cock-crow

## Adjectives
**iustus, iusta, iustum:** fair, right
**pugnax (pugnacis):** fighting, aggressive

## Verbs
**aggredior (aggredi), aggressus sum:** approach, attack
**clamo (clamare):** shout, exclaim
**converto (convertere), converti, conversus:** turn, turn around
**devoro (devorare):** consume, gulp down
**exclamo (exclamare), exclamavi, exclamatus:** shout, cry out
**incipio (incipere):** begin, start
**irruo (irruere), irrui:** rush in, rush into
**nascor (nasci), natus sum:** be born
**pasco (pascere):** graze, feed
**patior (pati), passus sum:** suffer, undergo
**persequor (persequi), persecutus sum:** chase, overtake
**reor (reri), ratus sum:** think, suppose

## Other
**aliquando:** sometime, sometime or other
**procul:** far off, at a distance
**propter:** because of, on account of
**quamobrem:** for what reason

# DE LEONE, ASINO ET GALLO

## Dramatis Personae

*Gallus*, the rooster, *Asinus*, the donkey, and *Leo*, the lion.

Gallus aliquando cum Asino pascebatur, Leone autem aggresso Asinum, Gallus exclamavit, et Leo, qui Galli vocem timet, fugere incipit. Asinus, ratus propter se fugere, aggressus est Leonem; ut vero procul a gallicinio persecutus est, conversus Leo Asinum devoravit, qui moriens clamabat, "Iusta passus sum; ex pugnacibus enim non natus parentibus, quamobrem in aciem irrui?"

## Grammar Notes

**gallus pascebatur.** The active form of the verb means to "feed, supply with food," while the passive form that you see here means "feed on, graze, browse."

**leone autem aggresso asinum.** Ablative absolute (see Fable 8) with the postpositive particle **autem** in second position (see Fable 16); the deponent verb is transitive and takes a direct object in the accusative: "when the lion attacked the donkey."

**propter se fugere.** Accusative plus infinitive construction in indirect statement (see Fable 7), with **leonem** as the implied subject of the infinitive, and **se** referring back to the donkey.

**asinus aggressus est leonem.** The deponent verb **aggressus est** is transitive and takes a direct object in the accusative (see Fable 9): "the donkey attacked the lion."

**ut vero persecutus est.** This is a temporal use of **ut,** meaning "as, as soon as" (see Fable 55); note the postpositive particle **vero** in second position (see the *Grammar Overview* for this fable); the subject of the verb is the donkey, and the lion is the implied object: **ut vero (asinus) persecutus est (leonem).**

**qui moriens clamabat.** The reference of the relative pronoun **qui** is **asinum** in the main clause: **qui (asinus) moriens clamabat.**

**iusta passus sum.** The deponent verb **passus sum** is transitive and takes a direct object in the accusative, with the neuter plural adjective **iusta,** used substantively as a noun.

**ex pugnacibus enim non natus parentibus.** The phrase **ex pugnacibus parentibus** wraps around the participle (see Fable 6); the placement of the postpositive **enim** shows that **ex pugnacibus** is treated as a single word unit (see Fable 20).

**quamobrem.** This is a compound word: **quam + ob + rem** (see Fable 76), with the noun phrase **quam rem** wrapped around the preposition.

Iratus herus canem verbis et verberibus increpabat.

# Fable 61.
# DE CANE VETULO ET MAGISTRO
## (Barlow 64)

## Introduction
### The Old Dog and His Master

This is a fable about a once valiant hunting dog who has lost his strength. In the version of the fable by G. F. Townsend, the dog tells his master: "I rather deserve to be praised for what I have been, than to be blamed for what I am." In his fifteenth-century version of the fable, Caxton provides this moral to the story: "Men ought not to dysprayse the auncyent; thow oughtest to loue and prayse the dedes whiche the haue done in theyr yongthe," in other words, "Men ought not to insult people who are old; you should love and praise the deeds that they have done in their youth." Based on the master's treatment of the dog in this story, what words would you use to express the moral of this fable? What are some of the ways in which this dog's situation can provide a model of human society?

For another story about old age, see the fable of the old lion and the donkey (Fable 45), or the old man who called upon Death (Fable 33). For a story about a master who is more perceptive than this dog's master, see the fable of the stag hidden in the stable (Fable 34).

## Grammar Overview
### The Predicate Dative

In this fable you will see the dative used in the predicate of a sentence to explain the purpose that something serves, what it is good for: *canis magno usui erat*, "the dog was (for) a big use" or, in more idiomatic English, "the dog was very useful." When you are dealing with a predicate dative, it is often easiest to find a predicative adjective or even a predicate noun to use in your English translation. For example, the statement *auxilio est*, "it is for a help," can be translated into English as "it is helpful" or "it is a help." Sometimes you will find two datives in the predicate: *canis erat emolumento hero*, "the dog was profitable (*emolumento*) for his master (*hero*)." There is a famous legal maxim in Latin that features two datives in the predicate: *Cui bono?* See if you can figure out why this famous Latin legal question is so helpful in figuring out who might have committed a crime. (For more uses of the dative in Latin, see the notes to Fable 64.)

# Vocabulary

## Nouns

**dens (dentis,** *m.***):** tooth, fang
**emolumentum (emolumenti,** *n.***):** benefit, profit
**magister (magistri,** *m.***):** master
**meritum (meriti,** *n.***):** service, reward
**usus (usus,** *m.***):** use, advantage
**velocitas (velocitatis,** *f.***):** rapidity, swiftness
**verber (verberis,** *n.***):** lash, whipping

## Adjectives

**durus, dura, durum:** hard, harsh
**imbellis, imbelle (imbellis):** unwarlike, defenseless
**longaevus, longaeva, longaevum:** aged, long in years
**multifarius, multifaria, multifarium:** numerous, diverse
**severus, severa, severum:** stern, unforgiving
**venaticus, venatica, venaticum:** for hunting, hunter's
**vetulus, vetula, vetulum:** aged, old

## Verbs

**apprehendo (apprehendere), apprehendi, apprehensus:** grab hold of, seize
**demitto (demittere), demisi, demissus:** let go, send away
**increpo (increpare):** rebuke, chide
**irascor (irasci), iratus sum:** grow angry, get mad
**pensito (pensitare):** ponder, reckon
**persequor (persequi):** reach, overtake
**praecello (praecellere), praecellui, praecelsus:** surpass, excel
**privo (privare), privavi, privatus:** deprive of

## Other

**fortuito:** accidentally, by chance
**male:** badly, poorly
**olim:** formerly, once upon a time
**quondam:** formerly, at one time

# DE CANE VETULO ET MAGISTRO

## Dramatis Personae

*Canis*, the dog, and *Herus*, the master.

Canis venaticus, qui quondam velocitate ceteris praecelluit et magno erat olim usui et emolumento Hero, iam longaevus et imbellis, fortuito cervum persequebatur et apprehensum (dentibus privatus) mox demisit. Quem iratus Herus verbis et verberibus increpabat. Cui Canis: "O dure et severe mihi Magister, qui multifaria mea merita tam male pensitaveris!"

## Grammar Notes

**velocitate ceteris praecelluit.** The verb **praecelluit** takes a dative complement, and the ablative **velocitate** explains in what way the dog had been better than all the rest.

**magno erat olim usui et emolumento hero.** The predicate datives **usui** and **emolumento** (see the *Grammar Overview* for this fable) express the dog's purpose for his master, **hero**: "once upon a time he was very useful and profitable for his master."

**cervum persequebatur.** The deponent verb **persequebatur** is transitive and takes a direct object in the accusative (see Fable 9).

**cervum . . . apprehensum demisit.** You might translate the passive participle with an active verb (see Fable 5): the dog caught the deer (**apprehensum**) and then let it go (**demisit**).

**dentibus privatus.** The participle **privatus** ("deprived of") takes an ablative complement.

**quem herus increpabat.** The referent of the relative pronoun **quem** is **canis** in the previous sentence (see Fable 4): **quem (canem) herus increpabat**.

**cui canis.** The referent of the relative pronoun **cui** is **herus** in the previous sentence, with an implied verb of speaking: **cui (hero) canis (inquit)**.

**qui pensitaveris.** The subjunctive, introduced by the relative pronoun **qui,** provides causal background information; according to the dog, this is why his master can be considered **durus et severus**.

Delphinus tam violento sequebatur impetu, ut arenis illideret.

# Fable 62.
# DE DELPHINO ET SMARIDE
## (Barlow 103)

## Introduction
### *The Dolphin and The Picarel*

The fable you are about to read concerns a tiny little fish who is called *smaris* in Latin, a "picarel" in English. Earlier, you saw a little picarel engaged in a life-or-death debate with a hungry fisherman (Fable 50). In this fable, you will see the little fish engaged in a life-or-death struggle with a dolphin. Although the little fish does not survive, he has some small pleasure at the end of the story seeing what happens to the dolphin. An ancient Greek version of the fable adds this moral: "People readily undergo a disaster when they can witness the destruction of those who are to blame." This moral is based on the point of view of the picarel—but what about the dolphin? If the dying dolphin were to pronounce a moral at the end of the story, what do you think he would say is the lesson he has learned?

For another story of how misery loves company, see the fable of the fox who lost her tail (Fable 51). For other stories about little creatures in a fight for their lives, see the wolf and the lamb at the stream (Fable 53), or the dove being chased by the hawk (Fable 18).

## Grammar Overview
### *Verbal Quotation Marks*

In modern written English, direct quotes are indicated with quotation marks at the beginning and at the end of the quotation. The ancient Romans, however, did not use quotation marks. Even today, you will find many Latin texts that are printed without the use of any quotation marks. I have added quotation marks to the Latin text in this book to make the stories easier to read, but that is an editorial choice on my part; the original seventeenth-century edition of these Latin stories did not include quotation marks. Latin does not really need the quotation marks, after all, because it relies instead on what you might call verbal punctuation, formulaic words such as *dicens* or *ait or inquit*, which indicate the presence of a direct quotation. So, as you read the fables, see what verbal clues you can find, in addition to the quotation marks, that alert you to the presence of a direct quotation. (For more about direct and indirect speech in Latin, see the notes to Fable 1.)

# Vocabulary
## Nouns
**arena (arenae,** *f.*): sand
**auctor (auctoris,** *m.*): author, originator
**delphinus (delphini,** *m.*): dolphin
**impetus (impetus,** *m.*): attack, charge
**pisciculus (pisciculi,** *m.*): little fish
**rupes (rupis,** *f.*): cliff, rock
**smaris (smaridis,** *m.*): picarel (tiny sea-fish)

## Adjectives
**defunctus, defuncta, defunctum:** dead, deceased
**moribundulus, moribundula, moribundulum:** dying
**violentus, violenta, violentum:** violent, impetuous

## Verbs
**capto (captare):** grab, grasp
**confugio (confugere), confugi:** flee, take refuge
**consolor (consolari), consolatus sum:** cheer, comfort
**haereo (haerere):** stick, cling
**illido (illidere):** strike, dash against
**persequor (persequi):** reach, overtake
**succumbo (succumbere):** succumb, lie down
**vito (vitare):** avoid, evade

## Other
**paululum:** a small amount, a short while
**prae:** in front of, in view of
**prius:** before, beforehand
**profecto:** certainly, as a matter of fact
**quod:** because, that

# DE DELPHINO ET SMARIDE

## Dramatis Personae

*Pisciculus*, the fish, and *Delphinus*, the dolphin.

Persequebatur Pisciculum Delphinus. Hunc ut vitaret,
Pisciculus ad rupem confugit. Quem ut captaret, Delphinus
tam violento sequebatur impetu, ut arenis illideret et haerens
morti succumberet. Quod cum vidisset Pisciculus, sibi paululum
consolatus est, moribundulus inquiens, "Dulcior mihi profecto
mea mors futura est quod prius auctorem meae mortis defunctum
prae oculis viderim."

## Grammar Notes

**persequebatur pisciculum.** The deponent verb **persequebatur** is transitive and takes a direct object in the accusative (see Fable 9).

**quem ut captaret.** The referent of the relative pronoun **quem** is **pisciculus** in the previous sentence: **quem (pisciculum) ut captaret**.

**violento sequebatur impetu.** The phrase **violento impetu** wraps around the verb (see Fable 6).

**arenis illideret.** The verb **illideret** takes a dative complement.

**morti succumberet.** The verb **succumberet** takes a dative complement.

**quod cum vidisset pisciculus.** The relative pronoun **quod** connects back to the previous sentence (see Fable 4), referring to the general situation described there, i.e., the dolphin being beached on the sand; the subjunctive, introduced by **cum**, gives causal background information as to why the fish cheered up (for the placement of **quod** before **cum**, see Fable 37).

**inquiens.** This is the present active participle of the defective verb **inquam,** used to indicate a direct quotation (see the *Grammar Overview* for this fable).

**futura est.** The future active participle with the verb **est** creates a future active periphrastic (see Fable 25).

**auctorem meae mortis defunctum.** This predicate adjective **defunctum** agrees with the predicate noun, i.e., the fish wants to see the dolphin (**auctorem meae mortis**) dead (**defunctum**).

**quod . . . viderim.** The subjunctive, introduced by **quod** ("because"), gives causal background information; according to the fish, this is why death comes more sweetly than it would otherwise.

*Cum vulpe habens commercium, dolos cave.*

*Quod est venturum, sapiens quasi praesens cavet.*

# Fable 63.
# DE VULPE IN PUTEO
## (Barlow 8)

## Introduction
### The Fox in The Well

In this fable, a goat and a fox are trapped in a well. These two animals did not "look before they leaped," as the English proverb goes. How will they get up out of the well? The fox has a great idea: she will jump on the horns of the goat, scramble up out of the well, and then help the goat make his escape. The version of the fable that you are about to read here does not explain the fox's plan in detail; the author probably assumed that the story was already familiar to his readers. Instead of focusing on the details of the escape plan, the author is more interested in what the fox does after she gets out of the well, while the goat is still trapped inside. Based on how things turn out for the fox and for the goat, what do you think are some of the lessons we could learn from this fable?

For another story about the fox in the well, see the fable of the wolf and the fox (Fable 22). For a story where the fox's tricks fail her, see the fable of the cat and the fox (Fable 72), or the fable of the fox and the rooster (Fable 47).

## Grammar Overview
### Correlatives in Latin

In Latin, there is an extensive series of word pairs, called correlatives, which are used to show relations of comparison. You might think of them as the *t-q* pairs: *tantum-quantum, talis-qualis, tam-quam* and *tot-quot*, etc. You choose the pair that corresponds to the nature of the comparison between the things that are being correlated. A relationship of quantity is expressed with *tantum-quantum*, "as (much) - as." A relationship of quality is expressed with *talis-qualis*, "(such) - as." The pair *tam-quam* is used to express degree: "(so) - as." The pair *tot-quot* is used to express number, "as (many) - as." English uses the word "as" to organize all these relationships, and does not have a series of paired words as Latin does to express these relationships (although English does have its own correlative adverbs; see Fable 65). In this fable you will see the correlative pair *tantum-quantum* featured in the punchline of the story, when the fox makes a delightful play on words comparing the quantity of the goat's wits to the quantity of his whiskers!

# Vocabulary
## Nouns
**caper (capri,** *m.***):** goat, billy-goat
**gaudium (gaudii,** *n.***):** joy, gladness
**hircus (hirci,** *m.***):** goat, billy-goat
**margo (marginis,** *f.***):** edge, rim
**mentum (menti,** *n.***):** chin
**pactum (pacti,** *n.***):** manner, agreement
**puteus (putei,** *m.***):** well, hole
**reditus (reditus,** *m.***):** return, going back
**saeta (saetae,** *f.***):** hair, bristle
**sensus (sensus,** *m.***):** awareness, sense

## Adjectives
**foedifragus, foedifraga, foedifragum:** treaty-breaking
**redux (reducis):** brought back, restored
**sitibundus, sitibunda, sitibundum:** thirsty

## Verbs
**circumspicio (circumspicere):** look around
**cursito (cursitare):** run about, race
**descendo (descendere), descendi, descensus:** go down, come down
**excogito (excogitare):** devise, invent
**exploro (explorare), exploravi, exploratus:** search out, test
**incuso (incusare):** accuse, blame
**obtempero (obtemperare), obtemperavi, obtemperatus:** obey, comply
**perbibo (perbibere), perbibi:** drink deeply, imbibe
**prosilio (prosilire):** leap forward

## Other
**ceterum:** besides, as for the rest
**enimvero:** to be sure, what is more
**etenim:** as a matter of fact, because
**prae:** in view of, because of
**prius:** before, earlier

# DE VULPE IN PUTEO

## Dramatis Personae

*Vulpes*, the fox, and *Caper* (*Hircus*), the goat.

Vulpes et Caper sitibundi in quendam puteum descendebant.
In quo cum perbibissent, Vulpes dixit circumspicienti reditum
Capro, "Bono animo esto, Caper! Excogitavi etenim quo pacto
uterque reduces simus." Obtemperavit consilio Caper, et Vulpes,
ex puteo prosiliens, prae gaudio in margine cursitabat. Ceterum,
cum ab Hirco ut foedifraga incusaretur, respondit, "Enimvero,
Hirce, si tantum tibi sensus esset in mente, quantum est
saetarum in mento, non prius in puteum descendisses, quam
de reditu exploravisses."

## Grammar Notes

**in quo cum perbibissent.** The referent of the relative pronoun **quo** is **puteum** in the previous sentence: **in quo (puteo);** the subjunctive, introduced by **cum**, gives causal background information as to why they were ready to get out of the well now.

**bono animo esto.** The form **esto** is the future imperative of **sum** (see Fable 11), with the predicate ablative **bono animo** functioning like a predicate adjective, "good-spirited, optimistic."

**quo pacto reduces simus.** The word **quo** introduces an indirect question with the subjunctive; **reduces** is a predicate adjective.

**uterque.** The pronoun is grammatically singular, but logically plural, referring to **uterque (nostrum),** "each of us two, both of us."

**obtemperavit consilio.** The verb **obtemperavit** takes a dative complement; the plan refers to the fox using the goat's horns to climb up and get out, so that he could then (supposedly) help the goat in turn to get out.

**cum ab hirco incusaretur.** The subjunctive, introduced by **cum**, gives causal background information; this is why the fox insulted the goat.

**ut foedifraga.** The phrase means "as a traitor."

**tantum sensus quantum saetarum.** Parallel construction (see the *Grammar Overview* for this fable), with partitive genitives (see Fable 30): **tantum** (so much) **sensus** (of wit), **quantum** (as much) **saetarum** (of whiskers) = "as much wit as whiskers."

*Personam, non faciem, gerit.*

*Calidum et frigidum ex eodem ore efflat.*

# Fable 64.
# DE SATYRO ET VIATORE
## (Barlow 74)

## Introduction
### The Satyr and The Wayfarer

The satyr is a famous character from Greek mythology, a wild creature who lives in the woods and mountains, with the upper body of a man but a lower body like that of a goat. In the fable you are about to read, a satyr rescues a man whom he finds frozen in the snow. He gives the man shelter, but then grows suspicious as he observes the man's behavior. In the end, the satyr tosses the man out because he is convinced that the man is a hypocrite and a liar, someone we might call "two-faced" in English, an idiom that is quite similar to the Latin phrase that the satyr uses when he accuses the man of having a "two-way mouth," an *os diversum*. What do you think: based on your own experience, is someone who "blows hot and cold," as this man seems to do, as dangerous as the satyr thinks that he is?

For another story about rescuing someone in the snow, see the fable of the frozen snake (Fable 35). For more stories about hypocrisy and lies, see the fable of the fox and the supposedly sour grapes (Fable 29), or the boy who cried "Wolf!" (Fable 12).

## Grammar Overview
### The Dative of Possession

Compared to other languages, English has a very broad sense of things we can "have" and things that are "mine" or "yours," etc. For example, in English, we talk about "my hands," "my feet," and so on, while in other languages, the idea that you possess or somehow own your body parts would seem very strange, as if those body parts could belong to anybody else but you! Likewise, we regularly say in English "I have two sisters and a brother," as if family members are things that we "have" in the same way we possess a material object. Latin often omits the possessive pronoun when it might be required usage in English, or it might express possession using the dative case instead, as in statements like *Filii duo mihi sunt,* "I have two sons," or *Nomen mihi est Julia,* "My name is Julia." In this fable you will see an example of a dative used with reference to a body part, when the satyr tells the wayfarer that he doesn't want someone in his house *cui tam diversum est os,* "who has [dative *cui*] a mouth that is so inconsistent."

# Vocabulary

## Nouns

**algor (algoris, *m.*):** cold, chill
**anhelitus (anhelitus, *m.*):** breath, panting
**antrum (antri, *n.*):** cave, hollow place
**nix (nivis, *f.*):** snow
**polenta (polentae, *f.*):** grain, polenta
**satyrus (satyri, *m.*):** satyr

## Adjectives

**diversus, diversa, diversum:** different, inconsistent

## Verbs

**accumbo (accumbere):** recline, sit down to dinner
**calefio (calefieri):** warm up, become warm
**eiicio (eiicere):** throw out, expel
**eneco (enecare), enecui, enectus:** kill, exhaust
**frigesco (frigescere):** grow cold, cool
**interrogo (interrogare), interrogavi, interrogatus:** question, inquire
**misereor (misereri), misertus sum:** pity, have mercy on
**nolo (nolle):** refuse, not want
**obruo (obruere):** cover up, bury
**percontor (percontari), percontatus sum:** inquire, ask
**refocillo (refocillare):** revive, warm to life
**sufflo (sufflare):** puff, blow

## Other

**continuo:** immediately, at once
**cur:** why
**postea:** afterwards

# DE SATYRO ET VIATORE

## Dramatis Personae

*Satyrus*, the satyr, and *Viator*, the wayfarer.

Satyrus Viatorem, nive obrutum atque algore enectum, misertus ducit in antrum suum. Refocillantem manus anhelitu oris percontatur causam; "Ut calefiant," inquit. Postea, cum accumberent, sufflat Viator in polentam. Quod cur ita faceret interrogatus "Ut frigescat," inquit. Tunc continuo Satyrus Viatorem eiiciens: "Nolo (inquit) in meo ut sis antro, cui tam diversum est os."

## Grammar Notes

**refocillantem manus.** The participle refers to the wayfarer: **(viatorem) refocillantem manus,** with **manus** an accusative plural, object of the participle.

**percontatur.** The satyr is the subject of this deponent verb, which takes a double accusative for the person who is being asked a question (**viatorem**) and the information requested (**causam**).

**ut calefiant.** The implied subject of this verb is the man's hands, **manus.**

**cum accumberent.** The subjunctive, introduced by **cum**, gives causal background information; this is why the man was now ready to eat his food.

**quod cur ita faceret.** The relative pronoun **quod** connects back to the previous sentence (see Fable 4), referring to the general situation described there, i.e., the man blowing on his food; **cur** introduces an indirect question with the subjunctive.

**in meo ut sis antro.** The phrase **in meo antro** wraps around the phrase, **ut sis** (see Fable 6).

**diversum.** This is a predicate adjective, agreeing with the noun **os.**

**cui est os.** The referent of the relative pronoun **cui** is you, the implied subject of **sis;** the dative here expresses possession (see the *Grammar Overview* for this fable): "whose mouth."

Constratus humi, se mortuum simulabat et spiritum totum compressit.

# Fable 65.
# DE URSO ET DUOBUS VIATORIBUS
## (Barlow 87)

## Introduction
### The Bear and The Two Wayfarers

This story shows what happens when two friends unexpectedly run into a bear. As you will see, one of the men "plays dead" in order to survive the bear's attack. The main point of the story, however, is what the bear's attack reveals about the nature of each of the two men and their supposed friendship. In Joseph Jacobs's version of this fable, the moral advises: "Never trust a friend who deserts you at a pinch." G. F. Townsend concludes that "Misfortune tests the sincerity of friends." After you see how the two friends react to the bear, what words would you use to express the moral of this fable?

For another story about false friends, see the fable of the animals who went hunting with a lion (Fable 73), or the wolf who offered his help to the sow in labor (Fable 26). For another story about a bear, see the fable of the bear who attacked the beehive (Fable 41).

## Grammar Overview
### Correlatives in English

As you saw in Fable 63, Latin has a series of correlatives, the *t-q* series (*tantum-quantum, talis-qualis*, etc.), which express relationships of quantity, quality, and so on. English also has a variety of correlative pairs that are used where Latin instead relies on the repetition of a single word, rather than a pair. Probably the most famous of these is the English pair "both-and," which is equivalent to the double use of *et* in Latin, as in the motto, *Et vi et virtute*, "Both by strength and by virtue." There is also the English pair "either-or," which is expressed in Latin with a double use of *vel* or double use of *aut*, as in this motto, *Aut inveniam viam aut faciam*, "Either I shall find a way or I will make one." The English negative "neither-nor" is expressed by double *nec* in Latin, as in this motto: *Nec temere nec timide*, "Neither rashly, nor timidly." In this fable you will see an example of the double use of Latin *alter*, "the one - the other," which is used to describe the different reactions of the two friends upon running into the bear.

# Vocabulary

## Nouns

**facies (faciei,** *f.***):** face, appearance
**foedus (foederis,** *n.***):** treaty, agreement
**humus (humi,** *f.***):** ground, soil
**socius (socii,** *m.***):** ally, partner
**spiritus (spiritus,** *m.***):** breath, spirit

## Adjectives

**falsus, falsa, falsum:** wrong, lying
**intactus, intacta, intactum:** untouched, intact
**perfidus, perfida, perfidum:** untrustworthy, treacherous
**posterus, postera, posterum:** after, future
**trepidus, trepida, trepidum:** fearful, anxious

## Verbs

**abeo (abire):** go away, depart
**admoveo (admovere):** bring near, move up
**caveo (cavere):** beware, watch out for
**comprimo (comprimere), compressi, compressus:** hold in, suppress
**conscendo (conscendere), conscendi, conscensus:** climb up, mount
**consterno (consternere), constravi, constratus:** stretch out, lay low
**descendo (descendere):** go down, come down
**incepto (inceptare):** begin, undertake
**moneo (monere):** warn, admonish
**percontor (percontari), percontatus sum:** inquire, ask
**simulo (simulare):** imitate, look like
**susurro (susurrare), susurravi:** whisper, mutter

## Other

**obviam:** in the way of, running into

# DE URSO ET DUOBUS VIATORIBUS

## Dramatis Personae

*Amici duo*, the two friends, and *Ursus*, the bear.

Amici duo, facto foedere, iter inceptantes, Urso obviam dabant.
Alter ex Amicis trepidus arborem conscendit. Alter autem,
constratus humi, se mortuum simulabat et spiritum totum
compressit. Accedens Ursus, ad faciem os admovens et mortuum
credens, abibat, intactum relinquens. Tandem descendebat ex
arbore Amicus et, Socium accedens, percontatus est quid illi
susurraverat Ursus. Cui ille respondit, "Monebat me Ursus, ut de
falsis et perfidis Amicis in posterum caverem."

## Grammar Notes

**facto foedere.** Ablative absolute construction (see Fable 8).

**obviam dabant.** The phrase **obviam dare** means "to meet, run into," and it takes a dative
complement: **urso.**

**alter . . . alter.** The double use of **alter** is equivalent to the English construction, "the one . . .
the other" (see the *Grammar Overview* for this fable).

**humi.** This is a locative form of the noun **humus,** meaning "on the ground."

**se mortuum.** Accusative plus infinitive construction (see Fable 7): **se mortuum (esse).**

**ad faciem.** This refers to the face of the man who is lying on the ground.

**mortuum credens.** Accusative plus infinitive construction, with the man lying on the
ground as the implied subject of the infinitive: **(eum) mortuum (esse) credens.**

**cui ille respondit.** The referent of the relative pronoun **cui** is **amicus** in the previous sentence (see Fable 4): **cui (amico) ille respondit.**

*Vis unita fortior.*

*Si vis regnare, divide.*

# Fable 66.
# DE LEONE ET QUATTUOR TAURIS
## (Barlow 3)

## Introduction
### The Lion and The Four Bulls

In this story, you will see the lion apply the principle of "divide and conquer" so that he can undermine the alliance of the bulls. Joseph Jacobs appended this English proverb to the fable: "United we stand, divided we fall." In a Greek version of the story, the lion says to each bull: "If you hand your partner over to me, I will keep you safe from harm." No details are provided in this Latin version of the story about exactly what the lion says to the bulls. What words do you think the lion used with the bulls to break up their alliance?

For a different story about someone who was able to divide and conquer, see the fable of the bear and the lion (Fable 48), or the sheepdogs and the sheep (Fable 13). For the virtues of solidarity, see the fable of the farmer and his quarrelsome sons (Fable 71).

## Grammar Overview
### The Postpositive Particles, Tamen and Ergo

You have already met with a wide range of postpositive particles in these Latin fables (see the notes to Fables 2, 16, 23, 32 and 60). In this fable, you will meet two more of these particles: *tamen* and *ergo*. You will often find *tamen* used to indicate a statement that comes as an unexpected surprise. For example, in this fable, the lion is very hungry but is surprisingly unable to attack the bulls because they are united: *coniunctos tamen aggredi non ausus est*. While *tamen* introduces something that is unexpected, the postpositive *ergo* does just the opposite, indicating an expected result, a logical outcome to the situation. The hungry lion comes up with a plan, just as you would expect: *hoc ergo consilium cepit*. In addition to serving as a postpositive particle, *ergo* can also be used as a conjunction standing first in a sentence or clause, as in this well-known statement: *Cogito, ergo sum*. Do you know which philosopher made this famous claim? (Hint: You may have studied his Cartesian coordinate system in your math class.)

# Vocabulary

## *Nouns*

**fames (famis,** *f.***):** hunger, famine
**foedus (foederis,** *n.***):** treaty, agreement
**salus (salutis,** *f.***):** health, safety
**societas (societatis,** *f.***):** alliance, company
**taurus (tauri,** *m.***):** bull

## *Adjectives*

**communis, commune (communis):** general, common
**fallax (fallacis):** deceitful, misleading
**grandis, grande (grandis):** great, large
**indignabundus, indignabunda, indignabundum:** indignant, outraged

## *Verbs*

**aggredior (aggredi):** approach, attack
**audeo (audere), ausus sum:** dare, venture
**coniungo (coniungere), coniunxi, coniunctus:** join, connect
**esurio (esurire):** hunger, be hungry
**ineo (inire), inii, initus:** go in, enter into
**lanio (laniare), laniavi, laniatus:** mangle, tear to pieces
**observo (observare):** watch, heed
**premo (premere), pressi, pressus:** press, press upon
**segrego (segregare):** remove, separate

## *Other*

**facile:** easily
**invicem:** alternately, mutually
**primum:** first, at first
**quamvis:** although, even if
**quattuor:** four

# DE LEONE ET QUATTUOR TAURIS

## Dramatis Personae

*Tauri*, the bulls, and *Leo*, the lion.

Quattuor fuere Tauri qui, inter se invicem societate inita,
foedus faciebant communem ipsorum esse salutem et commune
periculum. Hoc observavit esuriens et indignabundus Leo, qui
quamvis grandi premeretur fame, coniunctos tamen aggredi non
ausus est. Hoc ergo consilium cepit: primum verbis fallacibus
unum ab altero segregavit, deinde segregatos facile laniavit.

## Grammar Notes

**quattuor fuere tauri.** The phrase **quattuor tauri** wraps around the verb (see Fable 6), **fuere** (an alternate form of **fuerunt**), which is declarative: "there were four bulls."

**societate inita.** Ablative absolute construction (see Fable 8).

**communem esse salutem.** Accusative plus infinitive construction (see Fable 7), with the noun **salutem** as the subject and **communem** as predicate adjective.

**ipsorum esse salutem.** The noun phrase is wrapped around the infinitive; the pronoun **ipsorum** refers to the bulls: **ipsorum (taurorum) salutem.**

**commune periculum.** Accusative plus infinitive, parallel to **communem salutem** in the preceding statement: **commune (esse) periculum.**

**quamvis grandi premeretur fame.** The phrase **grandi fame** wraps around the verb, with the subjunctive expressing a supposition introduced by **quamvis** (see Fable 38).

**coniunctos tamen aggredi.** The deponent infinitive **aggredi** is transitive and takes a direct object in the accusative (see Fable 9); note the postpositive particle **tamen** in second position (see the *Grammar Overview* for this fable).

**hoc ergo consilium.** Note the postpositive particle **ergo** in second position (see the *Grammar Overview* for this fable).

*Quid leoni cum mure?*

*Amicus certus in re incerta cernitur.*

# Fable 67.
# DE LEONE ET MURE
## (Barlow 23)

## Introduction
### The Lion and The Mouse

In this fable, the lion makes a foolish mistake: he thinks that a creature so small as a mouse is not worthy of his attention in any way whatsoever. Little does he suspect that this mouse might be able to save his life! You will get a good example in this fable of why the mouse is called a "rodent" in English. The word "rodent" comes from the Latin verb *rodere,* meaning "to chew." You are going to see the little mouse engage in some heroic rodent action in this particular fable. Joseph Jacobs added this moral to the story: "Little friends may prove great friends." Sir Roger L'Estrange observes, "Great and Little have need one of another." If the lion were to pronounce the moral at the end of the story, what words do you think he would use to describe the lesson he has learned?

To find out how the lion repaid the mouse's favor, see the fable of the mouse who married a lion (Fable 37). For a different kind of story about gratitude, see the fable of the crane who helped a wolf (Fable 30), or the fable of the snake in the snow (Fable 35).

## Grammar Overview
### Diminutive Adjectives

As you learned in Fable 41 and Fable 43, Latin is rich in diminutives. It is even possible to create diminutive forms not just of nouns, but also of adjectives! So, in this fable the little mouse who is caught by the lion is *misellus,* a diminutive of the adjective *miser;* he is a "poor little" mouse. Yet when the lion thinks about killing this mouse, he realizes there is not much honor in killing *tantilla bestiola,* "such an itty-bitty little creature," where *bestiola* is a diminutive form of the noun *bestia,* and *tantilla* is a diminutive form of the adjective *tantus* (see Fable 56). Can you think of some other Latin adjectives that are diminutives? (Hint: Look up the etymology of the English words "rubella" and "novel" in the dictionary and see what you discover.)

# Vocabulary
## *Nouns*

**aestus** (**aestus,** *m.*): fire, heat wave
**bestiola** (**bestiolae,** *f.*): critter, little beast
**cuniculus** (**cuniculi,** *m.*): hole, hidden place
**cursus** (**cursus,** *m.*): running, race
**grex** (**gregis,** *m.*): flock, herd
**laqueus** (**laquei,** *m.*): snare, trap
**nex** (**necis,** *f.*): death, murder
**nodus** (**nodi,** *m.*): knot, node
**plaga** (**plagae,** *f.*): hunting net, trap
**seges** (**segetis,** *f.*): field of grain, crop
**tergum** (**tergi,** *n.*): back, rear
**umbra** (**umbrae,** *f.*): shade, shadow

## *Adjectives*

**captivus, captiva, captivum:** imprisoned, caught
**indignus, indigna, indignum:** unworthy, undeserving
**misellus, misella, misellum:** poor, unfortunate
**tantillus, tantilla, tantillum:** so small a quantity

## *Verbs*

**agnosco** (**agnoscere**): recognize, realize
**clamito** (**clamitare**): shout repeatedly, yell loudly
**comprehendo** (**comprehendere**): grasp, seize
**corrodo** (**corrodere**): gnaw away, chew up
**curro** (**currere**): run, race
**defetiscor** (**defetisci**), **defessus sum:** grow exhausted, get tired
**dimitto** (**dimittere**): let go, send away
**evado** (**evadere**): escape, get out
**exeo** (**exire**): go out, come out
**expergefacio** (**expergefacere**), **expergefeci, expergefactus:** wake up, arouse
**incido** (**incidere**): fall into, meet with
**irascor** (**irasci**), **iratus sum:** grow angry, get mad
**licet** (**licere**): it is permitted, allowed
**percurro** (**percurrere**): run through
**quiesco** (**quiescere**), **quievi, quietus:** rest, be inactive
**repo** (**repere**): creep, crawl
**reputo** (**reputare**): reflect, think over
**rugio** (**rugire**): roar, bellow
**supplico** (**supplicare**): plead, beg

# DE LEONE ET MURE

## Dramatis Personae

*Leo*, the lion, and *Mus*, the mouse.

Leo, aestu cursuque defessus, in umbra quiescebat. Murium autem grege tergum eius percurrente, expergefactus unum e multis comprehendit. Supplicat misellus, clamitans indignum se esse cui irascatur. Leo, reputans nihil laudis esse in nece tantillae bestiolae, captivum dimittit. Non multo post, Leo, dum per segetes currit, incidit in plagas; rugire licet, exire non licet. Rugientem Leonem Mus audit, vocem agnoscit, repit in cuniculos, et quaesitos laqueorum nodos invenit corroditque. Quo facto, Leo e plagis evadit.

## Grammar Notes

**murium autem grege percurrente.** Ablative absolute construction (see Fable 8) with **autem** in second position (see Fable 16).

**misellus.** The diminutive adjective (see the *Grammar Overview* for this fable) refers to the mouse: **misellus (mus)**.

**indignum se esse.** Accusative plus infinitive construction in indirect statement (see Fable 7), with **se** as the accusative subject and **indignum** as a predicate adjective.

**cui irascatur.** The subjunctive, introduced by the relative pronoun **cui,** explains the result of the mouse's unworthy status; he is not even the sort of creature a lion might get angry at.

**nihil laudis esse.** Accusative plus infinitive construction in indirect statement, with a partitive genitive construction (see Fable 30): **nihil** (nothing) **laudis** (of praise, glory) **esse** = "there is no glory."

**non multo post.** The ablative expresses the degree of difference in a comparison introduced by **post,** "not (by) much later."

**quaesitos nodos invenit corroditque.** You might translate the passive participle with an active verb (see Fable 5): the mouse searched for the knots (**quaesitos**), finds them (**invenit**) and chews through them (**corrodit**).

**quo facto.** Ablative absolute construction, in which the relative pronoun **quo** connects back to the previous sentence (see Fable 4), referring to the general situation described there, i.e., the mouse chewing through the knots.

Cervus, sedandi sitim gratia, ad fontem descendit.

# Fable 68.
# DE CERVO IN AQUAS INSPICIENTE
## (Barlow 106)

## Introduction
### The Stag Looking Into The Water

In modern terms, we could say that the stag in this story has a serious problem with "body image," being unable to see his true beauty when he looks in the reflecting mirror of the water. In the seventeenth-century version of this story by Sir Roger L'Estrange, here is what the poor stag says in the end: "What an unhappy fool was I, to take my friends for my enemies, and my enemies for my friends! I trusted to my head, that has betray'd me; and I found fault with my legs, that would have otherwise brought me off!" In Joseph Jacobs's version of the story, the stag says simply, "We often despise what is most useful to us." Imagine the scene when the hunter finally runs up and finds the deer in the thicket of trees: what words do you think the hunter would use to express the moral of the story?

For another story about a reflection, see the fable of the dog crossing the river (Fable 55). For more stories about stags, see the fable of the old dog and his master (Fable 61), or the stag who hid inside the stable (Fable 34).

## Grammar Overview
### Gratia

The basic meaning of the Latin noun *gratia* is favor or thanks, as in the idiom, *gratias agere*, "to thank, to offer thanks." In addition, there is an important idiomatic use of *gratia* in the ablative case with a genitive complement, meaning "for the sake of" or "on account of." So, in the fable you are about to read, the stag goes to the spring *sedandi sitim gratia*, "for the sake (ablative *gratia*) of allaying (genitive *sedandi*) his thirst (accusative *sitim*, object of the gerund)." You can find the ablative *gratia* construction in the commonly used Latin abbreviation, *e.g.*, meaning *exempli gratia*, "for (the sake of an) example." No doubt the most famous use of *gratia* with a genitive complement is in the logo of the Metro-Goldwyn-Mayer film studio, which features a roaring lion with the Latin motto: *Ars gratia artis*, "art (*ars*) for the sake (*gratia*, ablative) of art (*artis*)." Of course, whether a multibillion-dollar film studio can lay claim to such a high-minded motto is a separate question!

# Vocabulary

## Nouns

**cornu (cornus,** *n.***):** horn
**fons (fontis,** *m.***):** spring, source of water
**halitus (halitus,** *m.***):** breath, exhalation
**horror (horroris,** *m.***):** dread, terror
**praestantia (praestantiae,** *f.***):** excellence, superiority
**ruina (ruinae,** *f.***):** destruction, catastrophe
**salus (salutis,** *f.***):** health, safety
**sitis (sitis,** *f.***):** thirst
**tenuitas (tenuitatis,** *f.***):** slenderness, thinness
**tibiale (tibialis,** *n.***):** leg, shin
**velocitas (velocitatis,** *f.***):** rapidity, swiftness

## Adjectives

**moribundulus, moribundula, moribundulum:** dying
**praestans (praestantis):** excellent, outstanding
**ultimus, ultima, ultimum:** latest, last

## Verbs

**circumlatro (circumlatrare):** bark, bark around
**confugio (confugere), confugi:** flee, take refuge
**damno (damnare), damnavi, damnatus:** find guilty, condemn
**deprecor (deprecari), deprecatus sum:** abominate, disparage
**descendo (descendere), descendi, descensus:** go down, come down
**despecto (despectare):** look over, look down on
**detineo (detinere):** hold back, detain
**efflo (efflare):** breathe out, exhale
**ingruo (ingruere):** come at violently, advance threateningly
**inspicio (inspicere):** look at, look into
**laudo (laudare), laudavi, laudatus:** praise
**pario (parire), peperi, partus:** bear, produce
**sedo (sedare):** allay, calm

## Other

**magnopere:** particularly, especially
**maxime:** chiefly, especially
**misere:** sadly, wretchedly

# DE CERVO IN AQUAS INSPICIENTE

## Dramatis Persona

*Cervus*, the stag.

Cervus, sedandi sitim gratia, ad fontem descendit et, ibi totum corpus despectans, cornua magnopere praestantia laudavit, sed tibialium tenuitatem maxime deprecatus est. Sed mox canum circumlatrantium ingruebat horror et ille per tibialium velocitatem confugit ad silvas et ibi miserrime a cornibus detinebatur. Qui tum moribundulus sic ultimum efflavit halitum: "Me miserum, qui tibialium damnavi tenuitatem, quae mihi salutem, et cornuum laudavi praestantiam, quae mihi ruinam pepererunt."

## Grammar Notes

**sedandi sitim gratia.** The ablative **gratia** (for the sake of) takes a genitive complement, the gerund **sedandi**, while **sitim** is the direct object of the gerund (see the *Grammar Overview* for this fable).

**cornua magnopere praestantia laudavit.** The adjective **praestantia** and the noun **cornua** are a double predicate (see Fable 71): the stag praised his horns (as) especially beautiful.

**tibialium tenuitatem deprecatus est.** The deponent verb **deprecatus est** is transitive and takes a direct object in the accusative (see Fable 9).

**miserrime.** This is the superlative form of the adverb **misere** (see Fable 39).

**qui ultimum efflavit halitum.** The referent of the relative pronoun **qui** is **cervus** in the previous sentence: **qui (cervus) ultimum efflavit halitum;** the phrase **ultimum halitum** is wrapped around the verb (see Fable 6).

**moribundulus.** The diminutive adjective (see Fable 67) conveys a pathetic quality; the stag is not small in size, but he is in a sadly diminished state (see Fable 41).

**me miserum.** An exclamation using the accusative (see Fable 15).

**quae mihi salutem.** The referent of the relative pronoun **quae** is **tenuitatem**, and the verb is implied by the parallel construction: **quae (tenuitas) mihi salutem (peperit).**

**quae mihi ruinam pepererunt.** The referent of the relative pronoun **quae** is **cornuum**, which is neuter plural: **quae (cornua) mihi ruinam pepererunt.**

*Semper metuendo sapiens evitat malum.*

*Dum stertit cattus, nunquam sibi currit in os mus.*

# Fable 69.
# DE CATTO ET MURIBUS
## (Barlow 21)

## Introduction
### The Cat and The Mice

In the ancient Roman version of this fable, the story is not about a cat, but a weasel. This is because the ancient Romans kept weasels in their houses to chase the mice, instead of cats. As the centuries passed and people started keeping cats in their houses instead of weasels, they kept telling the same old fables, but they replaced the weasel characters with cats. Caxton's moral for this fable about the cat and the mice praises the wise old mouse with these words: "He is wyse that scapeth the wytte and malyce of euyll folke by wytte and not by force," which is to say, "He is wise who escapes the wit and malice of evil people by wit and not by force." After you see what happens at the end of the story, what do you think is the most important lesson we can learn from this fable?

For another story about a wise animal who is able to avoid danger, see the fable of the sow who kept her distance from the wolf (Fable 26), or the horse who escaped from the lion (Fable 54). For another story about cats and mice, see the fable of Venus and the cat (Fable 75).

## Grammar Overview
### The Future Passive Periphrastic

You have already seen an example of the future active periphrastic, where the future active participle is used with the verb "to be" in order to make a statement about the future (see Fable 25). There is also a future passive periphrastic where the future passive participle, also known as the gerundive (see Fable 54), is used with the verb "to be" in order to express the notion of obligation or necessity. Sometimes, in fact, this type of construction is called "the gerundive of necessity." The most famous example is Cato's slogan, *Carthago delenda est,* "Carthage must be destroyed." In this fable, you will see a quite different slogan: *non catto credendum est,* "it is not to be trusted to a cat" or, in more idiomatic English, "you mustn't trust a cat." If you wanted to specify that mice should not trust a cat, you would use a dative of agency: *muribus non catto credendum est.* Here is another example of this same construction, where a dative of agency is used with a gerundive of necessity: *Sors est sua cuique ferenda.* What do you think this saying could mean? (Hint: This word order might be easier to understand, *Cuique sors sua ferenda est.*)

# Vocabulary

## *Nouns*

**caedis (caedis, *f.*)**: slaughter, massacre
**disceptatio (disceptationis, *f.*)**: debate, dispute
**pactum (pacti, *n.*)**: manner, agreement
**paterfamilias (patrisfamilias, *m.*)**: head of the family
**pistor (pistoris, *m.*)**: baker

## *Adjectives*

**diuturnus, diuturna, diuturnum:** long-lasting, enduring
**occultus, occulta, occultum:** hidden, secret
**pauci, paucae, pauca:** few, small in number
**plurimus, plurima, plurimum:** most, very many
**senior, senius (senioris):** older, elder
**varius, varia, varium:** different, diverse
**vorabundus, vorabunda, vorabundum:** voracious, gulping

## *Verbs*

**concludo (concludere):** close, finish
**descendo (descendere):** go down, come down
**devoro (devorare):** consume, gulp down
**evito (evitare):** avoid, shun
**exclamo (exclamare), exclamavi, exclamatus:** shout, cry out
**fingo (fingere):** contrive, pretend
**ingredior (ingredi), ingressus sum:** enter, go into
**intellego (intellegere), intellexi, intellectus:** understand, realize
**provideo (providere):** foresee, provide for
**remaneo (remanere):** stay behind, remain

## *Other*

**caute:** carefully, thoroughly
**euge:** fine! bravo!
**interim:** meanwhile
**ne . . . quidem:** not . . . even

# DE CATTO ET MURIBUS

## Dramatis Personae

*Cattus*, the cat, and *Mures*, the mice.

Cattus, cum pistoris domum ingressus est, quam plurimos
invenit Mures et, nunc unum nunc alterum devorando, tam
caute patrifamilias providebat ut paucos relinqueret. Mures
interim, cum ante oculos habuissent diuturnam illorum caedem,
consilium ceperunt quo pacto Cattum vorabundum evitarent.
Post varias disceptationes concludebant tandem ut in locis
occultis altissimisque remanerent, ne descendendo in praedam
Catto venirent. Cattus, hoc consilio intellecto, se mortuum
fingebat, cum unus ex Murium senioribus ab alto exclamavit,
"Euge, amice! Non Catto credendum est, ne mortuo quidem."

## Grammar Notes

**cum domum ingressus est.** The deponent verb **ingressus est** is transitive and takes a direct object in the accusative (see Fable 9; for **cum** plus an indicative verb, see Fable 22).

**quam plurimos.** The phrase means "as many as could be" or "very many indeed."

**nunc unum nunc alterum devorando.** The gerund takes an accusative object (see Fable 14).

**patrifamilias.** This is the dative form of **paterfamilias,** a compound of two words, **pater** + **familias,** of which only the first word declines (see Fable 3).

**cum ante oculos habuissent caedem**. The subjunctive, introduced by **cum**, gives causal background information; this is why the mice needed to come up with a plan.

**quo pacto evitarent.** The word **quo** introduces an indirect question with the subjunctive.

**descendendo.** The gerund is in the ablative case (see Fable 48).

**consilio intellecto.** Ablative absolute construction (see Fable 8).

**se mortuum.** Accusative plus infinitive construction: **se mortuum (esse).**

**credendum est.** The future passive participle combined with the verb **est** results in a future passive periphrastic, also known as a "gerundive of necessity" (see the *Grammar Overview* for this fable). The subject is impersonal, hence the neuter singular form.

**ne mortuo quidem.** The phrase **ne . . . quidem** (see Fable 53) puts a strong emphasis on the word **mortuo.**

*Lupus hiat.*

*Quae volumus, et
credimus libenter.*

# Fable 70.
# DE NUTRICE ET LUPO
## (Barlow 69)

## Introduction
### *The Nanny and The Wolf*

In this fable, you will not only meet "Mr. Wolf" but also "Mrs. Wolf," who wants to know just why her husband has come home empty-handed, so to speak, when he was supposed to have been out hunting for food. In an ancient Greek version of this fable, the moral of the story is "There is no point in hoping for things that are not going to happen." Joseph Jacobs supplies this moral for the story: "Enemies' promises were made to be broken." What is the lesson you think we could learn from the wolf's mistake in this story?

For another story about the wolf who went away empty-handed, see the fable of the wise sow and the wolf (Fable 26). For more stories about hypocrisy, see the fable of the traveler in the house of the satyr (Fable 64), or the fable of the fox and the grapes (Fable 29).

## Grammar Overview
### *Inchoative Verbs*

As you saw in Fable 59, it is possible to use suffixes to create new Latin verbs. One such suffix is *-scere,* which is used to create inchoative verbs, that is, verbs that refer to a process of growing or becoming (the English word "inchoate," means "under development, taking shape"). So, for example, in the fable you are about to read, the crying baby finally grows quiet, *silescit.* The verb *silere* means "to be silent," but the verb *silescere* means "to become silent, to grow silent." A distinctive feature of these inchoative verbs is that the *-sc-* suffix only appears in the present stem, not in the perfect system. If you think about it, of course, that makes sense: the process of growing or becoming is something that unfolds over time, while the perfect system in Latin expresses completed action, not an unfolding process. So the verb *silesco* (*silescere*) has *siluit* as its third principle part, the same perfect stem as the verb *sileo* (*silere*). Can you think of any other examples of Latin verbs that contain this *-scere* suffix? (Hint: Think about the crescent moon, or about what happens in a convalescent home.)

# Vocabulary

## Nouns

**foris (foris,** *f.*): door, gate
**lupa (lupae,** *f.*): she-wolf
**nutrix (nutricis,** *f.*): nurse, nanny
**somnus (somni,** *m.*): sleep

## Adjectives

**gemebundus, gemebunda, gemebundum:** groaning, sighing
**ieiunus, ieiuna, ieiunum:** fasting, hungry
**inanis, inane (inanis):** empty, foolish

## Verbs

**abiicio (abiicere):** cast off, toss away
**fallo (fallere), fefelli, falsus:** deceive, beguile
**maneo (manere):** remain, stay
**minor (minari):** threaten, menace
**obrepo (obrepere):** creep over, sneak up
**ploro (plorare):** cry, wail
**praetereo (praeterire):** go by, pass by
**regredior (regredi):** go back, return
**sciscitor (sciscitari):** ask, inquire
**silesco (silescere):** grow quiet, fall silent
**taceo (tacere):** be silent, shut up
**trado (tradere), tradidi, traditus:** hand over, bestow

## Other

**forte:** by chance, accidentally
**ni:** if not, unless
**obviam:** in the way of, running into

# DE NUTRICE ET LUPO

## Dramatis Personae

*Nutrix*, the nurse, *Puer*, the boy and *Lupi*, the wolves.

Nutrix minatur Puerum plorantem: ni taceat, se Lupo illum tradituram. Lupus praeteriens id forte audit et spe praedae manet ad fores. Puer tandem, obrepente somno, silescit. Regreditur Lupus in silvas, ieiunus et inanis. Lupa obviam illi habens sciscitatur ubi sit praeda. Cui gemebundus Lupus: "Verba (inquit) mihi data sunt. Puerum plorantem abiicere Nutrix minabatur, sed fefellit."

## Grammar Notes

**minatur puerum.** The deponent verb **minatur** is transitive and takes a direct object in the accusative (see Fable 9).

**se illum tradituram.** Accusative plus infinitive construction in indirect statement (see Fable 7): **se illum tradituram (esse)**, with **se** as the accusative subject and **illum (puerum)** as the object.

**spe praedae.** The noun **praedae** is an objective genitive, complementing **spe** ("in hopes of").

**obrepente somno.** Ablative absolute construction (see Fable 8).

**obviam habens.** The phrase **obviam habere** means "to meet, run into," and takes a dative complement, **illi (lupo).**

**ubi sit praeda.** The word **ubi** introduces an indirect question with the subjunctive.

**cui lupus inquit.** The referent of the relative pronoun **cui** is **lupa** in the previous sentence (see Fable 4): **cui (lupae) lupus inquit**.

**mihi verba data sunt.** The phrase **verba dare** means "to cheat, deceive," with a dative complement: **mihi verba data sunt,** "I was deceived."

Agricola, filios suos videns quotidie litigantes, iussit fasciculum virgarum sibi afferri.

# Fable 71.
# DE AGRICOLA ET FILIIS
## (Barlow 62)

## Introduction
### The Farmer and His Sons

The version of the story you are about to read features a wise farmer and his quarrelsome sons. In the ancient Greek world, this same story was told about a legendary king of Scythia named Scilurus who, on his deathbed, used this example to teach his surviving sons—all eighty of them!—about the need to make peace amongst themselves and set aside their quarrels. Joseph Jacobs expressed the moral of the fable in three simple words: "Union gives strength." After you see just how the farmer teaches this lesson to his sons, what words would you use to express the moral of the fable?

For more stories about the need for solidarity, see the fable of the two friends on a journey (Fable 65), the union of the four bulls (Fable 66), or the fox who defeated the lion and the bear (Fable 48).

## Grammar Overview
### Double Predicate

In this fable, you will see a good example of what is called a "double predicate," with two nouns in apposition to one another in the predicate of the sentence. Here is how the father warns his sons about the dangers of quarreling: *aemulatio vos praedam inimicis praestabit*, "your rivalry will offer you to your enemies (as) prey." In idiomatic English, we often need to add a word like "as" to indicate the relationship between two predicate nouns. In Latin, however, the relationship between the nouns is expressed through the grammar of apposition itself. Remember also that, in Latin, nouns that are in apposition to each other must be in the same case (because they have the same grammatical role in the sentence), but they do not have to agree in number or in gender, in the way that nouns and adjectives must agree. The nouns *vos* and *praedam* are both in the accusative case, but they are not the same gender and number. The pronoun *vos* is masculine plural, while the noun *praedam* is feminine singular. The fact that they are both in the accusative case is all that is required for them to stand in apposition to each other, as a "double predicate" in this sentence.

# Vocabulary
## *Nouns*
**aemulatio (aemulationis,** *f.***):** rivalry, ambition
**agricola (agricolae,** *m.***):** farmer
**fasciculus (fasciculi,** *m.***):** little bundle, packet
**inimicus (inimici,** *m.***):** enemy, foe
**virga (virgae,** *f.***):** twig, rod

## *Adjectives*
**invictus, invicta, invictum:** undefeated, invincible
**opportunus, opportuna, opportunum:** useful, ready
**singuli, singulae, singula:** separate, individual
**unanimis, unanime (unanimis):** like-minded, in accord

## *Verbs*
**affero (afferre), attuli, allatus:** bring to, carry up
**colligo (colligare), colligavi, colligatus:** bind, tie together
**confringo (confringere):** break in two, shatter
**frango (frangere):** break, shatter
**litigo (litigare):** quarrel, squabble
**persto (perstare), perstiti, perstatus:** persevere, persist in
**praebeo (praebere):** present, offer
**praesto (praestare):** show, present
**solvo (solvere):** loosen, unbind
**trado (tradere), tradidi, traditus:** hand over, bestow

## *Other*
**facile:** easily
**minus:** less, not so well
**postea:** afterwards
**quotidie:** daily, each day
**sin:** if however, but if
**statim:** immediately, at once

# DE AGRICOLA ET FILIIS

## Dramatis Personae

*Agricola*, the farmer, and *Filii*, his sons.

Agricola, Filios suos videns quotidie litigantes, iussit fasciculum virgarum sibi afferri. Quae cum allatae essent, colligavit omnes in unum fasciculum, iussitque singulos Filiorum fasciculum capere et confringere. Illis vero confringere non valentibus, solvens postea fasciculum, tradidit singulas singulis eis frangendas, atque, illis statim facileque frangentibus, dixit, "Ita et vos, Filii mei, si unanimes perstiteritis, invictos vos hostibus praebebitis. Sin minus, ipsa vestra aemulatio opportunam vos praedam inimicis praestabit."

## Grammar Notes

**quae cum allatae essent.** The referent of the relative pronoun **quae** is **virgarum** in the previous sentence: **quae (virgae) cum allatae essent** (for the placement of the relative pronoun before **cum**, see Fable 37).

**colligavit omnes.** The adjective refers to the twigs: **omnes (virgas).**

**singulos filiorum.** The genitive plural is used with the distributive numeral, **singulos**: "each (of) his sons."

**illis vero confringere non valentibus.** Ablative absolute construction (see Fable 8); for the postpositive particle **vero,** see Fable 60.

**tradidit singulas singulis eis frangendas.** The word **singulis** agrees with **eis,** referring to the sons, while **singulas** refers to the twigs, and the gerundive **frangendas** expresses purpose: **tradidit singulas (virgas) singulis eis (filiis) frangendas.**

**illis frangentibus.** Ablative absolute construction, with the twigs as the implied object of the participle: **illis (virgas) frangentibus.**

**ita et vos.** For the adverbial use of **et** meaning "too," see Fable 17.

**sin minus.** The adverb **minus** refers to the situation just discussed: **sin minus (unanimes perstiteritis),** "but if (you persist in being) less (united) . . ."

**opportunam vos praedam inimicis praestabit.** The phrase **opportunam praedam** wraps around the pronoun (see Fable 6), with the noun phrase and the pronoun in apposition to one another in the predicate (see the *Grammar Overview* for this fable): "(your quarrel) will offer you to your enemies (as) ready prey."

*Ars varia vulpi.*

*Scit multa vulpes,*
*magnum echinus unicum.*

# Fable 72.
# DE CATTO ET VULPE
## (Barlow 20)

## Introduction
### The Cat and The Fox

In the fragmentary remains of the archaic Greek poet Archilochus, who was born sometime around 680 BCE, you can find this proverb about the fox and hedgehog: "The fox knows many things, but the hedgehog knows one big thing." What the hedgehog knows, of course, is how to roll itself up into a ball when it is attacked, so that it is defended by its spines all over. The fable you are about to read expresses the same idea about a cat, who knows just one trick, as opposed to the fox, who boasts about her many tricks. Joseph Jacobs applied this moral to the fable: "Better one safe way than a hundred on which you cannot reckon." If the fox were able to gasp out a few words at the end of the story, what do you think she would say is the lesson she has learned?

For an example of a cat playing a different kind of trick, see the fable of the old mouse and the cat (Fable 69). For another story where the fox's tricks fail her, see the fable of the fox and the rooster (Fable 47), or the fox and the stork (Fable 19).

## Grammar Overview
### Participles and Finite Verbs in Translation

One of the most common features of Latin style is the way that it likes to combine a participle with a finite verb, while English usually opts for two finite verbs instead. Take this Latin sentence, for example: *vulpes a canibus apprehensa laceratur.* Literally, this means "the fox, having been caught by the dogs, is torn to pieces." The English participle "having been caught" is grammatically equivalent to the Latin *apprehensa* but it sounds very formal and stilted by comparison. A more vivid alternative in English would be to replace the participle with a finite verb, joined to the other finite verb by a conjunction: "The fox is caught by the dogs and torn to pieces." You could also render the passive verb *laceratur* with an active verb in English: "The fox is caught by the dogs, and they tear her to pieces." You could even replace both passive verbs with active verbs in English: "The dogs catch the fox and tear her to pieces." As this example shows, there is a whole range of options to choose from when rendering Latin participles and Latin passive verbs in English, based on the goal you have in mind for your translation. (For a discussion of passive verb forms in Latin, see the notes to Fable 5.)

# Vocabulary
## *Nouns*
**amicitia (amicitiae,** *f.*): friendship
**astutia (astutiae,** *f.*): cleverness, trick
**latebra (latebrae,** *f.*): hiding place, lair
**numerus (numeri,** *m.*): number
**ramus (rami,** *m.*): branch, bough

## *Adjectives*
**contentus, contenta, contentum:** satisfied, content
**grandis, grande (grandis):** great, large
**odorus, odora, odorum:** keen-scented

## *Verbs*
**apprehendo (apprehendere), apprehendi, apprehensus:** grab hold of, seize
**appropinquo (appropinquare):** approach, draw near
**aufugio (aufugere):** run away, flee
**contraho (contrahere):** agree upon, contract
**curro (currere):** run, race
**despecto (despectare):** look over, look down on
**lacero (lacerare):** mangle, tear
**praeservo (praeservare):** keep safe, preesrve
**recenseo (recensere):** review, reckon
**replico (replicare), replicui, replicatus:** reply, unfold
**scando (scandere):** climb, mount
**sedeo (sedere):** sit, stay
**suggero (suggerere), suggessi, suggestus:** furnish, supply

## *Other*
**ast:** but, on the contrary
**confestim:** immediately, at once
**hic:** here, in this place
**illic:** in that place, over there
**secure:** safely, unconcernedly
**tantum:** only
**trepide:** fearfully, anxiously
**uspiam:** anywhere, somewhere

# DE CATTO ET VULPE

## Dramatis Personae

*Cattus*, the cat, and *Vulpes*, the fox.

Contrahebant inter se amicitias Cattus et Vulpes. Cui Vulpes astutiarum suarum grandem recensebat numerum. Cattus replicuit, "Ast ego uno tantum consilio et, quod natura ad meipsum praeservandum suggessit, contentus sum." Inter haec, odoram canum vim appropinquantium audiunt. Cattus confestim altissimos arboris scandebat ramos et secure despectans sedebat. Vulpes autem et hic et illic trepide currebat et, nulla aufugiendi spe relicta, nulla uspiam latebra inventa, a canibus apprehensa laceratur.

## Grammar Notes

**cui vulpes recensebat.** The referent of the relative pronoun **cui** is **cattus** in the previous sentence (see Fable 4): **cui (catto) vulpes recensebat**.

**grandem recensebat numerum.** The phrase **grandem numerum** wraps around the verb (see Fable 6).

**ego uno tantum consilio.** The predicate ablative functions like an adjective: **uno tantum consilio,** "I (am) just a one-plan (cat)."

**quod contentus sum.** The referent of the relative pronoun **quod** is the implied ablative complement of the verb: **contentus sum (eo) quod,** "I am contented with that which . . ."

**ad meipsum praeservandum.** The gerundive with the preposition **ad** expresses purpose (see Fable 54), and **meipsum** is an example of a compound word: **me + ipsum**.

**odoram canum vim.** The highly poetic phrase, **odora canum vis** ("the keen-scented pack of hounds"), comes from Vergil's *Aeneid*, Book IV.

**altissimos arboris scandebat ramos.** The phrase **altissimos arboris ramos** wraps around the verb.

**vulpes autem.** For the postpositive particle **autem,** see Fable 16.

**nulla aufugiendi spe.** The phrase **nulla spe** ("no hope of") wraps around the gerund in the genitive case (see Fable 78).

**nulla spe relicta . . . nulla latebra inventa.** Ablative absolute constructions (see Fable 8).

*Quid leone fortius?*

*Nunquam est fidelis cum potente societas.*

# Fable 73.
# DE LEONE ET QUIBUSDAM ALIIS QUADRUPEDIBUS
## (Barlow 22)

## Introduction
### *The Lion and Certain Other Animals*

The fable you are about to read is the origin of the famous phrase "the lion's share." Have you ever thought about just what that phrase means exactly? The lion's share does not mean the biggest part—instead, the lion's share means the WHOLE THING, because the lion is so greedy and so powerful that he takes whatever he wants. As a result, the "lion's share" does not actually involve any kind of sharing at all, as the lion's partners discover to their dismay. In his version of the story, Joseph Jacobs adds this moral: "You may share the labors of the great, but you will not share the spoil." Townsend simply comments, "Might makes right." What moral would you give to this story if you wanted to rebuke the lion for his greed? What if you wanted instead to criticize the sheep and the other animals for their foolishness in becoming partners with that lion?

For another story about a pact among partners, see the story of the four bulls (Fable 66), or the treaty between the sheep and the wolves (Fable 13). For another famous saying derived from an Aesop's fable, see the story of the "sour grapes" (Fable 29).

## Grammar Overview
### *Counting in Latin*

In this fable, you get a good lesson in counting in Latin, as the lion enumerates one by one the portions that he is going to claim for himself. He lays claim to the first part with the word *una*, meaning one part. He does not say *prima*, the first part, because he does not want to start off by suggesting that this is just one in a series of parts he will claim for himself. The lion acts as if he is going to play fair, taking just one part, *una*, like everybody else in the company. Next, the lion claims another part for himself, *altera*. This could give his partners some hope: if the lion is going to take one part, and then another part (*altera*), maybe that is all he will take! If the lion had said *secunda*, the second part, instead of *altera*, then the other animals might not entertain the same naive hope that perhaps the lion would be content with just two portions, *una et altera*. Yet of course the lion goes on, claiming the third part, *tertia*, and the fourth, *quarta*. With these ordinal numbers, the lion's plan is fully revealed: he is going to keep on enumerating the parts until he has taken them all, one after another—the proverbial "lion's share." (For more about counting in Latin, see the notes about numerical adverbs in Fable 12.)

# Vocabulary

## *Nouns*

**amicitia (amicitiae,** *f.***):** friendship

**quadrupes (quadrupedis,** *m/f.***):** animal, four-footed beast

**spolium (spolii,** *n.***):** spoils, booty

**venatio (venationis,** *f.***):** hunt, the chase

**venatus (venatus,** *m.***):** hunting

## *Adjectives*

**communis, commune (communis):** general, common

**praestans (praestantis):** excellent, outstanding

**quartus, quarta, quartum:** fourth

**reliquus, reliqua, reliquum:** rest, remaining

**singuli, singulae, singula:** separate, individual

**tacitus, tacita, tacitum:** silent, quiet

**tertius, tertia, tertium:** third

**vacuus, vacua, vacuum:** empty, empty-handed

## *Verbs*

**audeo (audere), ausus sum:** dare, venture

**concedo (concedere), concessi, concessus:** give up, grant

**convenio (convenire), conveni, conventus:** agree, meet

**discedo (discedere):** depart, march off

**divido (dividere):** divide, share

**incipio (incipere):** begin, start

**irrugio (irrugire):** roar, cry out

**muttio (muttire):** mutter, murmur

**pango (pangere), pepigi, pactus:** agree, settle upon

**pereo (perire), perii, peritus:** be lost, perish

**procumbo (procumbere):** sink down, lie down

**sudo (sudare):** sweat, perspire

**surgo (surgere):** rise up, get up

**tollo (tollere):** lift up, take away

**vendico (vendicare):** avenge, claim

## *Other*

**contra:** opposite, in opposition to

**denique:** finally, in the end

**ilicet:** right now, immediately

**item:** likewise

**porro:** further, furthermore

# DE LEONE ET QUIBUSDAM ALIIS QUADRUPEDIBUS

## Dramatis Personae

*Leo*, the lion, *Ovis*, the sheep, and *Quadrupedes*, the animals.

Convenere Leo et Ovis et alii Quadrupedes, pepigerantque inter se venationem fore communem. Itur venatum; procumbit cervus; spolia dividunt, singulas singulis partes tollere incipientibus. Irrugiens surgit Leo: "Una (inquit) pars mea est, quia sum dignissimus. Altera item mea est, quia viribus sum praestantissimus. Porro, quia in capiendo cervo plus sudaverim, tertiam mihi partem vendico. Quartam denique partem, nisi concesseritis, actum est de amicitia; ilicet periistis!" Reliqui, hoc audito, discedunt, vacui et taciti, non ausi muttire contra Leonem.

## Grammar Notes

**convenere.** This is an alternate form of **convenerunt**.

**venationem fore communem.** Accusative plus infinitive construction, with **fore** as the future infinitive of **esse** (see Fable 26); **venationem** is the accusative subject, and **communem** a predicate adjective.

**itur venatum.** The supine **venatum** combined with the verb of motion expresses purpose (see Fable 27), and the third person passive **itur** expresses the idea impersonally, "a hunt was gone on," i.e., they went hunting.

**singulas singulis partes tollere incipientibus.** The phrase **singulis incipientibus** is an ablative absolute construction (see Fable 8), with the participle taking a complementary infinitive phrase, **singulas partes tollere**.

**in capiendo cervo.** The gerundive **capiendo** agrees with the complement of the preposition, **cervo** (see Fable 54), "in catching the deer."

**quia . . . sudaverim.** The subjunctive is introduced by **quia** ("because"), giving causal background information; according to the lion, this is why he deserves the third portion.

**actum est de amicitia.** The idiomatic phrase **actum est de** means that something is "done" in the sense of "over and done with, finished."

**ilicet periistis.** You might translate this idiomatically as "you're as good as dead." The word **ilicet** (a compound of the imperative **i** + **licet**) was originally a formula used to dismiss someone from a meeting.

**hoc audito.** Ablative absolute construction (see Fable 8).

Ancillae gallum obtruncant, sperantes iam, necato illo, sese in medios dormituras dies.

# Fable 74.
# DE ANU ET ANCILLIS
## (Barlow 37)

## Introduction
### The Old Woman and Her Maids

You can put this fable in the category labeled, "Out of the frying pan, into the fire." Long before there were alarm clocks, there were roosters who crowed at the crack of dawn, rousing people to do their work. In this fable, you will find out what happens when some of the household maids decide they would rather sleep late in the morning. As often in Aesop's fables, their plan does not have the results that they expect! If one of the maids were to express the moral at the end of the story, what do you think she would say?

For other stories about unexpected outcomes, see the fable of the goose who laid the golden egg (Fable 56), or the mountains in labor (Fable 3). For another story about a rooster crowing, see the fable of the lion and the rooster (Fable 60).

## Grammar Overview
### Medius

The poor sleep-deprived servants in this fable dream of being able to slumber until noon, *in medios dies*, literally "until the middle (of the) days" or, more idiomatically, "until mid-day." There is also a compound word in Latin, *medidies* (*medi-dies*), which means "mid-day." You probably know this word *medidies* in its variant form, *meridies*, as in the phrase *ante meridiem* (A.M.), "before mid-day" and *post meridiem* (P.M.), "after mid-day." In Latin, the adjective *medius* is often used when in English we would use the noun "middle" instead. So, for example, the Latin phrase *in media via*, "in mid-road," would be rendered in English as "in the middle (of the) road." Probably the most famous example of this construction in Latin is *in medias res*, meaning "into the middle (of) things." As a literary technique, *in medias res* means plunging the audience into the middle of the plot, rather than beginning at the beginning. Take Vergil's *Aeneid*, for example. Does Vergil begin at the beginning, *ab ovo Ledae* (with the birth of Helen of Troy from the egg of her mother Leda), or does he start the story of Aeneas *in medias res*?

# Vocabulary
## *Nouns*

**ancilla (ancillae,** *f.*): maid, maidservant
**anus (anus,** *f.*): old woman
**cantus (cantus,** *m.*): song, tune
**hera (herae,** *f.*): mistress, lady of the house
**negotium (negotii,** *n.*): business
**taedium (taedii,** *n.*): weariness, tedium

## *Adjectives*

**complures, compluria (complurium**): many, a good number
**gallinaceus, gallinacea, gallinaceum:** poultry, barnyard
**intempestus, intempesta, intempestum:** unseasonable, untimely
**quotidianus, quotidiana, quotidianum:** daily, each day's

## *Verbs*

**alo (alere**): nourish, raise
**commoveo (commovere), commovi, commotus:** provoke, disturb
**dormio (dormire), dormivi, dormitus:** sleep
**excito (excitare**): stir up, arouse
**frustror (frustrari), frustratus sum:** disappoint, deceive
**interimo (interimere), interemi, interemptus:** kill, destroy
**lucesco (lucescere**): grow light, begin to shine
**neco (necare), necavi, necatus:** kill, slay
**obtrunco (obtruncare**): kill, cut down
**rescisco (rescicere), rescivi, rescitus:** learn, find out
**spero (sperare**): hope
**surgo (surgere**): rise up, get up

## *Other*

**antequam:** before, prior to
**deinceps:** next, thereafter
**quotidie:** daily, each day

# DE ANU ET ANCILLIS

## Dramatis Personae

*Anus*, the old woman, and *Ancillae*, the maids.

Anus quaedam domi habebat complures Ancillas, quas quotidie, antequam lucesceret, ad Galli gallinacei, quem domi alebat, cantum excitabat ad opus. Ancillae tandem, quotidiani negotii commotae taedio, Gallum obtruncant, sperantes iam, necato illo, sese in medios dormituras dies. Sed haec spes miseras frustrata est. Hera enim, ut interemptum Gallum rescivit, Ancillas intempesta nocte surgere deinceps iubet.

## Grammar Notes

**domi habebat ancillas.** The word **domi** is a locative form, meaning "in her home, at home."

**antequam lucesceret.** Like **cum**, you can find **antequam** used with both indicative and subjunctive verbs. Used with the subjunctive, as here, it puts more emphasis on the sense of unfulfilled expectation: the day would dawn eventually, but it had not dawned yet.

**ad galli gallinacei, quem domi alebat, cantum.** The phrase **ad galli gallinacei cantum** ("at cock-crow") wraps around the relative clause, **quem (gallum) domi alebat**.

**necato illo.** Ablative absolute construction (see Fable 8).

**sese dormituras.** This is an accusative plus infinitive construction in indirect statement (see Fable 7), with **sese** (alternate form of **se**) as the accusative subject: **sese dormituras (esse)**.

**in medios dies.** For this use of **medios**, see the *Grammar Overview* for this fable.

**miseras frustrata est.** The deponent verb **frustrata est** is transitive and takes a direct object in the accusative (see Fable 9); the feminine plural adjective, **miseras,** refers to the maids.

**hera enim.** For the postpositive particle **enim,** see Fable 2.

**ut interemptum gallum rescivit.** This is a temporal use of **ut,** meaning "as, as soon as" (see Fable 55), with an accusative plus infinitive construction: **interemptum (esse) gallum.**

**intempesta nocte.** The phrase means "in the dead of night."

Catta delicium erat adolescentis Veneremque oravit ut in feminam mutaret.

# Fable 75.
# DE CATTA IN FEMINAM MUTATA
## (Barlow 71)

## Introduction
### *The Cat Transformed Into a Woman*

Although the Latin fable you are about to read features a cat, the old Greek version of the story was about a weasel. (For more about weasels and cats, see Fable 69.) In applying a moral to this fable, Jacobs comments simply, "Nature will out." Of course, there are many other proverbial sayings in English that express the same idea, such as: "You can take the boy out of the country, but you can't take the country out of the boy." As you will see, it is none other than the goddess of love herself, Venus, who turns this cat into a woman. What words do you think Venus would use if she were to express the moral of the story at the end? And what about the young man and his cat: how would each of those characters describe the lesson they have learned?

For other stories of love gone wrong, see the fable of the mouse who married a lion (Fable 37), or the fable of the lion in love (Fable 20). For another story of divine intervention, see the fable of Hercules and the plow (Fable 11).

## Grammar Overview
### *The Implied Subject*

You have seen many examples of Latin sentences where the verb is implied, but not expressed, particularly when the verb is some form of the copula, "to be" (see Fable 13). It is also common for the subject of a Latin sentence to be implied, but not expressed directly. Consider, for example, this sentence from the fable you are about to read: *Venerem oravit.* There are two possible ways to understand this sentence. Either "she prayed to Venus" (meaning the cat) or "he prayed to Venus" (meaning the young man). Grammatically, the verb *oravit* requires only that the subject be third person singular, he or she. As a result, it is not grammar but context that will decide who really is the implied subject of the verb. In favor of the cat is the fact that the cat was the subject of the previous verb and Latin usually does not switch subjects without alerting you in some way (although that is a question of style, not grammar). In favor of the young man is the fact that the next sentence tells us that Venus took pity on the young man's desire, which seems to refer to the young man's desire to have the cat turned into a woman. So, as you read the opening sentences of this fable, consider the clues and decide what you think: who prayed to Venus—the cat, or the man?

# Vocabulary

## Nouns

**adolescens (adolescentis,** *m.***):** youth, young man
**adolescentulus (adolescentuli,** *m.***):** young man, youth
**amator (amatoris,** *m.***):** lover, admirer
**catta (cattae,** *f.***):** she-cat
**cupiditas (cupiditatis,** *f.***):** desire, greed
**dea (deae,** *f.***):** goddess
**delicium (delicii,** *n.***):** delight, source of joy
**facies (faciei,** *f.***):** face, appearance
**femina (feminae,** *f.***):** woman
**forma (formae,** *f.***):** shape, beauty
**medium (medii,** *n.***):** middle, center
**Venus (Veneris,** *f.***):** Venus (goddess of love)

## Adjectives

**formosus, formosa, formosum:** shapely, lovely
**speciosus, speciosa, speciosum:** attractive, appealing

## Verbs

**abduco (abducere), abduxi, abductus:** lead away, take
**aspicio (aspicere), aspexi, aspectus:** look at, notice
**constituo (constituere), constitui, constitutus:** establish, put in position
**converto (convertere), converti, conversus:** turn, turn around
**cupio (cupere):** want, desire
**experior (experiri):** test, try
**indignor (indignari), indignatus sum:** resent, be indignant
**misereor (misereri), misertus sum:** take pity, have mercy on
**muto (mutare), mutavi, mutatus:** change, alter
**obliviscor (oblivisci), oblitus sum:** forget
**persequor (persequi), persecutus sum:** chase, overtake

## Other

**denuo:** once more, a second time

# DE CATTA IN FEMINAM MUTATA

## Dramatis Personae

*Catta*, the cat, *Adolescens*, the young man, and *Venus*, the goddess of love.

Catta quaedam delicium erat formosi cuiusdam Adolescentis Veneremque oravit ut in feminam mutaret. Dea, miserta cupiditatis Adolescentuli, convertit Cattam in puellam. Quam, cum longe speciosa esset, Amator domum abduxit. Venus, experiri cupiens si, mutata facie, mutasset et mores, in medium constituit murem. Quem cum illa aspexit, oblita formae, murem ut caperet persecuta est. Qua super re indignata, Venus denuo eam in priorem Cattae formam mutavit.

## Grammar Notes

**catta quaedam**. While the noun **cattus** is the usual late Latin word for "cat," the feminine form can also be found, as here in this story.

**miserta cupiditatis**. The participle **miserta** ("take pity on") takes a genitive complement.

**cum longe speciosa esset**. The subjunctive, introduced by **cum**, gives causal background information; this is why the man takes the girl home with him.

**quam amator domum abduxit**. The referent of the relative pronoun **quam** is **puella** in the previous sentence (see Fable 4): **quam (puellam) amator domum abduxit**; this use of **domum** in the accusative means "to the house, homeward."

**si mutasset et mores**. The word **si** introduces an indirect question with the subjunctive; for the adverbial use of **et** meaning "also," see Fable 17.

**mutata facie**. Ablative absolute construction (see Fable 8).

**quem cum illa aspexit**. The referent of the relative pronoun **quem** is **murem** in the previous sentence (see Fable 37): **quem (murem) cum illa aspexit** (for **cum** plus the indicative, see Fable 24).

**oblita formae**. The participle **oblita** ("being forgetful of") takes a genitive complement.

**murem persecuta est**. The deponent verb **persecuta est** is transitive and takes a direct object in the accusative (see Fable 9).

**qua super re**. The phrase **qua re** wraps around the preposition, referring back to the events described previously (the woman chasing the mouse).

*Hospitium verendum.*

*Post tres dies piscis vilescit et hospes.*

# Fable 76.
# DE HERINACEIS VIPERAS
# HOSPITES EIICIENTIBUS
## (Barlow 40)

## Introduction
### The Hedgehogs Expelling The Vipers, Their Hosts

This unusual little story about the hedgehogs and the vipers is a fable invented by the Renaissance Latin author, Abstemius. Normally, you might expect that the vipers in this story would be the villains, but that is not the case. Instead, the vipers act very kindly towards the hedgehogs, and it is the hedgehogs who are the bad guys. As the vipers are finally driven out of their own home into the cold and snow, what do you think they might say is the lesson that they have learned from this story?

For another story about guests and hosts, see the fable of the fox and the stork (Fable 19), or the satyr and the traveler (Fable 64). For a story about a creature who did not act generously when winter was coming, see the fable of the ant and the cicada (Fable 16).

## Grammar Overview
### The Compound Word, Quare

You have already met several different Latin compound words, such as *quidpiam* (see Fable 3), *solummodo* (see Fable 46), and *quandoquidem* (see Fable 52). In this fable, you will meet another compound word: *quare*. The word *quare* was originally two words, *qua + re*, meaning, literally, "on account of which thing," or, more idiomatically, "for this reason." This is the usage you will see here in the story of the hedgehogs and the vipers: *quare viperae cesserunt hospitio*, "for this reason, the vipers gave up their lodging." In addition, *quare* can also be used interrogatively, to ask a question: "on account of which thing?" or, more idiomatically, "why?" A similar compound word, *quamobrem* (*quam + ob + rem*), can also be used to ask "on account of which thing?" or "why?" Can you think of another Latin question word that is a compound similar to *quare* and *quamobrem*? (Hint: How do you ask "how?" in Latin?)

# Vocabulary

## Nouns

**acumen (acuminis,** *n.***)**: sharpness, point
**caverna (cavernae,** *f.***)**: hole, den
**dolor (doloris,** *m.***)**: pain, grief
**frigus (frigoris,** *n.***)**: cold, frost
**herinaceus (herinacei,** *m.***)**: hedgehog
**hiems (hiemis,** *f.***)**: winter, winter time
**hospes (hospitis,** *m.***)**: host, guest, visitor
**hospitium (hospitii,** *n.***)**: hospitality, lodging
**spina (spinae,** *f.***)**: spine, thorn
**vipera (viperae,** *f.***)**: snake, viper

## Adjectives

**angustus, angusta, angustum:** narrow, steep
**blandus, blanda, blandum:** charming, coaxing
**proprius, propria, proprium:** one's own
**vehemens (vehementis):** violent, vigorous

## Verbs

**advento (adventare):** approach, arrive
**cedo (cedere), cessi, cessus:** retire, go away from
**concedo (concedere):** give up, grant
**eiicio (eiicere):** throw out, expel
**exeo (exire):** go out, come out
**maneo (manere):** remain, stay
**praesentio (praesentire):** feel in advance, anticipate
**provolvo (provolvere):** roll along, roll over
**pungo (pungere):** prick, puncture
**sentio (sentire), sensi, sensus:** perceive, feel
**torqueo (torquere):** twist, torment

## Other

**adversus:** against, opposite
**blande:** charmingly, coaxingly
**hic:** here, in this place
**huc:** here, to this place
**illuc:** to that place, there
**male:** badly, poorly
**nimis:** too much, very much
**quandoquidem:** since, seeing that
**quare:** for which reason, therefore

# DE HERINACEIS VIPERAS HOSPITES EIICIENTIBUS

## Dramatis Personae

*Herinacei*, the hedgehogs, and *Viperae*, the vipers.

Herinacei, hiemem adventare praesentientes, blande Viperas rogaverunt ut in propria illarum caverna adversus vim frigoris locum sibi concederent. Quod cum illae fecissent, Herinacei, huc atque illuc se provolventes, spinarum acumine Viperas pungebant et vehementi dolore torquebant. Illae, male secum actum videntes, blandis verbis orabant Herinaceos ut exirent, quandoquidem tam multis locus esset angustus nimis. Cui Herinacei: "Exeant (inquiunt) qui hic manere non possunt." Quare Viperae, sentientes ibi locum non esse, cesserunt hospitio.

## Grammar Notes

**hiemem adventare.** Accusative plus infinitive construction in indirect statement (see Fable 7).

**quod cum illae fecissent.** The relative pronoun **quod** connects back to the previous sentence (see Fable 4), referring to the general situation described there, i.e., the vipers inviting the hedgehogs into their home; for the placement of **quod** before **cum,** see Fable 37.

**male secum actum.** Accusative plus infinitive construction in indirect statement: **male secum actum (esse)**, "it had gone badly for them" (**secum** = **cum se**, "with them, for them").

**quandoquidem locus esset angustus.** The subjunctive, introduced by **quandoquidem** ("since"), gives causal background information; according to the vipers, this is why the hedgehogs need to move out.

**cui herinacei inquiunt.** The referent of the relative pronoun **cui** is the entire preceding statement (see Fable 4): "to (this) the hedgehogs say . . ."

**exeant qui hic manere non possunt.** The referent of the relative pronoun **qui** is the implied subject of the verb: **exeant (ei) qui hic manere non possunt;** the subjunctive expresses a wish or command, the result that the hedgehogs expect to happen.

**locum non esse.** Accusative plus infinitive construction in indirect statement: "there is no place."

**cesserunt hospitio.** The verb **cesserunt** ("go away from") takes an ablative complement.

*Quid libertate pretiosius?*

*Nemo nisi sapiens*
*liber est.*

# Fable 77.
# DE RANIS ET EARUM REGE
## (Barlow 36)

## Introduction
### The Frogs and Their King

The Roman poet Phaedrus told this story about the frogs and their king as an example of what happened in the city of Athens during the middle of the sixth century BCE, when the democratic form of government was replaced by a dictatorship under the rule of the tyrant Pisistratus, who actually had a good deal of popular support among the people of Athens. According to Phaedrus, Aesop used this fable to show the Athenians how dangerous it was to give up their democracy and accept the rule of a king instead: just look at what happened to the foolish frogs who did the same thing! Jacobs gives this moral to the fable: "Better no rule than cruel rule." If one of the frogs were to croak the moral of the story at the end, what do you think she would say?

For another story about the animals choosing a king, see the fable of the doves and the hawk (Fable 32). To see another foolish frog, look at the fable of the frog and the ox (Fable 14). For more stories about divine intervention, see the fable of Hercules and the plow (Fable 11), or Venus and the cat (Fable 75).

## Grammar Overview
### Negated Adjectives

Jupiter's final pronouncement at the end of this fable involves a Latin play on words, *clementem* and *inclementem*: since the frogs disparaged their *regem clementem*, their "merciful king," they will have to put up with a "merciless king," *regem inclementem*. The Latin prefix *in-* is a way you can negate an adjective in Latin, much like the way that the English prefix un- negates English adjectives. Here are some examples: *certus-incertus*, "certain-uncertain, *dignus-indignus*, "worthy-unworthy," and *felix-infelix*, "happy-unhappy." Probably the most confusing thing about the negating *in-* prefix is that there is also a verbal prefix *in-*, which means "in, into, at," which you can find in so many verbs: *inire*, "to go in," *inferre*, "to bring in," etc. So, be careful: when you find an *in-* prefix in Latin, you need to be clear about which of the two outwardly identical prefixes you are dealing with, the *in-* that negates adjectives, or the *-in* used for verb formation. Remember that sometimes adjectives are formed from verbal stems, so you cannot just assume that an adjectival word that starts with *in-* is negated. So, from this list of adjectival words that start with *in-*, can you tell which ones are examples of negation? *indulgens - innocens - ineptus - invisus - inimicus* (Hint: Three of them are negations, and two are not.)

# Vocabulary

## *Nouns*

**ciconia (ciconiae,** *f.***):** stork

**contemptus (contemptus,** *m.***):** scorn, disdain

**fluvius (fluvii,** *m.***):** river, stream

**fragor (fragoris,** *m.***):** noise, crash

**Iupiter (Iovis,** *m.***):** Jupiter (king of the gods)

**lusus (lusus,** *m.***):** amusement, game

**metus (metus,** *m.***):** fear, dread

**moles (molis,** *f.***):** mass, bulk

**palus (paludis,** *f.***):** swamp, marsh

**trabes (trabis,** *f.***):** tree-trunk, beam

**tyrannis (tyrannidis,** *f.***):** tyranny, regime

## *Adjectives*

**clemens (clementis):** merciful, gentle

**inclemens (inclementis):** unmerciful, harsh

**iners (inertis):** weak, helpless

**ingens (ingentis):** huge, enormous

**strenuus, strenua, strenuum:** vigorous, energetic

## *Verbs*

**abiicio (abiicere), abieci, abiectus:** cast off, toss away

**decerno (decernere), decrevi, decretus:** determine, resolve

**deiicio (deiicere), deieci, deiectus:** throw down, drop

**deprecor (deprecari), deprecatus sum:** abominate, disparage

**lacesso (lacessere):** provoke, harass

**perambulo (perambulare):** walk about, travel through

**quasso (quassare):** shake, batter

**queror (queri), questus sum:** complain, grumble

**sileo (silere):** be silent, keep quiet

**supplico (supplicare):** plead, beg

**terreo (terrere), terrui, territus:** scare, frighten

**veneror (venerari):** worship, revere

**voro (vorare):** swallow, devour

## *Other*

**frustra:** in vain, unsuccessfully

**obviam:** in the way of, running into

**prope:** near, nearly

**quidquid:** whatever, everything

**rursus:** again, in turn

# DE RANIS ET EARUM REGE

## Dramatis Personae

*Ranae*, the frogs, *Iupiter*, king of the gods, and *Ciconia*, the stork.

Gens Ranarum supplicabat sibi regem dari. Iupiter deiecit trabem,
cuius moles cum ingenti fragore quassabat fluvium. Territae,
silebant Ranae. Mox regem venerantur et tandem accedunt
propius; omni metu abiecto, iners rex lusui et contemptui est.
Lacessunt igitur Iovem rursus, orantes regem sibi dari qui strenuus
sit. Iupiter dat Ciconiam, quae, perambulans paludem, quidquid
Ranarum obviam fit, vorabat. De cuius tyrannide questae sunt,
sed frustra. Nam Iupiter non audit; decrevit enim ut, quae regem
clementem sunt deprecatae, iam ferant inclementem.

## Grammar Notes

**regem venerantur.** The deponent verb **venerantur** is transitive and takes a direct object in
the accusative (see Fable 9).

**propius.** This is the comparative form of the adverb, **prope.**

**metu abiecto.** Ablative absolute construction (see Fable 8).

**lusui et contemptui est.** The predicate datives express the purpose to which the frogs put
their king: he was an object of amusement and contempt (see Fable 61).

**lacessunt igitur Iovem.** For the postpositive particle **igitur,** see Fable 32.

**qui strenuus sit.** The subjunctive, introduced by the relative pronoun **qui,** explains the
result the frogs would like to see in response to their request for a king.

**quidquid ranarum obviam fit vorabat.** Partitive genitive **ranarum** (see Fable 30), with
the phrase **obviam fieri** ("to run into, get in the way of"), meaning that whatever frogs
(**quidquid ranarum**) got in the way of the stork (**obviam fit**), she devoured (**vorabat**).

**de cuius tyrannide.** The referent of the relative pronoun **cuius** is **ciconia** in the previous
sentence (see Fable 10 for the preposition standing first in the relative clause): **de cuius
(ciconiae) tyrannide**.

**decrevit enim.** For the postpositive particle **enim,** see Fable 2.

**quae regem sunt deprecatae.** The deponent verb **sunt deprecatae** is transitive and takes a
direct object in the accusative (see Fable 9).

Rana medicinae artem publice profitebatur.

# Fable 78.
# DE RANA ET VULPE
## (Barlow 4)

## Introduction
### The Frog and The Fox

This story of "Doctor Frog" provides an illustration of a proverb that is quoted in the *Gospel of Luke* in the New Testament: *Medice, cura teipsum;* "Physician, heal thyself!" As you read through the story, see what techniques the frog uses in order to persuade all the animals that she is truly an excellent doctor. One claim the frog makes is that she is more eminent than Hippocrates and Galen, the most famous physicians of the Greek and Roman worlds. Alone among the animals of the forest, it is the sly fox who sees through the frog's pretensions. How would you express the moral of this fable in order to emphasize the foolishness of the frog? What if you wanted instead to focus on the foolishness of the animals who believed what the frog was saying?

For another story about an animal physician, see the fable of the lion who pretended to be a doctor (Fable 54). For another story about the foolishness of frogs, see the fable of the frogs and their king (Fable 77), or the frog and the ox (Fable 14).

## Grammar Overview
### Gerunds in the Genitive Case

A gerund, like any noun, can be used in various cases. You have seen examples of the gerund in the ablative case (Fable 48), and in this fable you will see an example of the gerund put into the genitive case: *genus vivendi,* meaning "a type of living, a lifestyle." This particular phrase is similar to the phrase *modus vivendi,* "a way of living, a way of life," a Latin expression that is sometimes used in English even today. You can find a long list of genitive gerunds in the Biblical *Book of Ecclesiastes,* Chapter 3, which famously begins "To every thing there is a season, and a time to every purpose under heaven." The first item in the list is "a time to be born and a time to die," which reads in Latin: *tempus nascendi et tempus moriendi.* It's well worth taking a look at this passage from *Ecclesiastes* in its entirety, as you will find over twenty Latin gerunds listed there! There is one item in that list, in fact, which suits the fable you are about to read very nicely. The frog may not be much of a doctor, but at least she understands that there is *tempus tacendi, et tempus loquendi,* "a time to be silent, and a time to speak," as you will see at the end of the fable when the frog departs without a word, quietly sighing to herself.

# Vocabulary

## Nouns

**bestia (bestiae,** *f.***)**: beast, animal

**cachinnus (cachinni,** *m.***)**: cackle, chuckle

**corona (coronae,** *f.***)**: ring, crown

**Galenus (Galeni,** *m.***)**: Galen, famed Roman physician

**herba (herbae,** *f.***)**: herb, grass

**Hippocrates (Hippocratis,** *m.***)**: Hippocrates, famed Greek physician

**labrum (labri,** *n.***)**: lip

**medicina (medicinae,** *f.***)**: medicine

**medicus (medici,** *m.***)**: medical doctor, physician

**palus (paludis,** *f.***)**: swamp, marsh

**suspirium (suspirii,** *n.***)**: sigh, deep breath

## Adjectives

**circumstipatus, circumstipata, circumstipatum:** surrounded, crowded

**credulus, credula, credulum:** gullible, trusting

**gloriabundus, gloriabunda, gloriabundum:** triumphant, proud

**insulsus, insulsa, insulsum:** stupid, tedious

**lividus, livida, lividum:** bruise-colored, black-and-blue

**nobilis, nobile (nobilis):** respected, respectable

**pallidus, pallida, pallidum:** pale, yellow-green

**tacitus, tacita, tacitum:** silent, quiet

**vagus, vaga, vagum:** wandering, unreliable

**vanus, vana, vanum:** meaningless, useless

## Verbs

**abeo (abire)**: go away, depart

**acquiro (acquirere), acquisivi, acquisitus:** obtain, acquire

**adhibeo (adhibere)**: put, extend to

**blattero (blatterare)**: babble, yammer

**calleo (callere)**: know, have experience

**clamito (clamitare)**: shout repeatedly, yell loudly

**curo (curare)**: cure, heal

**excipio (excipere), excepi, exceptus:** take out, set aside

**gemo (gemere)**: moan, groan

**glorior (gloriari)**: boast, brag

**irrideo (irridere)**: mock, scoff at

**pertineo (pertinere)**: reach, relate to

**profiteor (profiteri)**: claim, declare

**resono (resonare)**: resound, echo

**respicio (respicere)**: regard, look at

**spero (sperare), speravi, speratus:** hope, expect

**valedico (valedicere)**: say goodbye to

## Other

**facile:** easily

**forsan:** perhaps

**minime:** barely, not at all

**prae:** in front of, before

**publice:** publicly

**quid:** why, for what reason

**quin:** why not, why don't

**solummodo:** only, alone

# DE RANA ET VULPE

## Dramatis Personae

*Rana*, the frog, and *Vulpes*, the fox.

Rana, paludibus valedicens, novo vivendi genere acquisito, in silvam gloriabunda sese tulit et, bestiarum coronis circumstipata, medicinae artem publice profitebatur, et in herbis, quae ad corpora curanda pertinent, nobiliorem se vel Galeno vel Hippocrate esse clamitabat. Credula bestiarum gens fidem facile adhibebat, Vulpe solummodo excepta, quae sic glorianti irridebat: "Insulsum vagumque animal! Quid tam vana blatteras? Quid artem nobilem prae te fers, quam minime calles? Livida pallidaque illa tua labra respice! Quin domi abi et teipsum cura, medice! Deinde ad nos redeas, meliora forsan de te speraturos." Nihil respondente Rana sed tacitis secum gemente suspiriis, tota bestiarum cachinnis resonabat silva.

## Grammar Notes

**novo vivendi genere acquisito.** Ablative absolute construction (see Fable 8), with the ablative noun phrase **novo genere** wrapping around the gerund that is in the genitive case (see the *Grammar Overview* for this fable).

**artem profitebatur.** The deponent verb **profitebatur** is transitive and takes a direct object in the accusative (see Fable 9).

**ad corpora curanda.** The gerundive with the preposition **ad** expresses purpose (see Fable 54).

**nobiliorem se esse.** Accusative plus infinitive construction in indirect statement (see Fable 7), with **se** as the accusative subject, and **nobiliorem** as a predicate adjective.

**vel Galeno vel Hippocrate.** Ablatives of comparison with **nobiliorem**; the double use of **vel** is equivalent to the English correlative conjunctions, "either . . . or" (see Fable 65).

**vulpe solummodo excepta.** Ablative absolute construction.

**quae sic glorianti irridebat.** The referent of the relative pronoun **quae** is the fox, and the participle **glorianti** agrees with the frog: **quae (vulpes) sic glorianti (ranae) irridebat.**

**quid blatteras?** The interrogative **quid** here means "why? for what reason?" (see Fable 21).

**Grammar Notes** continued on next page.

**prae te fers.** The idiom **prae se ferre** means "to profess, proclaim."

**quin domi abi et teipsum cura.** The word **quin** plus the imperative expresses the so-called interrogative imperative: "Why don't you go home and heal yourself?" (the pronoun **teipsum** is a compound, **te** + **ipsum**).

**redeas.** The subjunctive states a hypothetical possibility: the frog could come back again as a doctor—if she cures her own ailments first!

**meliora de te speraturos.** The future active participle agrees with **nos,** and **meliora** ("better things") is the accusative object of the participle.

**nihil respondente rana.** Ablative absolute construction, with **nihil** as the object of the participle.

**secum**. This is a compound word, in inverted order: **secum** = **cum** + **se** ("with herself, to herself").

**tacitis gemente suspiriis.** The phrase **tacitis suspiriis** wraps around the participle, **gemente,** which is part of an ablative absolute construction, parallel to **nihil respondente rana.**

**tota resonabat silva.** The noun phrase **tota silva** wraps around the verb.

*Medice, cura te ipsum!*

*Medico male est, si
nemini male est.*

*Morborum medicus
omnium mors ultimus.*

Sol et Aquilo certabant uter sit fortior.

# Fable 79.
# DE SOLE ET VENTO
## (Barlow 34)

## Introduction
### *The Sun and The Wind*

The ancient Romans and Greeks called the winds of the four directions by different names. The south wind was called Notus in Greek, or Auster in Latin; the east wind was Eurus in Greek, Vulturnus in Latin; the west wind was Zephyrus in Greek, Favonius in Latin—and the north wind, whom you will meet in this fable, was called Boreas in Greek, or Aquilo in Latin. A famous English proverb that you could apply to this contest between Boreas and the sun might be, "You can catch more flies with honey than with vinegar." Using more abstract vocabulary, Townsend put the moral of the fable this way: "Persuasion is better than force." If you imagine the defeated North Wind pronouncing the moral at the end of the story, what do you think he might say?

For another story about Boreas, see the fable of the reed and the oak tree (Fable 58). For other stories about contests, see the race between the tortoise and the hare (Fable 57), or between the tortoise and the eagle (Fable 39).

## Grammar Overview
### *Ubi-Unde-Uter*

Almost all of the question words in Latin—the interrogative pronouns, adjectives, and adverbs—begin with *qu-*, as you can see in these examples: *quis, quid, quomodo, quare*, etc. There are, however, a few important question words that start instead with *u-*. Probably the most common is *ubi*, which asks "where?" (or "when?"). There is also *unde*, which asks "from where?" ("whence?"). In this fable, you will meet up with the question word *uter*, which asks "which (of two)?" There is a common Latin adjective that is formed from the negation of the word *uter*: do you know what it is? (Hint: Think about the three different genders in Latin.)

# Vocabulary

## Nouns

**amictus (amictus,** *m.*): cloak, outer garment

**Aquilo (aquilonis,** *m.*): North wind

**Boreas** (*acc.* **Boream,** *m.*): North wind [Greek]

**mantica (manticae,** *f.*): knapsack, cloak

**nemus (nemoris,** *n.*): wood, forest

**nimbus (nimbi,** *m.*): cloud, rainstorm

**palma (palmae,** *f.*): palm, palm of victory

**radius (radii,** *m.*): ray

**turbo (turbinis,** *m.*): whirlwind, tornado

**ventus (venti,** *m.*): wind

**victoria (victoriae,** *f.*): victory

## Adjectives

**frondosus, frondosa, frondosum:** leafy, shady

**horrisonus, horrisona, horrisonum:** dreadful-sounding

**uter, utra, utrum (utrius):** which (of two)

## Verbs

**aestuo (aestuare):** become hot, boil

**aggredior (aggredi):** approach, attack

**anhelo (anhelare):** pant, gasp

**assumo (assumere):** take on, assume

**certo (certare):** contend, dispute

**contingit (contingere):** turn out, fall to

**convenio (convenire), conveni, conventus:** agree, meet

**desisto (desistere):** stop, cease

**duplico (duplicare):** fold over, bend double

**emolior (emoliri):** carry through, bring forth

**evinco (evincere), evici, evictus:** subdue, overcome

**excutio (excutere), excussi, excussus:** shake off, cast out

**experior (experiri):** test, try

**gradior (gradi):** walk, step

**incipio (incipere):** begin, start

**nequeo (nequire):** be unable, cannot

**obuicio (obuicere), obieci, obiectus:** cast off, throw

**progredior (progredi):** go forward, proceed

**resido (residere), resedi:** sit down, settle

**sudo (sudare):** sweat, perspire

## Other

**paulatim:** little by little

# DE SOLE ET VENTO

## Dramatis Personae

*Sol*, the sun, *Aquilo*, the north wind, and *Viator*, the wayfarer.

Sol et Aquilo certabant uter sit fortior. Conventum est experiri vires in Viatorem, ut palmam ferat qui excusserit Viatoris manticam. Boreas horrisono turbine Viatorem aggreditur. At ille non desistit, amictum gradiendo duplicans. Assumit vires Sol qui, nimbo paulatim evicto, totos emolitur radios. Incipit Viator aestuare, sudare, anhelare. Tandem progredi nequiens, sub frondoso nemore, obiecta mantica, resedit et ita Soli victoria contingebat.

## Grammar Notes

**uter sit fortior.** The word **uter** introduces an indirect question with the subjunctive.

**experiri vires.** The deponent infinitive **experiri** is transitive and takes a direct object in the accusative (see Fable 9).

**ut palmam ferat qui excusserit.** The implied subject of the verb **ferat** supplies the referent of the relative pronoun: **ut palmam ferat (is) qui excusserit.**

**viatorem aggreditur.** The deponent verb **aggreditur** is transitive and takes a direct object in the accusative.

**amictum gradiendo duplicans.** The participial phrase **amictum duplicans** wraps around the gerund in the ablative case, **gradiendo**, which describes how the man kept moving: "pacing; walking step by step."

**nimbo evicto.** Ablative absolute construction (see Fable 8).

**totos emolitur radios.** The phrase **totos radios** wraps around the verb (see Fable 6), which is transitive and takes a direct object in the accusative.

**obiecta mantica.** Ablative absolute construction.

*Libertas optima rerum.*

*Liber inops servo divite felicior.*

# Fable 80.
# DE CANE ET LUPO
## (Barlow 97)

## Introduction
### The Dog and The Wolf

This fable poses an age-old question: is it better to live free, without a lot of material security, or is it worth surrendering some of your freedom in return for creature comforts? The wolf in this fable has no doubts about where he stands on this question. In G. F. Townsend's version of the story, the wolf declares: "The weight of this chain is enough to spoil the appetite." Joseph Jacobs adds this moral to the story: "Better starve free than be a fat slave." When you compare your situation to that of the dog and the wolf in this fable, what do you think: are you living more like the dog, or like the wolf?

For more stories about material possessions, see the fable of the city mouse and the country mouse (Fable 4), or the rooster who found a gemstone (Fable 38). For another story about a dog and his master, see the fable of the old dog who caught a deer (Fable 61).

## Grammar Overview
### Ne!

In this fable, the wolf speaks very forcefully at the end of the fable, using the interjection *ne* to express his feelings. Although it might seem like this *ne* should be a negative word, the interjection *ne* is actually a strongly affirming exclamation in Latin: "Indeed! That's for sure!" It is sometimes written as *nae*, although this is considered an incorrect spelling. So, you need to be careful not to confuse the affirmative interjection *ne* with the negative conjunction *ne*. From context, though, you can usually tell the difference, especially if the editor of the text has been kind enough to provide you with an exclamation mark to indicate the presence of an interjection, as you will see here. Although the ancient Romans did not use exclamation marks in their writing, modern editions of Latin texts often employ exclamation marks to indicate exclamatory interjections. So, when you are punctuating a text in Latin, or when you are punctuating a text in English translated from Latin, you need to think about when you might choose to use an exclamation mark. It's not just a matter of grammar; it's a matter of style.

# Vocabulary

## Nouns

**catena (catenae,** *f.***):** chain, bond
**cibus (cibi,** *m.***):** food
**cicatrix (cicatricis,** *f.***):** scar
**collis (collis,** *m.***):** hill
**collum (colli,** *n.***):** neck
**cruditas (cruditatis,** *f.***):** rawness, wound
**fustis (fustis,** *m.***):** club, stick
**indicium (indicii,** *n.***):** sign, evidence
**ius (iuris,** *n.***):** right, law
**libertas (libertatis,** *f.***):** freedom
**mensa (mensae,** *f.***):** table
**nemus (nemoris,** *n.***):** wood, forest
**paries (parietis,** *m.***):** wall
**pascuum (pascui,** *n.***):** pasture
**victus (victus,** *m.***):** food, sustenance

## Adjectives

**ieiunus, ieiuna, ieiunum:** fasting, hungry
**impastus, impasta, impastum:** unfed, hungry
**indulgens (indulgentis):** mild, lenient
**macilentus, macilenta, macilentum:** thin, lean
**pinguis, pingue (pinguis):** fat, sleek
**praesens (praesentis):** at hand, in person
**privatus, privata, privatum:** personal, private
**saginatus, saginata, saginatum:** fattened, well-fed
**satur, satura, saturum:** well-fed, stuffed
**saucius, saucia, saucium:** wounded, injured

## Verbs

**accido (accidere), accidi:** occur, happen
**attono (attonare), attonui, attonitus:** daze, strike with lightning
**claudo (claudere), clausi, clausus:** close, shut
**comparo (comparare):** procure, buy
**contundo (contundere):** beat, bruise
**evado (evadere):** get out, turn out to be
**fruor (frui):** use, enjoy
**invideo (invidere):** envy, begrudge
**malo (malle):** prefer, want more
**miror (mirari), miratus sum:** be amazed, marvel at
**occurro (occurrere):** run into, meet
**paeniteo (paenitere):** displease, regret
**percontor (percontari), percontatus sum:** inquire, ask
**perspicio (perspicere):** examine, observe
**perstringo (perstringere):** tie up, make tight
**porrigo (porrigere):** extend, offer
**possideo (possidere):** seize, hold

## Other

**interdum:** sometimes
**intra:** within, inside
**ne:** surely, indeed
**paulisper:** for a short time
**prope:** near, nearly
**quomodo:** how
**quotidie:** daily, each day
**tantummodo:** only, merely
**tot:** many, so many

# DE CANE ET LUPO

## Dramatis Personae

*Canis*, the dog, and *Lupus*, the wolf.

Saginato Cani occurrit Lupus macilentus, miratus quomodo ille, qui intra parietes privatos clauderetur, tam pinguis evaderet, et ipse tam macilentus foret, qui tot nemora, colles, et pascua de iure suo possideret, ex quibus victum sibi compararet. Respondit Canis se indulgentissimum habuisse herum, qui cibos illi quotidie de mensa sua porrigebat. Attonitus stetit paulisper Lupus sed, propius cicatrices et collum saucium perspiciens, percontatus est unde haec cruditas acciderit. Respondit Canis haec tantummodo esse catenae indicia, qua interdum perstringebatur. Cui Lupus: "Ne! Tuae non invideo fortunae, nec meae paeniteo. Malim enim, ieiunus et impastus, praesenti frui libertate, quam satur catenis perstringi et fustibus contundi."

## Grammar Notes

**cani occurrit lupus.** The verb **occurrit** ("run into to") takes a dative complement.

**quomodo ille tam pinguis evaderet.** The word **quomodo** introduces an indirect question with the subjunctive; **pinguis** is a predicate adjective, agreeing with the subject, **ille (canis).**

**qui clauderetur.** The subjunctive, introduced by the relative pronoun **qui,** provides causal background information; according to the wolf, this is why it is so surprising that the dog is fat.

**ipse tam macilentus foret.** The pronoun refers to the wolf, **ipse (lupus),** with **foret** as an alternative subjunctive form of **esset** (see Fable 26), continuing the indirect question introduced by **quomodo,** with the predicate **tam macilentus** parallel to **tam pinguis.**

**qui possideret ex quibus compararet.** The subjunctives provide causal background information; according to the wolf, this is why it is so surprising that he, the wolf, is thin.

**se habuisse herum.** Accusative plus infinitive construction in indirect statement (see Fable 7), with **se** as the accusative subject, and **herum** as the object.

**Grammar Notes** continued on next page.

**indulgentissimum habuisse herum**. The noun phrase, **indulgentissimum herum,** wraps around the infinitive (for this use of the superlative, see Fable 39).

**unde haec cruditas acciderit.** The word **unde** introduces an indirect question with the subjunctive.

**haec esse indicia.** Accusative plus infinitive construction in indirect statement; **haec** is the accusative subject (neuter plural), and **indicia** is the predicate noun (neuter plural).

**cui lupus.** The referent of the relative pronoun **cui** is **canis** in the previous sentence (see Fable 4), with an implied verb of speaking: **cui (cani) lupus (inquit).**

**ne! tuae non invideo fortunae.** For the interjection **ne**, see the *Grammar Overview* for this fable; the phrase **tuae fortunae** wraps around the verb, **non invideo,** which takes a dative complement.

**nec meae paeniteo.** The verb **paeniteo** takes a genitive complement, and you can replace the word **nec** with the words **et non** (see Fable 18): **et meae (fortunae) non paeniteo.**

**malim enim ieiunus et impastus.** The subjunctive is part of an implied hypothetical statement: "I would prefer (if I had a choice)," and the adjectives **ieiunus** and **impastus** agree with the subject of the verb; for the postpositive particle **enim,** see Fable 2.

**praesenti frui libertate.** The noun phrase, **praesenti libertate,** wraps around the infinitive **frui**, which takes an ablative complement.

**satur.** Like **ieiunus** and **impastus,** this adjective agrees with the subject of **malim**.

**quam perstringi et contundi.** The word **quam** coordinates a comparison introduced by **malim** (= **magis** + **velim**), with the infinitives **frui** and **perstringi et contundi** as the things being compared.

*Omnes homines aut liberi sunt aut servi.*

# GLOSSARY

For specialized vocabulary lists (lists by roots, lists by word type, etc.) and online vocabulary activities, visit the website at *LatinViaFables.com*.

## A

**ā** or **ab** (*prep. + abl.*): from; by (*agent*)

**abdūcō** (**abdūcere**, *verb*), **abdūxī**, **abductus**: lead away, take

**abeō** (**abīre**, *irregular verb*), **abīvī** or **abiī**, **abitus**: go away, depart

**abesse**, *see* **absum**

**abigō** (**abigere**, *verb*), **abēgī**, **abactus**: drive away, expel

**abiiciō** (**abiicere**, *verb*), **abiēcī**, **abiectus**: cast off, toss away

**abnuō** (**abnuere**, *verb*), **abnuī**, **abnuitus**: refuse, decline

**abrōdō** (**abrōdere**, *verb*), **abrōsī**, **abrōsus**: gnaw away, chew off

**abscondō** (**abscondere**, *verb*), **abscondī**, **asconditus**: hide, conceal

**absentia** (**absentiae**, *f.*): absence

**absolūtus, absolūta, absolūtum** (*adj.*): finished, complete

**absorbeō** (**absorbēre**, *verb*), **absorbuī**, **absorptus**: swallow up, engulf

**absum** (**abesse**, *irregular verb*), **āfuī**: be away, be absent

**absūmō** (**absūmere**, *verb*), **absūmpsī**, **absūmptus**: consume, destroy

**accēdō** (**accēdere**, *verb*), **accessī**, **accessus**: come near, approach

**accidō** (**accidere**, *verb*), **accidī**: occur, happen

**accipiter** (**accipitris**, *m.*): hawk

**accumbō** (**accumbere**, *verb*), **accubuī**, **accubitus**: recline, sit down to dinner

**accurrō** (**accurrere**, *verb*), **accurrī**, **accursus**: run to, run up

**acerbus, acerba, acerbum** (*adj.*) harsh, bitter

**acervus** (**acervī**, *m.*): heap, pile

**aciēs** (**aciēī**, *f.*): sharp edge, battle line

**acquīrō** (**acquīrere**, *verb*), **acquisīvī**, **acquisītus**: obtain, acquire

**ācriter** (*adv.*): sharply, pointedly

**actus**, *see* **agō**

**aculeus** (**aculeī**, *m.*): sting, goad

**acūmen** (**acūminis**, *n.*): sharpness, point

**acuō** (**acuere**, *verb*), **acuī**, **acūtus**: sharpen

**ad** (*prep. + acc.*): to, towards

**adaptō** (**adaptāre**, *verb*), **adaptāvī**, **adaptātus**: modify, fit to

**adeō** (**adīre**, *irregular verb*), **adīvī** or **adiī**, **aditus**: go to, approach

**adeptus**, *see* **adipiscor**

**adesse**, *see* **adsum**

**adhibeō** (**adhibēre**, *verb*), **adhibuī**, **adhibitus**: put, extend to

**adiī** or **adīvī**, *see* **adeō**

**adiiciō** (**adiicere**, *verb*), **adiēcī**, **adiectus**: throw to, toss towards

**adipiscor** (**adipiscī**, *deponent verb*), **adeptus sum**: get, win

**adiuvō** (**adiuvāre**, *verb*), **adiūvī**, **adiūtus**: help, aid

**adminiculum** (**adminiculī**, *n.*): prop, support

**admoneō** (**admonēre**, *verb*), **admonuī**, **admonitus**: suggest, prompt

**admoveō** (**admovēre**, *verb*), **admōvī**, **admōtus**: bring near, move up

**adolescēns** (**adolescentis**, *m.*): youth, young man

**adolescentulus** (**adolescentulī**, *m.*): young man, youth

**adorior** (**adorīrī**, *deponent verb*), **adortus sum**: assail, attack adproperō (adproperāre, *verb*), adproperāvī, adproperātus: hasten, hurry towards

adsum (adesse, *irregular verb*), affuī: be present, attend

adveniō (advenīre, *verb*), advēnī, adventus: come to, arrive

adventō (adventāre, *verb*), adventāvī, adventātus: approach, arrive

adventus (adventūs, *m.*): arrival, coming

adversor (adversārī, *deponent verb*), adversātus sum: oppose, be against

adversus (*prep.* + *acc.*): against, opposite

aedēs (aedis, *f.*): temple, shrine

aegrōtō (aegrōtāre, *verb*), aegrōtāvī, aegrōtātus: be ill, sick

aegrōtus, aegrōta, aegrōtum (*adj.*): ailing, sick

aemulātiō (aemulātiōnis, *f.*): rivalry, ambition

aequō (aequāre, *verb*), aequāvī, aequātus: equal, level

aerumnōsus, aerumnōsa, aerumnōsum (*adj.*): troubled, full of difficulty

aestās (aestātis, *f.*): summer, summer heat

aestimō (aestimāre, *verb*), aestimāvī, aestimātus: assess, consider

aestuō (aestuāre, *verb*), aestuāvī, aestuātus: become hot, boil

aestus (aestūs, *m.*): fire, heat wave

aetās (aetātis, *f.*): age, stage of life

afferō (afferre, *irregular verb*), attulī, allātus: bring to, carry up

afficiō (afficere, *verb*), affēcī, affectus: afflict, weaken

affor (affārī, *deponent verb*), affātus sum: speak to, address

affuī, *see* adsum

afuī, *see* absum

ager (agrī, *m.*): field

aggredior (aggredī, *deponent verb*), aggressus sum: approach, attack

agitō (agitāre, *verb*), agitāvī, agitātus: drive, guide

agmen (agminis, *n.*): army, marching column

agnoscō (agnoscere, *verb*), agnōvī, agnitus: recognize, realize

agnus (agnī, *m.*): lamb

agō (agere, *verb*), ēgī, actus: conduct, do, carry out the role

agricola (agricolae, *m.*): farmer

aiō (*defective verb*): say; ait: he/she says; aiunt: they say

āla (ālae, *f.*): wing

alauda (alaudae, *f.*): crested lark

algor (algōris, *m.*): cold, chill

aliēnus, aliēna, aliēnum (*adj.*): belonging to another, foreign

aliquandō (*adv.*): sometime, sometime or other

aliquis, aliquid (alicūius, *pron.*): someone, some (also aliquī, aliqua, aliquod, *adj.*)

alius, alia, aliud (alīus, *adj.*): another, other

allātus, *see* afferō

alliciō (allicere, *verb*), allexī, allectus: entice, lure

alō (alere, *verb*), aluī, alitus: nourish, raise

alter, altera, alterum (alterīus, *adj.*): other, another

altus, alta, altum (*adj.*): high, tall, deep

alveāre (alveāris, *n.*): beehive

amābilis, amābile (amābilis, *adj.*): lovable, amiable

amātor (amātōris, *m.*): lover, admirer

amātōrius, amātōria, amātōrium (*adj.*): amorous, in love

ambāgēs (ambāgis, *f.*): long story, convoluted words

ambō, ambae, ambō (*number, pron.*): both, two together

amīcitia (amīcitiae, *f.*): friendship

amictus (amictūs, *m.*): cloak, outer garment

amīcus (amīcī, *m.*): friend

amnis (amnis, *m.*): river, stream

**amō** (**amāre**, *verb*), **amāvī, amātus**: love

**amplius** (*adv.*): more, any more

**anceps** (**ancipitis**, *adj.*): two-headed, doubtful

**ancilla** (**ancillae**, *f.*): maid, maidservant

**anguis** (**anguis**, *m.*): snake, serpent

**angustus, angusta, angustum** (*adj.*): narrow, steep

**anhēlitus** (**anhēlitūs**, *m.*): breath, panting

**anhēlō** (**anhēlāre**, *verb*), **anhēlāvī, anhēlātus**: pant, gasp

**animadvertō** (**animadvertere**, *verb*), **animadvertī, animadversus**: notice, pay attention to

**animal** (**animālis**, *n.*): animal, living being

**animāns** (**animantis**, *n.*): animal, living being

**animōsus, animōsa, animōsum** (*adj.*): courageous, energetic

**animus** (**animī**, *m.*): mind, spirit

**annītor** (**annītī**, *deponent verb*), **annīxus sum**: lean upon, strive

**annus** (**annī**, *m.*): year

**ansa** (**ansae**, *f.*): handle

**anser** (**anseris**, *m.*): goose

**ante** (*prep. + acc.*): before, in front of

**antequam** (*conj.*): before, prior to

**antrum** (**antrī**, *n.*): cave, hollow place

**anus** (**anūs**, *f.*): old woman

**anxictās** (**anxietātis**, *f.*): worry, anxiety

**anxius, anxia, anxium** (*adj.*): uneasy, worried

**apage** (*interjection*): begone, away with

**aper** (**aprī**, *m.*): wild boar

**apicula** (**apiculae**, *f.*): bee, little bee

**apis** (**apis**, *f.*): bee

**appāreō** (**appārēre**, *verb*), **appāruī, appāritus**: appear, show up

**applaudō** (**applaudere**, *verb*), **applausī, applausus**: clap, applaud

**apprehendō** (**apprehendere**, *verb*), **apprehendī, apprehēnsus**: grab hold of, seize

**appropinquō** (**appropinquāre**, *verb*), **appropinquāvī, appropinquātus**: approach, draw near

**aptus, apta, aptum** (*adj.*): suitable, proper

**aqua** (**aquae**, *f.*): water

**aquila** (**aquilae**, *f.*): eagle

**Aquilō** (**Aquilōnis**, *m.*): North wind

**āra** (**ārae**, *f.*): altar

**arātrum** (**arātrī**, *n.*): plow

**arbor** (**arboris**, *f.*): tree

**arēna** (**arēnae**, *f.*): sand

**armātus, armāta, armātum** (*adj.*): armor-clad, spurred

**armentum** (**armentī**, *n.*): herd, cattle

**arō** (**arāre**, *verb*), **arāvī, arātus**: plow

**arrēpō** (**arrēpere**, *verb*), **arrēpsī, arrēptus**: creep up to

**arripiō** (**arripere**, *verb*), **arripuī, arreptus**: assail, jump at

**ars** (**artis**, *f.*): art, artifice, skill

**artus, arta, artum** (*adj.*): narrow, tight

**arundō** (**arundinis**, *f.*): reed

**ascendō** (**ascendere**, *verb*), **ascendī, ascēnsus**: climb up, go up

**asellus** (**asellī**, *m.*): donkey, little donkey

**asinus** (**asinī**, *m.*): donkey

**asper, aspera, asperum** (*adj.*): violent, rough

**aspiciō** (**aspicere**, *verb*), **aspexī, aspectus**: look at, notice

**assūmō** (**assūmere**, *verb*), **assūmpsī, assūmptus**: take on, assume

**ast** (*conj.*): but, on the contrary

**astūtia** (**astūtiae**, *f.*): cleverness, trick

**at** (*conj.*): but, but yet

**atque** or **ac** (*conj.*): and, and moreover, than

**attendō** (**attendere**, *verb*), **attendī, attentus**: pay attention to

**attingō** (**attingere**, *verb*), **attigī, attactus**: touch, reach

**attollō** (**attollere**, *verb*): raise up, lift on high

**attonō (attonāre,** *verb*), **attonuī, attoni-tus:** daze, strike with lightning

**attulī,** *see* **afferō**

**auceps (aucupis,** *m.*): fowler, birdcatcher

**auctor (auctōris,** *m.*): author, originator

**auctōritās (auctōritātis,** *f.*): authority, prestige

**audeō (audēre,** *semi-deponent verb*), **ausus sum:** dare, venture

**audiō (audīre,** *verb*), **audīvī, audītus:** hear

**aufugiō (aufugere,** *verb*), **aufūgī:** run away, flee

**augur (auguris,** *m.*): prophet, seer

**augurium (auguriī,** *n.*): omen, sign

**aureus, aurea, aureum (***adj.***):** gold, golden

**auricula (auriculae,** *f.*): ear, little ear

**auris (auris,** *f.*): ear

**aurum (aurī,** *n.*): gold

**auspex (auspicis,** *m.*): seer, guide

**ausus,** *see* **audeō**

**aut (***conj.***):** or

**autem (***conj.***):** but, moreover

**autumō (autumāre,** *verb*), **autumāvī, autumātus:** assert, reckon

**auxilium (auxiliī,** *n.*): help

**avārus, avāra, avārum (***adj.***):** greedy, grasping

**avicula (aviculae,** *f.*): bird, little bird

**avidē (***adv.***):** eagerly, insatiably

**avidus, avida, avidum (***adj.***):** eager, insatiable

**avis (avis,** *f.*): bird

**avolō (avolāre,** *verb*), **avolāvī, avolātus:** fly away, fly off

# B

**basilica (basilicae,** *f.*): great hall, court

**bellātor (bellātōris,** *m.*): warrior, combatant

**bellum (bellī,** *n.*): war, combat

**bene (***adv.***):** well, good

**benefactor (benefactōris,** *m.*): benefactor

**beneficium (beneficiī,** *n.*): kindness, favor

**benevolentia (benevolentiae,** *f.*): goodwill, kindness

**bestia (bestiae,** *f.*): beast, animal

**bestiola (bestiolae,** *f.*): critter, little beast

**bibō (bibere,** *verb*), **bibī:** drink

**bis (***adv.***):** twice, on two occasions

**blandē (***adv.***):** charmingly, coaxingly

**blandus, blanda, blandum (***adj.***):** charming, coaxing

**blatterō (blatterāre,** *verb*), **blatterāvī, blatterātus:** babble, yammer

**bonus, bona, bonum (***adj.***):** good

**Boreās (***acc.*** Boream,** *m.*): North wind [Greek]

**bōs (bovis,** *m.*): ox, bull

**breviter (***adv.***):** shortly, briefly

**brūma (brūmae,** *f.*): winter weather, cold

**Brūtus (Brūtī,** *m.*): Brutus (Marcus Junius Brutus)

# C

**cachinnus (cachinnī,** *m.*): cackle, chuckle

**caedis (caedis,** *f.*): slaughter, massacre

**caelum (caelī,** *n.*): sky, heaven

**calculus (calculī,** *m.*): reckoning, calculation

**calefīō (calefierī,** *irregular verb*), **calefac-tus sum:** warm up, become warm

**calidus, calida, calidum (***adj.***):** warm, hot

**calleō (callēre,** *verb*), **calluī:** know, have experience

**calx (calcis,** *f.*): heel, foot, hoof

**campana (campanae,** *f.*): bell

**canis (canis,** *m/f.*): dog

**canōrus, canōra, canōrum (***adj.***):** melodious, resonant

**cantō (cantāre,** *verb*), **cantāvī, cantātus:** sing

**cantus (cantūs,** *m.*): song, tune

**caper (caprī,** *m.*): goat, billy-goat

**capiō (capere,** *verb*), **cēpī, captus:** get, seize

captīvus, captīva, captīvum (*adj.*): imprisoned, caught

captō (captāre, *verb*), captāvī, captātus: grab, grasp

caput (capitis, *n.*): head, person, life

careō (carēre, *verb*), caruī: lack

carō (carnis, *f.*): flesh, meat

carrus (carrī, *m.*): wagon

Carthāgō (Carthāginis, *f.*): Carthage

cārus, cāra, cārum (*adj.*): dear, precious

cassus, cassa, cassum (*adj.*): hollow, fruitless

cāsus (cāsūs, *m.*): chance, accident

catēna (catēnae, *f.*): chain, bond

catta (cattae, *f.*): she-cat

cattus (cattī, *m.*): cat

catulus (catulī, *m.*): puppy, whelp

cauda (caudae, *f.*): tail

causa (causae, *f.*): reason, cause

cautē (*adv.*): carefully, thoroughly

cautus, cauta, cautum (*adj.*): careful, cautious

caveō (cavēre, *verb*), cāvī, cautus: beware, watch out for

caverna (cavernae, *f.*): hole, den

cēdō (cēdere, *verb*), cessī, cessus: yield, give way; retire, go away from

cedrus (cedrī, *f.*): cedar tree

cēna (cēnae, *f.*): dinner, meal

cēnō (cēnāre, *verb*), cēnāvī, cēnātus: dine, eat

cēpī, *see* capiō

cernō (cernere, *verb*), crēvī, crētus: see, discern

certāmen (certāminis, *n.*): contest, competition

certō (certāre, *verb*), certāvī, certātus: contend, dispute

certus, certa, certum (*adj.*): fixed, sure

cervus (cervī, *m.*): deer, stag

cessī, *see* cēdō

cēterum (*adv.*): besides, as for the rest, moreover

cēterus, cētera, cēterum (*adj.*): rest, other

cibus (cibī, *m.*): food

cicāda (cicādae, *f.*): cricket

cicātrix (cicātrīcis, *f.*): scar

cicōnia (cicōniae, *f.*): stork

cieō (ciēre, *verb*), cīvī, citus: set in motion, produce

circumcircā (*adv.*): round about, all around

circumferō (circumferre, *irregular verb*), circumtulī, circumlātus: cast about, move in circles

circumlātrō (circumlātrāre, *verb*), circumlātrāvī, circumlātrātus: bark, bark around

circumspiciō (circumspicere, *verb*), circumspexī, circumspectus: look around

circumstīpātus, circumstīpāta, circumstīpātum (*adj.*): surrounded, crowded

circumstō (circumstāre, *verb*), circumstetī: surround, stand around

circumvagor (circumvagārī, *deponent verb*), circumvagātus sum: wander around, roam

circumvolō (circumvolāre, *verb*), circumvolāvī, circumvolātus: fly around, flit

citus and cīvī, *see* cieō

clāmitō (clāmitāre, *verb*), clāmitāvī, clāmitātus: shout repeatedly, yell loudly

clāmō (clāmāre, *verb*), clāmāvī, clāmātus: shout, exclaim

clāmor (clāmōris, *m.*): shouting, outcry

clāmōsus, clāmōsa, clāmōsum (*adj.*): shouting, noisy

clangor (clanglōris, *m.*): blare, clang

clārus, clāra, clārum (*adj.*): clear, bright

claudō (claudere, *verb*), clausī, clausus: close, shut, conclude, finish

clēmens (clēmentis, *adj.*): merciful, gentle

coepī (coepisse, *perfect verb*), coeptus: begin, start

cōgitō (cōgitāre, *verb*), cōgitāvī, cōgitātus: think, ponder

cognoscō (cognoscere, *verb*), cognōvī, cognitus: learn, find out

cōgō (cōgere, *verb*), coēgī, coactus: compel, drive

cohabitō (cohabitāre, *verb*), cohabitāvī, cohabitātus: live together

collābor (collābī, *deponent verb*), collapsus sum: fall down, slip down

colligō (colligāre, *verb*), colligāvī, colligātus: bind, tie together

collis (collis, *m.*): hill

collum (collī, *n.*): neck

coluber (colubrī, *m.*): snake, serpent

columba (columbae, *f.*): dove, pigeon

comedō (comedere, *verb*), comēdī, comēsus: eat, consume

comes (comitis, *m.*): companion, parter

commercium (commerciī, *n.*): business, dealing

commodum (commodī, *n.*): convenience, advantage

commoveō (commovēre, *verb*), commōvī, commōtus: provoke, disturb

commūnis, commūne (commūnis, *adj.*): general, common

commūtō (commūtāre, *verb*), commūtāvī, commūtātus: change, exchange

comparō (comparāre, *verb*), comparāvī, comparātus: procure, buy, provide

complūrēs, complūria (complūrium, *adj.*): many, a good number

comprehendō (comprehendere, *verb*), comprehendī, comprehēnsus: grasp, seize

comprimō (comprimere, *verb*), compressī, compressus: hold in, suppress

cōnātus (cōnātūs, *m.*): effort, attempt (see also **conor**)

concēdō (concēdere, *verb*), concessī, concessus: give up, grant

concertō (concertāre, *verb*), concertāvī, concertātus: fight over, argue over

concitō (concitāre, *verb*), concitāvī, concitātus: urge, spur

conclūdō (conclūdere, *verb*), conclūsī, conclūsus: close, finish

concussiō (concussiōnis, *f.*): shaking, rough blow

condoleō (condolēre, *verb*), condoluī, condolitus: empathize, feel pain with another

confestim (*adv.*): immediately, at once

conficiō (conficere, *verb*), confēcī, confectus: consume, exhaust

confringō (confringere, *verb*), confrēgī, confractus: break in two, shatter

confugiō (confugere, *verb*), confūgī: flee, take refuge

cōniciō (cōnicere, *verb*), coniēcī, coniectus: hurl, make go, put together, conjecture

coniungō (coniungere, *verb*), coniunxī, coniunctus: join, connect

cōnor (cōnārī, *deponent verb*), cōnātus sum: try, attempt, endeavor

conscendō (conscendere, *verb*), conscendī, conscēnsus: climb up, mount

conscius, conscia, conscium (*adj.*): aware of, accomplice in

consilium (consiliī, *n.*): advice, suggestion

consōlor (consōlārī, *deponent verb*), consōlātus sum: cheer, comfort

conspiciō (conspicere, *verb*), conspexī, conspectus: observe, witness

conspicor (conspicārī, *deponent verb*), conspicātus sum: notice, observe

consternō (consternere, *verb*), constrāvī, constrātus: stretch out, lay low

constituō (constituere, *verb*), constituī, constitūtus: establish, put in position

constō (constāre, *verb*), constitī: consist of, stand upon

consuescō (consuescere, *verb*), consuēvī, consuētus: be in the habit of, get used to

**consulō** (**consulere**, *verb*), **consuluī, consultus**: advise, offer advice

**contemnō** (**contemnere**, *verb*), **contempsī, contemptus**: scorn, disparage

**contemptus** (**contemptūs**, *m.*): scorn, disdain

**contentus, contenta, contentum** (*adj.*): satisfied, content

**conterō** (**conterere**, *verb*), **contrīvī, contrītus**: crush, grind into bits

**contiguus, contigua, contiguum** (*adj.*): near, touching

**contineo** (**continēre**, *verb*), **continuī, contentus**: confine, stay

**contingit** (**contingere**, *impersonal verb*), **contigit, contactum est**: turn out, fall to

**continuō** (*adv.*): immediately, at once

**contrā** (*adv.*, also *prep. + acc.*): opposite, in opposition to

**contrahō** (**contrahere**, *verb*), **contraxī, contractus**: agree upon, contract

**contrīvī**, *see* **conterō**

**contundō** (**contundere**, *verb*), **contudī, contūsus**: beat, bruise

**convalescō** (**convalescere**, *verb*), **convaluī**: get well, grow strong

**conveniō** (**convenīre**, *verb*), **convēnī, conventus**: agree, meet

**convertō** (**convertere**, *verb*), **convertī, conversus**: turn, turn around

**cōpia** (**cōpiae**, *f.*): abundance, plenty

**cor** (**cordis**, *m.*): heart, mind

**coriārius** (**coriāriī**, *m.*): tanner, leatherworker

**corium** (**coriī**, *n.*): skin, leather

**cornix** (**cornīcis**, *f.*): crow, she-crow

**cornu** (**cornūs**, *n.*): horn

**corōna** (**corōnae**, *f.*): ring, crown

**corpus** (**corporis**, *n.*): body

**corripiō** (**corripere**, *verb*), **corripuī, correptus**: seize, carry off

**corrōdō** (**corrōdere**, *verb*), **corrōsī, corrōsus**: gnaw away, chew up

**crās** (*adv.*): tomorrow

**crēdō** (**crēdere**, *verb*), **crēdidī, crēditus**: believe, think

**crēdulus, crēdula, crēdulum** (*adj.*): gullible, trusting

**creō** (**creāre**, *verb*), **creāvī, creātus**: create, make

**crepō** (**crepāre**, *verb*), **crepuī, crepitus**: burst, snap

**crescō** (**crescere**, *verb*), **crēvī, crētus**: grow, increase

**cruciō** (**cruciāre**, *verb*), **cruciāvī, cruciātus**: torment, torture

**crūdēlitās** (**crūdēlitātis**, *f.*): roughness, cruelty

**crūditās** (**crūditātis**, *f.*): rawness, wound

**cucurrī**, *see* **currō**

**cum** (*conj.*, also *prep. + abl.*): when, since, because; with

**cunīculus** (**cunīculī**, *m.*): hole, hidden place

**cupiditās** (**cupiditātis**, *f.*): desire, greed

**cupidus, cupida, cupidum** (*adj.*): desiring, longing for

**cupiō** (**cupere**, *verb*), **cupīvī, cupītus**: want, desire

**cupressus** (**cupressī**, *f.*): cypress tree

**cūr** (*adv.*): why

**cūra** (**cūrae**, *f.*): care, worry

**cūriōsē** (*adv.*): carefully, diligently

**cūrō** (**cūrāre**, *verb*), **cūrāvī, cūrātus**: cure, heal

**currō** (**currere**, *verb*), **cucurrī, cursus**: run, race

**cursitō** (**cursitāre**, *verb*), **cursitāvī, cursitātus**: run about, race

**cursus** (**cursūs**, *m.*): running, race

**custōdia** (**custōdiae**, *f.*): guard, protection

**custōs** (**custōdis**, *m.*): guardian, watcher

# D

**damnō (damnāre,** *verb*), **damnāvī, damnātus**: find guilty, condemn

**daps (dapis,** *f.*): feast, meal

**datus,** *see* **dō**

**dē** (*prep.* + *abl.*): down from, about

**dea (deae,** *f.*): goddess

**deambulō (deambulāre,** *verb*), **deambulāvī, deambulātus**: go for a walk, walk around

**dēbeō (dēbēre,** *verb*), **dēbuī, dēbitus**: owe, ought

**dēcēdō (dēcēdere,** *verb*), **dēcessī, dēcessus**: depart, withdraw

**dēcernō (dēcernere,** *verb*), **dēcrēvī, dēcrētus**: determine, resolve

**dēcipiō (dēcipere,** *verb*), **dēcēpī, dēceptus**: trick, deceive

**dēclīnō (dēclīnāre,** *verb*), **dēclīnāvī, dēclīnātus**: swerve, bend

**dēcoquō (dēcoquere,** *verb*), **dēcoxī, dēcoctus**: melt down, consume

**dēcrēvī,** *see* **dēcernō**

**dēcumbō (dēcumbere,** *verb*), **dēcubuī**: lie, lie down

**decus (decoris,** *n.*): distinction, honor

**dēdecus (dēdecoris,** *n.*): dishonor, disgrace

**dedī,** *see* **dō**

**deesse,** *see* **desum**

**dēfatīgō (dēfatīgāre,** *verb*), **dēfatīgāvī, dēfatīgātus**: tire out, exhaust

**dēfēcī,** *see* **dēficiō**

**dēfetiscor (dēfetiscī,** *deponent verb*), **dēfessus sum**: grow exhausted, get tired

**dēficiō (dēficere,** *verb*), **dēfēcī, dēfectus**: falter, defect

**dēfīgō (dēfīgere,** *verb*), **dēfīxī, dēfīxus**: fix, pin down

**dēfuī,** *see* **dēsum**

**dēfunctus, dēfuncta, dēfunctum** (*adj.*): dead, deceased

**dēiiciō (dēiicere,** *verb*), **dēiēcī, dēiectus**: throw down, drop

**deinceps** (*adv.*): next, thereafter

**deinde** (*adv.*): afterwards, then

**dēleō (dēlēre,** *verb*), **dēlēvī, dēlētus**: erase, wipe out

**dēlicātulus, dēlicātula, dēlicātulum** (*adj.*): charming, dainty

**dēlicium (dēliciī,** *n.*): delight, source of joy

**dēligō (dēligere,** *verb*), **dēlēgī, dēlectus**: pick, select

**dēlitescō (dēlitescere,** *verb*), **dēlituī**: lurk in, seek shelter in

**delphīnus (delphīnī,** *m.*): dolphin

**dēmittō (dēmittere,** *verb*), **dēmīsī, dēmissus**: let go, send away

**dēnique** (*adv.*): finally, in the end

**dens (dentis,** *m.*): tooth, fang

**dēnuō** (*adv.*): once more, a second time

**dēpascor (dēpascī,** *deponent verb*), **dēpastus sum**: graze on, eat up

**dēpendeō (dēpendēre,** *verb*), **dēpendī**: hang, hang down

**dēpōnō (dēpōnere,** *verb*), **dēposuī, dēpositus**: put away, set aside

**dēportō (dēportāre,** *verb*), **dēportāvī, dēportātus**: bring to, carry along

**dēprecor (dēprecārī,** *deponent verb*), **dēprecātus sum**: abominate, disparage

**dēprehendō (dēprehendere,** *verb*), **dēprehendī, dēprehēnsus**: seize, pounce on

**dēprīvō (dēprīvāre,** *verb*), **dēprīvāvī, dēprīvātus**: deprive of

**dēprōmō (dēprōmere,** *verb*), **dēprōmpsī, dēprōmptus**: fetch, bring out

**dērīdeō (dērīdēre,** *verb*), **dērīsī, dērīsus**: laugh at, make fun of

**dēscendō (dēscendere,** *verb*), **dēscendī, dēscēnsus**: go down, come down

**dēsīderium (dēsīderiī,** *n.*): longing, desire

**dēsignō (dēsignāre,** *verb*), **dēsignāvī, dēsignātus**: select, appoint

**dēsipiō (dēsipere,** *verb*), **dēsipuī**: act foolishly

**dēsistō** (**dēsistere**, *verb*), **dēstitī**, **dēstitus**: stop, cease

**dēspectō** (**dēspectāre**, *verb*): look over, look down on

**dēspiciō** (**dēspicere**, *verb*), **dēspexī**, **dēspectus**: look down on, despise

**dēstituō** (**dēstituere**, *verb*), **dēstituī**, **dēstitūtus**: leave without, desert

**dēsum** (**dēesse**, *irregular verb*), **dēfuī**: lack, have not

**dētegō** (**dētegere**, *verb*), **dētexī**, **dētectus**: uncover, lay bare

**dētineō** (**dētinēre**, *verb*), **dētinuī**, **dētentus**: hold back, detain

**dētrahō** (**dētrahere**, *verb*), **dētraxī**, **dētractus**: drag down, take off

**dētruncō** (**dētruncāre**, *verb*), **dētruncāvī**, **dētruncātus**: cut off, lop off

**deus** (**deī**, *m.*): god

**dēvorō** (**dēvorāre**, *verb*), **dēvorāvī**, **dēvorātus**: consume, gulp down

**dextra** (**dextrae**, *f.*): right hand

**dīcō** (**dīcere**, *verb*), **dixī**, **dictus**: say

**dictitō** (**dictitāre**, *verb*), **dictitāvī**, **dictitātus**: say, repeat

**dies** (**diēī**, *m.*): day, daylight

**differō** (**differre**, *irregular verb*), **distulī**, **dīlātus**: put off, delay

**difficilis, difficile** (**difficilis**, *adj.*): difficult, hard

**dīgnōscō** (**dīgnōscere**, *verb*): distinguish, recognize

**dignus, digna, dignum** (*adj.*): worthy, deserving

**dīlātus**, *see* **differō**

**dīligenter** (*adv.*): carefully, diligently

**dīmittō** (**dīmittere**, *verb*), **dīmīsī**, **dīmissus**: let go, send away

**dīripiō** (**dīripere**, *verb*), **dīripuī**, **dīreptus**: seize, tear off

**discēdō** (**discēdere**, *verb*), **discessī**, **discessus**: depart, march off

**disceptātiō** (**disceptātiōnis**, *f.*): debate, dispute

**discō** (**discere**, *verb*), **didicī**: learn

**discordia** (**discordiae**, *f.*): disagreement, dispute

**disiiciō** (**disiicere**, *verb*), **disiēcī**, **disiectus**: toss aside, break up

**dispereō** (**disperīre**, *irregular verb*), **disperīvī** or **disperiī**: perish, be lost

**dispōnō** (**dispōnere**, *verb*), **disposuī**, **dispositus**: put in order, arrange

**dissipō** (**dissipāre**, *verb*), **dissipāvī**, **dissipātus**: scatter, disperse

**dissolūtus, dissolūta, dissolūtum** (*adj.*): careless, loose

**distendō** (**distendere**, *verb*), **distendī**, **distentus**: spread out, extend

**distulī**, *see* **differō**

**diūturnus, diūturna, diūturnum** (*adj.*): long-lasting, enduring

**dīversus, dīversa, dīversum** (*adj.*): different, inconsistent

**dīves** (**dīvitis**, *adj.*): rich, wealthy

**dīvidō** (**dīvidere**, *verb*), **dīvīsī**, **dīvīsus**: divide, share

**dō** (**dare**, *verb*), **dedī**, **datus**: give

**doceō** (**docēre**, *verb*), **docuī**, **doctus**: teach

**dolor** (**dolōris**, *m.*): pain, grief

**dolus** (**dolī**, *m.*): trick, treachery

**dominus** (**dominī**, *m.*): master, owner

**domus** (**domūs**, *f.*): home, house

**dōnec** (*conj.*): until

**dormiō** (**dormīre**, *verb*), **dormīvī**, **dormītus**: sleep

**drāma** (**drāmatis**, *n.*): drama, play

**dubitō** (**dubitāre**, *verb*), **dubitāvī**, **dubitātus**: doubt, be uncertain

**dubium** (**dubiī**, *n.*): doubt

**dūcō** (**dūcere**, *verb*), **dūxī**, **ductus**: lead, bring

**dūdum** (*adv.*): a while ago

**dulcis, dulce** (**dulcis**, *adj.*): sweet

**dum** (*conj.*): while

**dumtaxat** (*adv.*): only, precisely

**duo, duae, duo** (*adj.*): two

duplicō (duplicāre, *verb*), duplicāvī, duplicātus: fold over, bend double

dūrus, dūra, dūrum (*adj.*): hard, harsh

dux (ducis, *m.*): leader, commander

dūxī, *see* dūcō

# E

echīnus (echinī, *m.*): hedgehog

ēdentulus, ēdentula, ēdentulum (*adj.*): toothless

ēditus, ēdita, ēditum (*adj.*): high, rising

ēdō (ēdere, *verb*), ēdidī, ēditus: bring forth, put out

ēdūcō (ēdūcere, *verb*), ēdūxī, ēductus: draw out, take out

efflō (efflāre, *verb*), efflāvī, efflātus: breathe out, exhale

effringō (effringere, *verb*), effrēgī, effractus: break open, smash

effugiō (effugere, *verb*), effūgī: escape, flee

effundō (effundere, *verb*), effūdī, effūsus: pour out

egeō (egēre, *verb*), eguī: need, require

ēgī, *see* agō

ego (*personal pronoun*): I

ēgregiē (*adv.*): exceptionally, admirably well

ēheu (*interjection*): alas, woe

ēiiciō (ēiicere, *verb*), ēiēcī, ēiectus: throw out, expel

ēlābor (ēlābī, *deponent verb*), ēlapsus sum: slip, slide

ēlātrō (ēlātrāre, *verb*), ēlātrāvī, ēlātrātus: bark, bark out

ēligō (ēligere, *verb*), ēlēgī, ēlectus: choose, select

ēlūdō (ēlūdere, *verb*), ēlūsī, ēlūsus: frustrate, cheat

ēmōlior (ēmōlīrī, *deponent verb*), ēmōlītus sum: carry through, bring forth

ēmolumentum (ēmolumentī, *n.*): benefit, profit

ēnecō (ēnecāre, *verb*), ēnecuī, ēnectus: kill, exhaust

enim (*conj.*): for, that is to say

enimvērō (*conj.*): to be sure, what is more

eō (īre, *irregular verb*), īvī or iī, itus: go

epulor (epulārī, *deponent verb*), epulātus sum: feast, dine lavishly

equus (equī, *m.*): horse

ergo (*adv. and conj.*): therefore, then

ērigō (ērigere, *verb*), ērexī, ērectus: raise, erect

ēripiō (ēripere, *verb*), ēripuī, ēreptus: snatch away, take

errō (errāre, *verb*), errāvī, errātus: make a mistake, be wrong

ēsuriō (ēsurīre, *verb*): hunger, be hungry

et (*conj. and adv.*): and; even also

etenim (*conj.*): as a matter of fact, because

etiam (*adv.*): even, also

euge (*interjection*): fine! bravo!

Eurus (Eurī, *m.*): East wind

ēvādō (ēvādere, *verb*), ēvāsī, ēvāsus: escape, get out, turn out to be

ēvellō (ēvellere, *verb*), ēvellī, ēvulsus: pluck, tear out

ēveniō (ēvenīre, *verb*), ēvēnī, ēventus: come forth, turn out

ēvincō (ēvincere, *verb*), ēvīcī, ēvictus: subdue, overcome

ēvītō (ēvītāre, *verb*), ēvītāvī, ēvītātus: avoid, shun

ex (*prep. + abl.*): out, from

exāmen (exāminis, *n.*): swarm

exanimātus, exanimāta, exanimātum (*adj.*): deprived of air, deprived of life

excidō (excidere, *verb*), excidī: perish, disappear

excieō (exciēre, *verb*), excīvī, excitus: rouse, summon

excipiō (excipere, *verb*), excēpī, exceptus: take out, set aside

excitō (excitāre, *verb*), excitāvī, excitātus: stir up, arouse from

**exclāmō** (**exclāmāre**, *verb*), **exclāmāvī**, **exclāmātus**: shout, cry out

**exclūdō** (**exclūdere**, *verb*), **exclūsī**, **exclūsus**: thrust out, hatch

**excōgitō** (**excōgitāre**, *verb*), **excōgitāvī**, **excōgitātus**: devise, invent

**excoriō** (**excoriāre**, *verb*), **excoriāvī**, **excoriātus**: flay, strip

**excors** (**excordis**, *adj.*): brainless, lacking understanding

**excurrō** (**excurrere**, *verb*), **excurrī**, **excursus**: run out, sally forth

**excutiō** (**excutere**, *verb*), **excussī**, **excussus**: shake off, cast out

**exemplum** (**examplī**, *n.*): example, model

**exeō** (**exīre**, *irregular verb*), **exīvī** or **exiī**, **exitus**: go out, come out

**exerceō** (**exercēre**, *verb*), **exercuī**, **exercitus**: conduct, carry out

**exhauriō** (**exhaurīre**, *verb*), **exhausī**, **exhaustus**: drain, empty, drink up

**existimō** (**existimāre**, *verb*), **existimāvī**, **existimātus**: value, estimate

**expectō** (**expectāre**, *verb*), **expectāvī**, **expectātus**: await, anticipate

**expediō** (**expedīre**, *verb*), **expedīvī**, **expedītus**: unfold, explain

**expergefacio** (**expergēfacere**, *verb*), **expergēfēcī**, **expergēfactus**: wake up, arouse

**expergiscor** (**expergiscī**, *deponent verb*), **experrectus sum**: wake up, awake

**experior** (**experīrī**, *deponent verb*), **expertus sum**: test, try

**expleō** (**explēre**, *verb*), **explēvī**, **explētus**: satisfy, fulfill

**explicō** (**explicāre**, *verb*), **explicāvī**, **explicātus**: unfold, untangle

**explōrō** (**explōrāre**, *verb*), **explōrāvī**, **explōrātus**: search out, test

**expostulō** (**expostulāre**, *verb*), **expostulāvī**, **expostulātus**: complain, remonstrate

**exprobrō** (**exprobrāre**, *verb*), **exprobrāvī**, **exprobrātus**: reproach with, criticize

**expugnō** (**expugnāre**, *verb*), **expugnāvī**, **expugnātus**: assault, conquer

**extendō** (**extendere**, *verb*), **extendī**, **extēnsus**: stretch out, spread

**extō** (**extāre**, *verb*): stand out, protrude

**extollō** (**extollere**, *verb*): raise up, praise

**extrā** (*adv.* and *prep.* + *acc.*): outside, beyond

**extrahō** (**extrahere**, *verb*), **extraxī**, **extractus**: pull out, extract

**exultō** (**exultāre**, *verb*), **exultāvī**, **exultātus**: jump about, rejoice

**exuō** (**exuere**, *verb*), **exuī**, **exūtus**: take off, strip

**exuviae** (**exuviārum**, *f.*): skin, something that is shed

# F

**fabricō** (**fabricāre**, *verb*), **fabricāvī**, **fabricātus**: make, fashion

**fābula** (**fābulae**, *f.*): story, tale, talk

**faciēs** (**faciēī**, *f.*): face, appearance

**facile** (*adv.*): easily

**facilis, facile** (**facilis**, *adj.*): easy

**faciō** (**facere**, *verb*), **fēcī, factus**: make, do

**factus**, *see* **faciō** *or* **fiō**

**fācundus, fācunda, fācundum** (*adj.*): eloquent

**faenum** (**faenī**, *n.*): hay

**fallax** (**fallācis**, *adj.*): deceitful, misleading

**fallō** (**fallere**, *verb*), **fefellī, falsus**: deceive, beguile

**falsus, falsa, falsum** (*adj.*): wrong, lying

**falx** (**falcis**, *f.*): sickle, scythe

**famēlicus, famēlica, famēlicum** (*adj.*): starving, hungry

**famēs** (**famis**, *f.*): hunger, famine

**fasciculus** (**fasciculī**, *m.*): little bundle, packet

**fascis** (**fascis**, *m.*): bundle, packet

**fateor** (**fatērī**, *deponent verb*), **fassus sum**: admit, confess

**fatīgō (fatīgāre,** *verb*), **fatīgāvī, fatīgātus:**
exhaust, tire

**fatiscō (fatiscere,** *verb*): give way, wear out

**faux (faucis,** *f.*): gullet, throat

**fax (facis,** *f.*): torch, firebrand

**fēcī,** *see* **faciō**

**fefellī,** *see* **fallō**

**fel (fellis,** *n.*): gall, bile

**fēlix (fēlīcis,** *adj.*): happy, lucky

**fēmina (fēminae,** *f.*): woman

**fera (ferae,** *f.*): wild beast, animal

**fēriae (fēriarum,** *f.*): holidays, vacation

**fermē** (*adv.*): nearly, almost

**ferō (ferre,** *irregular verb*), **tulī, lātus:**
carry, bear

**fētus (fētūs,** *m.*): offspring, young

**fidēlis, fidēle (fidēlis,** *adj.*): loyal, reliable

**fidēs (fideī,** *f.*): faith, trust, security

**fīdō (fīdere,** *semi-deponent verb*), **fīsus**
**sum:** put trust in, believe in

**fīgō (fīgere,** *verb*), **fīxī, fīxus:** fasten, fix

**fīlia (fīliae,** *f.*): daughter

**fīlius (fīliī,** *m.*): son

**fingō (fingere,** *verb*), **finxī, fictus:** contrive, pretend

**fīnis (fīnis,** *m.*): end, limit

**fiō (fierī,** *irregular verb*), **factus sum:**
become, be, happen

**firmus, firma, firmum** (*adj.*): firm, steady

**fīsus,** *see* **fīdō**

**fīxī,** *see* **fīgō**

**flagellō (flagellāre,** *verb*), **flagellāvī,**
**flagellātus:** whip, flog

**flamma (flammae,** *f.*): flame, blaze

**flātus (flātūs,** *m.*): blowing, breeze

**flectō (flectere,** *verb*), **flexī, flexus:** bend,
bow

**fluitō (fluitāre,** *verb*), **fluitāvī, fluitātus:**
flow, float

**flūmen (flūminis,** *n.*): stream, river

**fluvius (fluviī,** *m.*): river, stream

**fluxus, fluxa, fluxum** (*adj.*): fluid, transient

**focus (focī,** *m.*): hearth, fireplace

**fodīna (fodīnae,** *f.*): pit, mine

**fodiō (fodere,** *verb*), **fōdī, fossus:** dig

**foedifragus, foedifraga, foedifragum**
(*adj.*): treaty-breaking

**foedus (foederis,** *n.*): treaty, agreement

**fons (fontis,** *m.*): spring, source of water

**fonticulus (fonticulī,** *m.*): little spring,
fountain

**forās** (*adv.*): out, out of doors

**foris (foris,** *f.*): door, gate

**forīs** (*adv.*): outside, out of doors

**forma (formae,** *f.*): shape, beauty

**formīca (formīcae,** *f.*): ant

**formōsus, formōsa, formōsum** (*adj.*):
shapely, handsome, lovely

**forsan** (*adv.*): perhaps

**forte** (*adv.*): by chance, accidentally

**fortis, forte (fortis,** *adj.*): strong

**fortuītō** (*adv.*): accidentally, by chance

**fortūna (fortūnae,** *f.*): luck, fortune

**fovea (foveae,** *f.*): pit, snare

**fragilis, fragile (fragilis,** *adj.*): frail,
breakable

**fragor (fragōris,** *m.*): noise, crash

**frangō (frangere,** *verb*), **frēgī, fractus:**
break, shatter

**frāterculus (frāterculī,** *m.*): little brother

**fremebundus, fremebunda, fremebun-**
**dum** (*adj.*): roaring, murmuring

**frēnum (frēnī,** *n.*): bridle, harness

**fricō (fricāre,** *verb*), **fricuī, frictus:** rub,
scratch

**frīgescō (frīgescere,** *verb*), **frixī:** grow
cold, cool

**frīgidus, frīgida, frīgidum** (*adj.*): cold, cool

**frīgus (frīgoris,** *n.*): cold, frost

**frondōsus, frondōsa, frondōsum** (*adj.*):
leafy, shady

**fruor (fruī,** *deponent verb*), **fructus sum:**
use, enjoy

**frustrā** (*adv.*): in vain, unsuccessfully

**frustror** (**frustrārī,** *deponent verb*), **frustrātus sum**: disappoint, deceive

**fuga** (**fugae,** *f.*): flight, escape

**fugiō** (**fugere,** *verb*), **fūgī, fugitus**: run away, flee

**fugō** (**fugāre,** *verb*), **fugāvī, fugātus**: chase away, put to flight

**fulgurāns** (**fulgurantis,** *adj.*): glittering, flashing

**fundus** (**fundī,** *m.*): bottom, base

**fūnis** (**fūnis,** *m.*): rope, cord

**fūr** (**fūris,** *m.*): thief, robber

**fūrax** (**fūrācis,** *adj.*): thieving

**fustis** (**fustis,** *m.*): club, stick

**fūtilis, fūtile** (**fūtilis,** *adj.*): worthless, useless

# G

**Galēnus** (**Galēnī,** *m.*): Galen, famed Roman physician

**gallicinium** (**galliciniī,** *n.*): cock-crow

**gallināceus, gallinācea, gallināceum** (*adj.*): poultry, barnyard

**gallus** (**gallī,** *m.*): rooster

**garrulus, garrula, garrulum** (*adj.*): talkative, chattering

**gaudeō** (**gaudēre,** *semi-deponent verb*), **gāvīsus sum**: be glad, rejoice

**gaudium** (**gaudiī,** *n.*): joy, gladness

**gemebundus, gemebunda, gemebundum** (*adj.*): groaning, sighing

**gemma** (**gemmae,** *f.*): jewel, gem

**gemmārius** (**gemmāriī,** *m.*): jeweller

**gemō** (**gemere,** *verb*), **gemuī, gemitus**: moan, groan

**gens** (**gentis,** *f.*): tribe, nation

**genus** (**generis,** *n.*): kind, type

**gerō** (**gerere,** *verb*), **gessī, gestus**: carry on, manage

**glōriābundus, glōriābunda, glōriābundum** (*adj.*): triumphant, proud

**glōrior** (**glōriārī,** *deponent verb*), **glōriātus sum**: boast, brag

**gradior** (**gradī,** *deponent verb*), **gressus sum**: walk, step

**grandescō** (**grandescere,** *verb*): grow, increase

**grandis, grande** (**grandis,** *adj.*): great, large

**grānum** (**grānī,** *n.*): grain, seed

**grātia** (**grātiae,** *f.*): favor, pleasantness, thanks

**grātīs** (*adv.*): freely, at no cost

**grātus, grāta, grātum** (*adj.*): agreeable, acceptable

**gravātus, gravāta, gravātum** (*adj.*): weighed down

**gravis, grave** (**gravis,** *adj.*): weighty, serious

**graviter** (*adv.*): heavily, seriously

**gressus,** *see* **gradior**

**grex** (**gregis,** *m.*): flock, herd

**grūs** (**gruis,** *f.*): crane

**gustō** (**gustāre,** *verb*), **gustāvī, gustātus**: taste, enjoy

**guttur** (**gutturis,** *n.*): throat, gullet

# H

**habeō** (**habēre,** *verb*), **habuī, habitus**: have

**haereō** (**haerēre,** *verb*), **haesī, haesus**: stick, cling

**hālitus** (**hālitūs,** *m.*): breath, exhalation

**hāmātus, hāmāta, hāmātum** (*adj.*): hooked

**hasta** (**hastae,** *f.*): spear, javelin

**haud** (*adv.*): by no means, no way

**haudquāquam** (*adv.*): not

**hauriō** (**haurīre,** *verb*), **hausī, haustus**: drain, drink

**hera** (**herae,** *f.*): mistress, lady of the house

**herba** (**herbae,** *f.*): herb, grass

**Herculēs** (**Herculis,** *m.*): Hercules

**herināceus** (**herināceī,** *m.*): hedgehog

**herus** (**herī,** *m.*): master, owner

**heus** (*interjection*): hey!

**hic, haec, hoc** (**hūius,** *adj. and pronoun*): this

**hīc** (*adv.*): here, in this place

**hiems** (**hiemis**, *f.*): winter, winter time

**hinc** (*adv.*): from here, from this place

**hinnītus** (**hinnītūs**, *m.*): neighing, whinny

**hinnulus** (**hinnulī**, *m.*): deer, fawn

**hiō** (**hiāre**, *verb*), **hiāvī, hiātus**: gape, be open-mouthed

**Hippocrātēs** (**Hippocrātis**, *m.*): Hippocrates, famed Greek physician

**hircus** (**hircī**, *m.*): goat, billy-goat

**hirundō** (**hirundinis**, *f.*): swallow, martin

**hodiē** (*adv.*): today, this day

**homō** (**hominis**, *m.*): person, man

**hordeum** (**hordeī**, *n.*): barley, barley-corn

**horrisonus, horrisona, horrisonum** (*adj.*): dreadful-sounding

**horror** (**horrōris**, *m.*): dread, terror

**hortor** (**hortārī**, *deponent verb*), **hortātus sum**: encourage, urge

**hospes** (**hospitis**, *m.*): host, guest, visitor

**hospitium** (**hospitiī**, *n.*): hospitality, lodging

**hostis** (**hostis**, *m/f.*): enemy, stranger

**hūc** (*adv.*): here, to this place

**humus** (**humī**, *f.*): ground, soil

# I

**iaceō** (**iacēre**, *verb*), **iacuī, iacitus**: lie, lie down

**iactō** (**iactāre**, *verb*), **iactāvī, iactātus**: boast about, brandish

**iactūra** (**iactūrae**, *f.*): loss, damage

**iam** (*adv.*): already, now

**iamiam** (*adv.*): already, now

**ibī** (*adv.*): there

**īcō** (**īcere**, *verb*), **īcī, ictus**: strike, stab

**ictus** (**ictūs**, *m.*): hit, blow

**īdem, eadem, idem** (**ēiusdem**, *adj.* and *pronoun*): the same

**ideō** (*adv.*): for this reason, therefore

**iēiūnus, iēiūna, iēiūnum** (*adj.*): fasting, hungry

**igitur** (*conj.*): therefore

**ignāvus, ignāva, ignāvum** (*adj.*): lazy, useless

**ignis** (**ignis**, *m.*): fire

**iī** or **īvī**, *see* **eō**

**īlicet** (*adv.*): right now, immediately

**ille, illa, illud** (**illīus**, *adj.* and *pronoun*): that

**illīc** (*adv.*): in that place, over there

**illicō** (*also spelled* **īlicō**; *adv.*): immediately, on the spot

**illīdō** (**illīdere**, *verb*), **illīsī, illīsus**: strike, dash against

**illigō** (**illigāre**, *verb*), **illigāvī, illigātus**: tie on, fasten

**illinc** (*adv.*): from there, from that place

**illūc** (*adv.*): to that place, there

**illūdō** (**illūdere**, *verb*), **illūsī, illūsus**: fool, dupe

**imbellis, imbelle** (**imbellis**, *adj.*): unwarlike, defenseless

**immātūrus, immātūra, immātūrum** (*adj.*): unripe, untimely

**immemor** (**immemoris**, *adj.*): unmindful, forgetful

**immisceō** (**immiscēre**, *verb*), **immiscuī, immixtus**: mix in, mingle with

**immolātiō** (**immolātiōnis**, *f.*): sacrifice, offering of victim

**immolō** (**immolāre**, *verb*), **immolāvī, immolātus**: sacrifice, offer as victim

**impactus**, *see* **impingō**

**impastus, impasta, impastum** (*adj.*): unfed, hungry

**impediō** (**impedīre**, *verb*), **impedīvī, impeditus**: hinder, obstruct

**imperium** (**imperiī**, *n.*): rule, supreme power

**impetus** (**impetūs**, *m.*): attack, charge

**impingō** (**impingere**, *verb*), **impēgī, impactus**: thrust, strike against

**implōrō** (**implōrāre**, *verb*), **implōrāvī, implōrātus**: beg for; call for, call upon

**impōnō** (**impōnere**, *verb*), **imposuī, impositus**: put on, set

**importūnus, importūna, importūnum**
(*adj.*): inconvenient, annoying

**imprōvīsus, imprōvīsa, imprōvīsum**
(*adj.*): unexpected, unforeseen

**impūnē** (*adv.*): unpunished, without harm

**in** (*prep.*): in (*abl.*), into (*acc.*)

**inānis, ināne** (**inānis**, *adj.*): empty, foolish

**incendium** (**incendiī**, *n.*): fire, conflagration

**inceptō** (**inceptāre**, *verb*), **inceptāvī,**
**inceptātus**: begin, undertake

**inceptum** (**inceptī**, *n.*): undertaking,
beginning

**incertus, incerta, incertum** (*adj.*): uncertain, unsure

**incidō** (**incidere**, *verb*), **incidī, incāsus**:
fall into, meet with

**incipiō** (**incipere**, *verb*), **incēpī, inceptus**:
begin, start

**inclēmens** (**inclēmentis**, *adj.*): unmerciful,
harsh

**inclīnō** (**inclīnāre**, *verb*), **inclīnāvī,**
**inclīnātus**: bend, lower

**incolumis, incolumc** (**incolumis**, *adj.*):
unharmed, safe

**increpō** (**increpāre**, *verb*), **increpuī, in-**
**crepitus**: rebuke, chide

**incruentus, incruenta, incruentum**
(*adj.*): bloodless, without casualties

**incūsō** (**incūsāre**, *verb*), **incūsāvī,**
**incūsātus**: accuse, blame

**inde** (*adv.*): from there, thereupon, thence

**indēfatīgābilis, indēfatīgābile**
(**indēfatīgābilis**, *adj.*): untiring, tireless

**indicium** (**indiciī**, *n.*): sign, evidence

**indicō** (**indicāre**, *verb*), **indicāvī,**
**indicātus**: point out, show

**indignābundē** (*adv.*): indignantly, angrily

**indignābundus, indignābunda,**
**indignābundum** (*adj.*): indignant,
outraged

**indignor** (**indignārī**, *deponent verb*),
**indignātus sum**: resent, be indignant

**indignus, indigna, indignum** (*adj.*): unworthy, undeserving

**indulgēns** (**indulgentis**, *adj.*): mild,
lenient

**indulgeō** (**indulgēre**, *verb*), **indulsī, indul-**
**tus**: be kind, lenient

**induō** (**induere**, *verb*), **induī, indūtus**: put
on, dress in

**ineō** (**inīre**, *irregular verb*), **inīvī** or **iniī,**
**initus**: go in, enter into

**ineptus, inepta, ineptum** (*adj.*): foolish,
silly

**inermis, inerme** (**inermis**, *adj.*): unarmed,
harmless

**iners** (**inertis**, *adj.*): weak, helpless

**infēlix** (**infēlīcis**, *adj.*): unhappy, unlucky

**inferō** (**inferre**, *irregular verb*), **intulī,**
**inlātus**: bring in, inflict

**inficiō** (**inficere**, *verb*), **infēcī, infectus**:
corrupt, poison

**infortūnium** (**infortūniī**, *n.*): misfortune,
bad luck

**infrā** (*adv.* and *prep.* + *acc.*): below, beneath, downstream

**ingemō** (**ingemere**, *verb*), **ingcmuī, in-**
**gemitus**: groan, moan

**ingens** (**ingentis**, *adj.*): huge, enormous,
mighty

**ingrātus, ingrāta, ingrātum** (*adj.*): ungrateful, unpleasant

**ingredior** (**ingredī**, *deponent verb*), **in-**
**gressus sum**: enter, go into

**ingruō** (**ingruere**, *verb*), **ingruī**: come at
violently, advance threateningly

**inguen** (**inguinis**, *n.*): groin, muscle

**iniectō** (**iniectāre**, *verb*), **iniectāvī,**
**iniectātus**: lay on, put in

**iniī** or **inīvī**, *see* **ineō**

**inimīcus** (**inimīcī**, *m.*): enemy, foe

**iniūria** (**iniūriae**, *f.*): injury, injustice

**inlātus**, *see* **inferō**

**innectō** (**innectere**, *verb*), **innexuī, in-**
**nexus**: weave, devise

**innocēns** (**innocentis**, *adj.*): harmless,
innocent

**inopia** (**inopiae**, *f.*): lack, poverty

**inops** (**inopis**, *adj.*): poor, destitute

**inquam** (*defective verb*): say. **inquit**: he says; **inquiunt**: they say

**insequor** (**insequī**, *deponent verb*), **insecūtus sum**: pursue, chase after

**inserviō** (**inservīre**, *verb*), **inservīvī**, **inservītus**: look after, take care of

**insideō** (**insidēre**, *verb*), **insēdī**, **insessus**: sit on, settle upon

**insidiae** (**insidiārum**, *f.*): ambush, snare

**insidior** (**insidiārī**, *deponent verb*), **insidiātus sum**: lie in wait, ambush

**insignis, insigne** (**insignis**, *adj.*): conspicuous, remarkable

**insolitus, insolita, insolitum** (*adj.*): unusual, unaccustomed

**inspiciō** (**inspicere**, *verb*), **inspexī**, **inspectus**: look at, look into

**insulsus, insulsa, insulsum** (*adj.*): stupid, tedious

**insultus** (**insultūs**, *m.*): jumping, insulting

**intactus, intacta, intactum** (*adj.*): untouched, intact

**integer, integra, integrum** (*adj.*): entire, complete

**intellegō** (**intellegere**, *verb*), **intellexī**, **intellectus**: understand, realize

**intempestus, intempesta, intempestum** (*adj.*): unseasonable, untimely

**intentus, intenta, intentum** (*adj.*): attentive, eager

**inter** (*prep. + acc.*): between, among, during

**interdum** (*adv.*): sometimes

**intereā** (*adv.*): meanwhile

**interficiō** (**interficere**, *verb*), **interfēcī**, **interfectus**: kill, do away with

**interim** (*adv.*): meanwhile

**interimō** (**interimere**, *verb*), **interēmī**, **interemptus**: kill, destroy

**interlābor** (**interlābī**, *deponent verb*), **interlapsus sum**: glide away, slip by

**interrogō** (**interrogāre**, *verb*), **interrogāvī**, **interrogātus**: question, inquire

**intonō** (**intonāre**, *verb*), **intonuī**, **intonātus**: thunder, boom

**intrā** (*prep. + acc.*): within, inside

**intrō** (**intrāre**, *verb*), **intrāvī**, **intrātus**: enter, enter into

**introeō** (**introīre**, *irregular verb*), **introīvī** or **introiī**, **introitus**: go into, enter

**intulī**, *see* **inferō**

**intumescō** (**intumescere**, *verb*), **intumuī**: swell up, puff up

**inūtilis, inūtile** (**inūtilis**, *adj.*): useless

**inveniō** (**invenīre**, *verb*), **invēnī**, **inventus**: find, discover

**invicem** (*adv.*): alternately, mutually

**invictus, invicta, invictum** (*adj.*): undefeated, invincible

**invideō** (**invidēre**, *verb*), **invīdī**, **invīsus**: envy, begrudge

**invidia** (**invidiae**, *f.*): envy, grudge

**invidus, invida, invidum** (*adj.*): envious, hateful

**invīsus, invīsa, invīsum** (*adj.*): hated, despised

**invītō** (**invītāre**, *verb*), **invītāvī**, **invītātus**: invite

**invocō** (**invocāre**, *verb*), **invocāvī**, **invocātus**: call upon, pray for

**involō** (**involāre**, *verb*), **involāvī**, **involātus**: fly into, rush at

**iocus** (**iocī**, *m.*): jest, joke

**ipse, ipsa, ipsum** (**ipsīus**, *adj.* and *pronoun*): the very one, himself

**īrascor** (**īrascī**, *deponent verb*), **īrātus sum**: grow angry, get mad

**irrētiō** (**irrētīre**, *verb*), **irrētīvī**, **irrētītus**: entangle, catch in a net

**irrīdeō** (**irrīdēre**, *verb*), **irrīsī**, **irrīsus**: mock, scoff at

**irrītō** (**irrītāre**, *verb*), **irrītāvī**, **irrītātus**: annoy, irritate

**irrūgiō** (**irrūgīre**, *verb*): roar, cry out

**irruō** (**irruere**, *verb*), **irruī**: rush in, rush into

**is, ea, id** (**eius**, *adj.* and *pronoun*): he/she/it, this one

**iste, ista, istud** (**istīus**, *adj.* and *pronoun*): that, that there of yours ita (*adv.*): thus, therefore

item (*adv.*): likewise

iter (itineris, *n.*): journey, path

iterō (iterāre, *verb*), iterāvī, iterātus: repeat

iterum (*adv.*): again, a second time

iubeō (iubēre, *verb*), iussī, iussus: command, order

iūdex (iūdicis, *m.*): judge

iugum (iugī, *n.*): yoke

iunceus, iuncea, iunceum (*adj.*): made of rushes

Iūpiter (Iovis, *m.*): Jupiter (king of the gods)

iūre (*adv.*): justly, deservedly

iūs (iūris, *n.*): right, law

iussī, *see* iubeō

iustus, iusta, iustum (*adj.*): fair, right

iuvenis (iuvenis, *m.*): young man, youth

ivī, *see* eō

# L

labor (labōris, *m.*): effort, work

labōrō (labōrāre, *verb*), labōrāvī, labōrātus: work, exert effort

lābrum (lābrī, *n.*): lip

lacerō (lacerāre, *verb*), lacerāvī, lacerātus: mangle, tear

lacessō (lacessere, *verb*), lacessīvī, lacessītus: provoke, harass

laedō (laedere, *verb*), laesī, laesus: hurt, injure

laetābundus, laetābunda, laetābundum (*adj.*): rejoicing, cheerful

laniō (laniāre, *verb*), laniāvī, laniātus: mangle, tear to pieces

lapillulus (lapillulī, *m.*): pebble, tiny stone

lapis (lapidis, *m.*): stone

laqueus (laqueī, *m.*): snare, trap

lascīvus, lascīva, lascīvum (*adj.*): playful, unrestrained

latebra (latebrae, *f.*): hiding place, lair

lateō (latēre, *verb*), latuī: be hidden, lurk

lātrō (lātrāre, *verb*), lātrāvī, lātrātus: bark

lātus, *see* ferō

laudō (laudāre, *verb*), laudāvī, laudātus: praise

laus (laudis, *f.*): praise, glory

lautē (*adv.*): lavishly, sumptuously

lautitia (lautitiae, *f.*): luxurious lifestyle, elegance

leaena (leaenae, *f.*): lioness

lectus (lectī, *m.*): bed

lēgātus (lēgātī, *m.*): envoy, deputy

legō (legere, *verb*), lēgī, lectus: gather, collect

leō (leōnis, *m.*): lion

leōnīnus, leōnīna, leōnīnum (*adj.*): lion's, of a lion

lepus (leporis, *m.*): hare, rabbit

levis, leve (levis, *adj.*): slight, slight, trivial

leviter (*adv.*): lightly, slightly

levō (levāre, *verb*), levāvī, levātus: lift up, elevate, alleviate, lighten

lex (lēgis, *f.*): law, principle

libenter (*adv.*): gladly, with pleasure

līber, lībera, līberum (*adj.*): free, independent

līberī (līberōrum, *m.*): children

līberō (līberāre, *verb*), līberāvī, līberātus: set free, release

lībertās (lībertātis, *f.*): freedom

licet (licēre, *impersonal verb*), licuit, licitum est: it is permitted, allowed

licet (*conj.*): even if, although

lignum (lignī, *n.*): wood, timber

lingō (lingere, *verb*), linxī, linctus: lick

lingua (linguae, *f.*): tongue

līnum (līnī, *n.*): flax, flax seed

liquidō (*adv.*): clearly, plainly

liquidus, liquida, liquidum (*adj.*): liquid

lītigō (lītigāre, *verb*), lītigāvī, lītigātus: quarrel, squabble

līvidus, līvida, līvidum (*adj.*): bruise-colored, black-and-blue

locus (locī, *m.*): place

longaevus, longaeva, longaevum (*adj.*): aged, long in years

longē (*adv.*): far, at length, greatly

loquor (**loquī**, *deponent verb*), **locūtus sum**: speak

lūbricus, lūbrica, lūbricum (*adj.*): slippery, tricky

lūceō (**lūcēre**, *verb*), **lūxī**: shine, be apparent

lūcescō (**lūcescere**, *verb*): grow light, begin to shine

lucrum (**lucrī**, *n.*): gain, profit

lūculentē (*adv.*): splendidly, excellently

lugeō (**lugēre**, *verb*), **lūxī, luctus**: lament, grieve over

lupa (**lupae**, *f.*): she-wolf

lupulus (**lupulī**, *m.*): wolf-cub, little wolf

lupus (**lupī**, *m.*): wolf

luscinia (**lusciniae**, *f.*): nightingale

lūsus (**lūsūs**, *m.*): amusement, game

lutum (**lutī**, *n.*): mud, clay

lūx (**lūcis**, *f.*): light

lūxī, *see* lūceō

lympha (**lymphae**, *f.*): water

# M

macilentus, macilenta, macilentum (*adj.*): thin, lean

macula (**maculae**, *f.*): spot, stain

magister (**magistrī**, *m.*): master

magnopere (*adv.*): particularly, especially

magnus, magna, magnum (*adj.*): great, large

māior, māius (**māiōris**, *adj.*): greater

male (*adv.*): badly, poorly

mālō (**mālle**, *irregular verb*), **māluī**: prefer, want more

mālum (**mālī**, *n.*): apple, fruit

mālus (**mālī**, *f.*): apple tree

malus, mala, malum (*adj.*): bad, unlucky

mandō (**mandāre**, *verb*), **mandāvī, mandātus**: entrust, commit

māne (*adv.*): in the morning

maneō (**manēre**, *verb*), **mānsī, mānsus**: remain, stay

mantica (**manticae**, *f.*): cloak, outer garment, knapsack

manus (**manūs**, *f.*): hand

margō (**marginis**, *f.*): edge, rim

Mars (**Martis**, *m.*): god of war, battle

māter (**mātris**, *f.*): mother

mātrimōnium (**mātrimōniī**, *n.*): marriage

mātūrescō (**mātūrescere**, *verb*), **mātūruī**: mature, ripen

maximē (*adv.*): chiefly, especially

medēla (**medēlae**, *f.*): cure, healing

medicīna (**medicīnae**, *f.*): medicine

medicus (**medicī**, *m.*): medical doctor, physician

meditor (**meditārī**, *deponent verb*), **meditātus sum**: ponder, plan

medium (**mediī**, *n.*): middle, center

medius, media, medium (*adj.*): middle, medium

mel (**mellis**, *n.*): honey

melior, melius (**meliōris**, *adj.*): better

mendīcō (**mendīcāre**, *verb*), **mendīcāvī, mendīcātus**: beg, be a beggar

mens (**mentis**, *f.*): mind, brain

mensa (**mensae**, *f.*): table, counter

mentum (**mentī**, *n.*): chin

merīdiēs (**merīdiēī**, *f.*): noon, midday

meritum (**meritī**, *n.*): service, reward

messis (**messis**, *f.*): harvest, crop

metō (**metere**, *verb*), **messuī, messus**: reap, harvest

metuō (**metuere**, *verb*), **metuī**: fear, be afraid

metus (**metūs**, *m.*): fear, dread

meus, mea, meum (*adj.*): my, mine

micō (**micāre**, *verb*), **micuī**: sparkle, gleam

mīlvus (**mīlvī**, *m.*): kite [a bird]

minimē (*adv.*): barely, not at all, least of all

minitor (**minitārī**, *deponent verb*), **minitātus sum**: threaten, menace

**minor** (**minārī**, *deponent verb*), **minātus sum**: threaten, menace

**minus** (*adv.*): less, not so well

**mīrābilis, mīrābile** (**mīrābilis**, *adj.*): amazing, astonishing

**mīror** (**mīrārī**, *deponent verb*), **mīrātus sum**: be amazed, marvel at

**mīrus, mīra, mīrum** (*adj.*): wondrous, strange

**misellus, misella, misellum** (*adj.*): poor, unfortunate

**miser, misera, miserum** (*adj.*): wretched, unfortunate

**miserē** (*adv.*): sadly, wretchedly

**misereor** (**miserērī**, *deponent verb*), **misertus sum**: take pity, have mercy on

**miseria** (**miseriae**, *f.*): wretchedness, suffering

**mittō** (**mittere**, *verb*), **mīsī, missus**: send

**modicus, modica, modicum** (*adj.*): modest, small

**modus** (**modī**, *m.*): means, measure, way

**mōlēs** (**mōlis**, *f.*): mass, bulk

**mōlīmen** (**mōlīminis**, *n.*): effort, vehemence

**mōlior** (**mōlīrī**, *deponent verb*), **mōlītus sum**: construct, build; struggle, strive

**mollis, molle** (**mollis**, *adj.*): soft, tender

**momordī**, *see* **mordeō**

**moneō** (**monēre**, *verb*), **monuī, monitus**: warn, admonish

**mons** (**montis**, *m.*): mountain

**monstrum** (**monstrī**, *n.*): portent, unnatural thing

**mora** (**morae**, *f.*): delay, pause

**morbus** (**morbī**, *m.*): disease, illness

**mordax** (**mordācis**, *adj.*): biting

**mordeō** (**mordēre**, *verb*), **momordī, morsus**: bite

**moribundulus, moribundula, moribundulum** (*adj.*): dying

**morior** (**morī**, *deponent verb*), **mortuus sum**: die

**moror** (**morārī**, *deponent verb*), **morātus sum**: delay, entertain

**mors** (**mortis**, *f.*): death

**morsus**, *see* **mordeō**

**mortuus**, *see* **morior**

**mōs** (**mōris**, *m.*): custom, habit; (*pl.*) character

**moveō** (**movēre**, *verb*), **mōvī, mōtus**: move, stir

**mox** (*adv.*): soon, then

**multifārius, multifāria, multifārium** (*adj.*): numerous, diverse

**multum** (*adv.*): much, greatly, a lot

**multus, multa, multum** (*adj.*): much, many, great

**mūs** (**mūris**, *m/f.*): mouse

**mūtō** (**mūtāre**, *verb*), **mūtāvī, mūtātus**: change, alter

**muttiō** (**muttīre**, *verb*), **muttivī, muttītus**: mutter, murmur

**mūtus, mūta, mūtum** (*adj.*): silent, mute

# N

**nactus**, *see* **nanciscor**

**nam** (*conj.*): for, for instance

**nanciscor** (**nanciscī**, *deponent verb*), **nactus sum**: find, stumble on

**narrō** (**narrāre**, *verb*), **narrāvī, narrātus**: tell, relate

**nascor** (**nascī**, *deponent verb*), **nātus sum**: be born

**nātūra** (**nātūrae**, *f.*): nature, birth

**nātus** (**nātī**, *m.*): son, child (*see also* **nascor**)

**nē ... quidem** (*adv.*): not ... even

**nē** (*conj.*): in order not to, so that not

**nē** (*interjection*): surely, indeed

**nec** or **neque** (*conj.*): nor, neither, and not

**necesse** (*indeclinable adj.*): necessary, inevitable

**necessitās** (**necessitātis**, *f.*): necessity, inevitability

**necō** (**necāre**, *verb*), **necāvī, necātus**: kill, slay

**nēdum** (*conj.*): still less, much less

negligēns (negligentis, *adj.*): careless, indifferent

negligenter (*adv.*): carelessly, indifferently

negōtium (negōtiī, *n.*): business

nēmō (nēminis, *m.*): nobody

nemus (nemoris, *n.*): wood, forest

nēquāquam (*adv.*): no way, by no means

neque, *see* nec

nequeō (nequīre, *verb*), nequivī, nequītus: be unable, cannot

neuter, neutra, neutrum (neutrīus, *adj.*): neither, not either

nex (necis, *f.*): death, murder

nī (*conj.*): if not, unless

nīdulāns (nīdulantis, *adj.*): nesting

nīdus (nīdī, *m.*): nest

nihil (*indeclinable noun*): nothing

nimbus (nimbī, *m.*): cloud, rainstorm

nimis (*adv.*): too much, very much

nimium (*adv.*): too much, excessively

nisi (*conj.*): unless, except

nix (nivis, *f.*): snow

nōbilis, nōbile (nōbilis, *adj.*): respected, respectable

nōbilitās (nōbilitātis, *f.*): respectability, excellence

nocēns (nocentis, *m.*): criminal, guilty person

nōdus (nōdī, *m.*): knot, node

nola (nolae, *f.*): bell

nōlō (nōlle, *irregular verb*), nōluī: refuse, not want

nōmen (nōminis, *m.*): name

nōn (*adv.*): not

noscō (noscere, *verb*), nōvī, nōtus: get to know, be familiar with

noster, nostra, nostrum (*adj.*): our, ours

nota (notae, *f.*): mark, sign

notō (notāre, *verb*), notāvī, notātus: observe, notice

Notus (Notī, *m.*): South wind

nōtus, *see* nosco

novellus, novella, novellum (*adj.*): fresh, new

nōvī, *see* noscō

novus, nova, novum (*adj.*): new

nox (noctis, *f.*): night

nūbis (nūbis, *m.*): cloud

nullus, nulla, nullum (nullīus, *adj.*): none, not any

num (*adv.*): introduces question expecting negative answer

numerō (numerāre, *verb*), numerāvī, numerātus: number, count

numerus (numerī, *m.*): number

nunc (*adv.*): now

nunquam (*adv.*): never, not ever

nūper (*adv.*): recently, just now

nupta (nuptae, *f.*): bride

nutriō (nutrīre, *verb*), nutrīvī, nutrītus: nourish, tend

nūtrix (nūtrīcis, *f.*): nurse, nanny

# O

ō (*interjection*): o, oh

ob (*prep. + acc.*): on account of

obambulō (obambulāre, *verb*), obambulāvī, obambulātus: traverse, walk about

obiiciō (obiicere, *verb*), obiēcī, obiectus: cast off, throw

oblātus, *see* offerō

oblīviscor (oblīviscī, *deponent verb*), oblitus sum: forget

obrēpō (obrēpere, *verb*), obrēpsī, obrēptus: creep over, sneak up

obruō (obruere, *verb*), obruī, obrutus: cover up, bury

obsecrō (obsecrāre, *verb*), obsecrāvī, obsecrātus: implore, beseech

obsequium (obsequiī, *n.*): servility, service

observō (observāre, *verb*), observāvī, observātus: watch, heed

obses (obsidis, *m.*): hostage, guarantee

obsistō (obsistere, *verb*), obstitī, obstitus: oppose, withstand

obsōnium (obsōniī, *n.*): food

obstō (obstāre, *verb*), obstitī, obstātus: oppose, hinder

obtemperō (obtemperāre, *verb*), obtemperāvī, obtemperātus: obey, comply

obtruncō (obtruncāre, *verb*), obtruncāvī, obtruncātus: kill, cut down

obtulī, *see* offerō

obviam (*adv.*): in the way of, running into

occīdō (occīdere, *verb*), occīdī, occīsus: kill, slaughter

occultus, occulta, occultum (*adj.*): hidden, secret

occurrō (occurrere, *verb*), occurrī, occursus: run into, meet

ocellus (ocellī, *m.*): eye, little eye

oculus (oculī, *m.*): eye

ōdē (*acc.* ōdēn, *f.*): ode, song [Greek]

odium (odiī, *n.*): hatred

odōrus, odōra, odōrum (*adj.*): keen-scented

offendō (offendere, *verb*), offendī, offēnsus: bump into, stumble upon

offerō (offere, *irregular verb*), obtulī, oblātus: offer, present

officium (officiī, *n.*): duty, obligation

ōlim (*adv.*): formerly, once upon a time

omnimodō (*adv.*): in every way, entirely

omnīnō (*adv.*): altogether, completely

omnis, omne (omnis, *adj.*): all, every

onus (oneris, *n.*): burden, load

onustus, onusta, onustum (*adj.*): laden, burdened

opera (operae, *f.*): work, effort

oportet (oportēre, *impersonal verb*), oportuit: it is right; ought

oppōnō (oppōnere, *verb*), opposuī, oppositus: oppose, counter

opportūnus, opportūna, opportūnum (*adj.*): useful, ready

opprobrium (opprobriī, *n.*): reproach, shame

ops (opis, *f.*): help, means

optimus, optima, optimum (*adj.*): best

optō (optāre, *verb*), optāvī, optātus: choose, wish for

opus (operis, *n.*): need, work

ordō (ordinis, *m.*): order, row

ornāmentum (ornāmentī, *n.*): decoration, trappings

ornātus (ornātūs, *m.*): decoration, apparel

ornātus, ornāta, ornātum (*adj.*): decorated, adorned

ōrō (ōrāre, *verb*), ōrāvī, ōrātus: ask, pray

ōs (ōris, *n.*): mouth, snout

os (ossis, *n.*): bone

oscitanter (*adv.*): lazily, listlessly

ostentō (ostentāre, *verb*), ostentāvī, ostentātus: show, display

ovis (ovis, *f.*): sheep

ōvum (ōvī, *n.*): egg

# P

pactum (pactī, *n.*): manner, agreement

pactus, *see* pangō

paene (*adv.*): almost, mostly

paeniteō (paenitēre, *verb*), paenituī: displease, regret, feel regret

pallidus, pallida, pallidum (*adj.*): pale, yellow-green

palma (palmae, *f.*): palm, palm of victory

palumbēs (palumbis, *m.*): ringdove, wood-pigeon

palūs (palūdis, *f.*): swamp, marsh

pangō (pangere, *verb*), pepigī, pactus: agree, settle upon

pānis (pānis, *m.*): bread, loaf

pār (paris, *adj.*): equal, like

parcō (parcere, *verb*), pepercī: be sparing, show consideration

pardus (pardī, *m.*): panther, leopard

parens (parentis, *m/f.*): parent

**pāreō** (**pārēre**, *verb*), **pāruī, pāritus**: obey, comply

**pariēs** (**parietis,** *m.*): wall

**pariō** (**parīre**, *verb*), **peperī, partus**: bear, produce

**parō** (**parāre**, *verb*), **parāvī, parātus**: prepare, supply, get

**pars** (**partis,** *f.*): part, portion

**parturiō** (**parturīre**, *verb*), **parturīvī**: give birth, be in labor

**partus** (**partūs,** *m.*): birth, labor (*see also* **pariō**)

**parvus, parva, parvum** (*adj.*): small, little

**pascō** (**pascere**, *verb*), **pāvī, pastus**: graze, feed

**pascuum** (**pascuī,** *n.*): pasture

**passus,** *see* **patior**

**pastor** (**pastōris,** *m.*): shepherd

**pastus** (**pastūs,** *m.*): pasture, feeding ground

**pater** (**patris,** *m.*): father

**paterfamiliās** (**patrisfamiliās,** *m.*): head of the family

**patienter** (*adv.*): patiently, tolerantly

**patior** (**patī,** *deponent verb*), **passus sum**: suffer, undergo

**patrimōnium** (**patrimōniī,** *n.*): inheritance

**paucī, paucae, pauca** (*adj.*): few, small in number

**paulātim** (*adv.*): little by little

**paulisper** (*adv.*): for a short time

**paululum** (*adv.*): a small amount, a short while

**pāvō** (**pāvōnis,** *m.*): peacock

**pavor** (**pavōris,** *m.*): terror, panic

**pāx** (**pācis,** *f.*): peace, harmony

**pectus** (**pectoris,** *n.*): chest, heart

**pecūnia** (**pecūniae,** *f.*): money

**pēior, pēius** (**pēiōris,** *adj.*): worse

**pellicula** (**pelliculae,** *f.*): skin, hide

**pellis** (**pellis,** *f.*): skin, hide

**pendeō** (**pendēre**, *verb*), **pependī**: depend

**penetrō** (**penetrāre**, *verb*), **penetrāvī, penetrātus**: enter, penetrate

**penitus** (*adv.*): thoroughly, completely

**penna** (**pennae,** *f.*): feather, wing

**pensitō** (**pensitāre**, *verb*), **pensitāvī, pensitātus**: ponder, reckon

**penum** (**penī,** *n.*): provisions, food

**pepercī,** *see* **parcō**

**peperī,** *see* **pariō**

**pepigī,** *see* **pangō**

**per** (*prep. + acc.*): through, by, by way of

**perambulō** (**perambulāre**, *verb*), **perambulāvī, perambulātus**: walk about, travel through

**perbibō** (**perbibere**, *verb*), **perbibī**: drink deeply, imbibe

**perbonus, perbona, perbonum** (*adj.*): very good

**percellō** (**percellere**, *verb*), **perculī, perculsus**: strike down, dismay

**percipiō** (**percipere**, *verb*), **percēpī, perceptus**: perceive, notice

**percontor** (**percontārī,** *deponent verb*), **percontātus sum**: inquire, ask

**perculsus,** *see* **percellō**

**percurrō** (**percurrere**, *verb*), **percurrī, percursus**: run through

**perditē** (*adv.*): helplessly, hopelessly

**perdix** (**perdīcis,** *f.*): partridge

**perdō** (**perdere**, *verb*), **perdidī, perditus**: lose, destroy

**pereō** (**perīre**, *irregular verb*), **perīvī** or **periī, peritus**: be lost, perish

**perfidus, perfida, perfidum** (*adj.*): untrustworthy, treacherous

**pergrandis, pergrande** (**pergrandis,** *adj.*): very great, very large

**perīculum** (**perīculī,** *n.*): danger, hazard, trial

**perlustrō** (**perlustrāre**, *verb*), **perlustrāvī, perlustrātus**: scan, scrutinize

**permagnus, permagna, permagnum** (*adj.*): very great, important

**perscrūtor** (**perscrūtārī,** *deponent verb*), **perscrūtātus sum**: search through, investigate

**persequor** (**persequī**, *deponent verb*), **persecūtus sum**: chase, reach, overtake

**persōna** (**persōnae**, *f.*): mask; character, personality

**perspiciō** (**perspicere**, *verb*), **perspexī**, **perspectus**: examine, observe

**perstō** (**perstāre**, *verb*), **perstitī**, **perstātus**: persevere, persist in

**perstringō** (**perstringere**, *verb*), **perstrinxī**, **perstrictus**: tie up, make tight

**pertaesus, pertaesa, pertaesum** (*adj.*): tired, disgusted

**pertineō** (**pertinēre**, *verb*), **pertinuī**: reach, relate to

**perveniō** (**pervenīre**, *verb*), **pervēnī**, **perventus**: reach, arrive at

**pēs** (**pedis**, *m.*): foot

**petō** (**petere**, *verb*), **petīvī**, **petītus**: ask, request

**phalerae** (**phalerārum**, *f.*): ornaments, decorations

**piget** (**pigēre**, *impersonal verb*), **piguit**, **pigitum est**: disgusts, irks

**pilus** (**pilī**, *m.*): hair, fur

**pinguis, pingue** (**pinguis**, *adj.*): fat, sleek

**pīnus** (**pīnī**, *f.*): pine tree

**pirum** (**pirī**, *n.*): pear (fruit)

**pirus** (**pirī**, *f.*): pear tree

**piscātor** (**piscātōris**, *m.*): fisherman

**pisciculus** (**pisciculī**, *m.*): little fish

**piscis** (**piscis**, *m.*): fish

**pistor** (**pistōris**, *m.*): baker

**pius, pia, pium** (*adj.*): dutiful, conscientious

**placeō** (**placēre**, *verb*), **placuī**, **placitus**: please, satisfy

**plaga** (**plagae**, *f.*): hunting net, trap

**plēnus, plēna, plēnum** (*adj.*): full

**plērumque** (*adv.*): often, for the most part

**plōrō** (**plōrāre**, *verb*), **plōrāvī**, **plōrātus**: cry, wail

**plūrimus, plūrima, plūrimum** (*adj.*): most, very many

**plūs** (*adv.*): more

**poena** (**poenae**, *f.*): penalty, punishment

**pol** (*interjection*): by Pollux, really!

**polenta** (**polentae**, *f.*): grain, polenta

**polliceor** (**pollicērī**, *deponent verb*), **pollicitus sum**: promise

**pōnō** (**pōnere**, *verb*), **posuī**, **positus**: place, put

**popīna** (**popīnae**, *f.*): cookshop, bistro

**populāris** (**populāris**, *m/f.*): fellow, compatriot

**populor** (**populārī**, *deponent verb*), **populātus sum**: lay waste, strip

**populus** (**populī**, *m.*): people, nation

**porrigō** (**porrigere**, *verb*), **porrexī**, **porrectus**: extend, offer

**porrō** (*adv.*): further, furthermore

**portiuncula** (**portiunculae**, *f.*): small part, tiny portion

**portō** (**portāre**, *verb*), **portāvī**, **portātus**: carry, bring

**possideō** (**possidēre**, *verb*), **possēdī**, **possessus**: seize, hold

**possum** (**posse**, *irregular verb*), **potuī**: be able, can

**post** (*prep. + acc.*): after, behind

**posteā** (*adv.*): afterwards

**posterus, postera, posterum** (*adj.*): after, future

**posthabeō** (**posthabēre**, *verb*), **posthabuī**, **posthabitus**: disregard, think unimportant

**postquam** (*conj.*): after, since

**postremō** (*adv.*): at last, finally

**postrēmus, postrēma, postrēmum** (*adj.*): last, endmost

**postulō** (**postulāre**, *verb*), **postulāvī**, **postulātus**: demand, require

**posuī**, *see* **pōnō**

**potens** (**potentis**, *adj.*): powerful, capable

**potentia** (**potentiae**, *f.*): power

**potuī**, *see* **possum**

**pōtus** (**pōtūs**, *m.*): drink, beverage

**prae** (*prep. + abl.*): in front of, before; in view of, because of

**praebeō** (**praebēre**, *verb*), **praebuī**, **praebitus**: present, offer

**praecellō** (**praecellere**, *verb*), **praecelluī**, **praecelsus**: surpass, excel

**praeceps** (**praecipitis**, *adj.*): headlong, precipitous

**praecipitō** (**praecipitāre**, *verb*), **praecipitāvī**, **praecipitātus**: throw headlong, cast down

**praeclārus, praeclāra, praeclārum** (*adj.*): splendid, famous

**praeda** (**praedae**, *f.*): prey, plunder

**praedulcis, praedulce** (**praedulcis**, *adj.*): very sweet

**praegravātus, praegravāta, praegravātum** (*adj.*): weighed down, burdened

**praegravis, praegrave** (**praegravis**, *adj.*): very weighty, very serious

**praepōnō** (**praepōnere**, *verb*), **praeposuī**, **praepositus**: put in front, prefer

**praesens** (**praesentis**, *adj.*): at hand, in person

**praesentia** (**praesentiae**, *f.*): presence

**praesentiō** (**praesentīre**, *verb*), **praesēnsī**, **praesēnsus**: feel in advance, anticipate

**praesēpe** (**praesēpis**, *n.*): manger, stall

**praeservō** (**praeservāre**, *verb*), **praeservāvī**, **praeservātus**: keep safe, preesrve

**praesidium** (**praesidiī**, *n.*): protection, defense

**praestāns** (**praestantis**, *adj.*): excellent, outstanding

**praestantia** (**praestantiae**, *f.*): excellence, superiority

**praestō** (**praestāre**, *verb*), **praestitī, praestitus**: show, present

**praetendō** (**praetendere**, *verb*), **praetendī, praetentus**: stretch out, spread

**praetereō** (**praeterīre**, *irregular verb*), **praeterīvī** or **praeteriī, praeteritus**: go by, pass by

**praeterquam** (*prep. + acc.*): except, besides

**prātum** (**prātī**, *n.*): meadow, meadow grass

**precor** (**precārī**, *deponent verb*), **precātus sum**: entreat, pray

**prehendō** (**prehendere**, *verb*), **prehendī, prehēnsus**: grab, take in hand

**premō** (**premere**, *verb*), **pressī, pressus**: press, press upon

**pretiōsus, pretiōsa, pretiōsum** (*adj.*): valuable, precious

**pretium** (**pretiī**, *n.*): prize, price, reward

**prex** (**precis**, *f.*): prayer, request

**prīmum** (*adv.*): first, at first

**prīmus, prīma, prīmum** (*adj.*): first

**principium** (**principiī**, *n.*): beginning

**prior, prius** (**priōris**, *adj.*): preceding, previous

**prius** (*adv.*): before, beforehand, earlier

**prīvātus, prīvāta, prīvātum** (*adj.*): personal, private

**prīvō** (**prīvāre**, *verb*), **prīvāvī, prīvātus**: deprive of

**prō** (*prep. + abl.*): in exchange for

**probē** (*adv.*): rightly, thoroughly

**procul** (*adv.*): far off, far from, at a distance

**prōculcō** (**prōculcāre**, *verb*), **prōculcāvī, prōculcātus**: trample on

**prōcumbō** (**prōcumbere**, *verb*), **prōcubuī, prōcubitus**: sink down, lie down

**prōdō** (**prōdere**, *verb*), **prōdidī, prōditus**: reveal, betray

**profectō** (*adv.*): certainly, as a matter of fact

**profiteor** (**profitērī**, *deponent verb*), **professus sum**: claim, declare

**profundus, profunda, profundum** (*adj.*): deep

**prōgredior** (**prōgredī**, *deponent verb*), **prōgressus sum**: go forward, proceed

**prōlēs** (**prōlis**, *f.*): offspring, young

**prōmissum** (**prōmissī**, *n.*): promise

**prōmittō** (**prōmittere**, *verb*), **prōmīsī, prōmissus**: promise

**prōmptē** (*adv.*): willingly, readily

**prōmptus, prōmpta, prōmptum** (*adj.*): willing, ready

**prope** (*adv.*): near, nearly

**propitius, propitia, propitium** (*adj.*): favorable, well-disposed

**prōpōnō** (**prōpōnere**, *verb*), **prōposuī, prōpositus**: put forward, propose

**proprius, propria, proprium** (*adj.*): one's own

**propter** (*prep. + acc.*): because of, on account of

**prōsiliō** (**prōsilīre**, *verb*), **prōsiluī**: leap forward

**prōsternō** (**prōsternere**, *verb*), **prōstrāvī, prōstrātus**: stretch out, lay low

**prōvideō** (**prōvidēre**, *verb*), **prōvīdī, prōvīsus**: foresee, provide for

**prōvolō** (**prōvolāre**, *verb*), **prōvolāvī, prōvolatus**: fly forth, dash forward

**prōvolvō** (**prōvolvere**, *verb*), **prōvolvī, prōvolūtus**: roll along, roll over

**pūblicē** (*adv.*): publicly

**pudet** (**pudēre**, *impersonal verb*), **puduit, puditum est**: shames, makes ashamed

**pudor** (**pudōris**, *m.*): shame, embarrassment

**puella** (**puellae**, *f.*): girl

**puer** (**puerī**, *m.*): boy

**puerpera** (**puerperae**, *f.*): female in labor

**pugna** (**pugnae**, *f.*): fight, battle

**pugnax** (**pugnācis**, *adj.*): fighting, aggressive

**pugnō** (**pugnāre**, *verb*), **pugnāvī, pugnātus**: fight, do battle

**pulchritūdō** (**pulchritūdinis**, *f.*): beauty

**pullus** (**pullī**, *m.*): chick, young bird

**pulpāmentum** (**pulpāmentī**, *n.*): flesh, meat

**pungō** (**pungere**, *verb*), **pupugī, punctus**: prick, puncture

**puteus** (**puteī**, *m.*): well, hole

**putō** (**putāre**, *verb*), **putāvī, putātus**: think, reckon

# Q

**quadrupēs** (**quadrupedis**, *m./f.*): animal, four-footed beast

**quaerō** (**quaerere**, *verb*), **quaesīvī, quaesītus**: search out, seek

**quam** (*adv. and conj.*): how, how much, as; than

**quamobrem** (*adv.*): for what reason

**quamquam** (*conj.*): although

**quamvis** (*adv. and conj.*): although, even if

**quandoquidem** (*conj.*): since, seeing that

**quantus, quanta, quantum** (*adj.*): how great, how much, however much

**quārē** (*adv.*): for which reason, therefore

**quartus, quarta, quartum** (*adj.*): fourth

**quasi** (*conj.*): as if

**quassō** (**quassāre**, *verb*), **quassāvī, quassātus**: shake, batter

**quater** (*adv.*): four times

**quattuor** (*number*): four

**~que** (*enclitic conj.*): and

**quercus** (**quercūs**, *f.*): oak, oak tree

**querimōnia** (**querimōniae**, *f.*): complaint, grievance

**queror** (**querī**, *deponent verb*), **questus sum**: complain, grumble

**quī, quae, quod** (**cūius**, *adj. and pron.*): which, that

**quia** (*conj.*): because

**quīcumque, quaecumque, quodcumque** (**cūiuscumque**, *adj.*): whatever, whatsoever

**quid** (*adv.*): why, for what reason

**quīdam, quaedam, quiddam** (**cūiusdam**): a, a certain (*pronoun*; also **quīdam, quaedam, quoddam**, *adj.*)

**quidem** (*adv.*): indeed

**quidquid** (*pronoun*): whatever, everything

**quiescō** (**quiescere**, *verb*), **quiēvī, quiētus**: rest, be inactive

**quīlibet, quaelibet, quodlibet** (**cūiuslibet**, *adj.*): whatever, every

**quīn** (*adv.*): why not, why don't

**quinquiēs** (*adv.*): five times

**quippe** (*adv.*): obviously, as you see, inasmuch

**quis, quid** (**cūius**, *pronoun*): who, what

**quispiam, quidpiam** (**cūiuspiam**, *pronoun*): something, anything

**quisque, quidque** (**cūiusque**, *pronoun*): everybody, each person

**quō** (*adv.*): to where, whither

**quod** (*conj.*): because, that, as for the fact that

**quōmodo** (*adv.*): how

**quondam** (*adv.*): formerly, at one time

**quotīdiānus, quotīdiāna, quotīdiānum** (*adj.*): daily, each day's

**quotīdiē** (*adv.*): daily, each day

# R

**racēmus** (**racēmī**, *m.*): bunch, cluster

**radius** (**radiī**, *m.*): ray

**rāmus** (**rāmī**, *m.*): branch, bough

**rāmusculus** (**rāmusculī**, *m.*): twig, tiny branch

**rāna** (**rānae**, *f.*): frog

**rapīna** (**rapīnae**, *f.*): robbery, plunder

**rapiō** (**rapere**, *verb*), **rapuī, raptus**: grab, snatch

**ratus**, *see* **reor**

**recēdō** (**recēdere**, *verb*), **recessī, recessus**: go away, depart

**recenseō** (**recensēre**, *verb*), **recensuī, recensus**: review, reckon

**recipiō** (**recipere**, *verb*), **recēpī, receptus**: regain, recover

**recūsō** (**recūsāre**, *verb*), **recūsāvī, recūsātus**: refuse, decline

**reddō** (**reddere**, *verb*), **reddidī, redditus**: return, give back

**redeō** (**redīre**, *irregular verb*), **redīvī** or **rediī, reditus**: return, go back

**reditus** (**reditūs**, *m.*): return, going back

**redux** (**reducis**, *adj.*): brought back, restored

**referō** (**referre**, *irregular verb*), **retulī** (**rettulī**), **relātus**: return, carry back

**refocillō** (**refocillāre**, *verb*), **refocillāvī, refocillātus**: revive, warm to life

**regnō** (**regnāre**, *verb*), **regnāvī, regnātus**: rule, be king

**regredior** (**regredī**, *deponent verb*), **regressus sum**: go back, return

**relātus**, *see* **referō**

**relinquō** (**relinquere**, *verb*), **relīquī, relictus**: leave, abandon

**reliquia** (**reliquiae**, *f.*): remains, vestiges

**reliquus, reliqua, reliquum** (*adj.*): rest, remaining

**remaneō** (**remanēre**, *verb*), **remānsī, remānsus**: stay behind, remain

**removeō** (**removēre**, *verb*), **remōvī, remōtus**: put away, put aside

**renuō** (**renuere**, *verb*), **renuī**: refuse, shake head no

**reor** (**rērī**, *deponent verb*), **ratus sum**: think, suppose

**reperiō** (**reperīre**, *verb*), **repperī, repertus**: find, discover

**replicō** (**replicāre**, *verb*), **replicuī, replicātus**: reply, unfold

**rēpō** (**rēpere**, *verb*), **rēpsī, rēptus**: creep, crawl

**repōnō** (**repōnere**, *verb*), **reposuī, repositus**: store, put up

**reptilis, reptile** (**reptilis**, *adj.*): creeping, crawling

**repugnō** (**repugnāre**, *verb*), **repugnāvī, repugnātus**: fight back

**reputō** (**reputāre**, *verb*), **reputāvī, reputātus**: reflect, think over

**rēs** (**reī**, *f.*): thing, business

**resciscō** (**rescicere**, *verb*), **rescīvī, rescītus**: learn, find out

**resīdō** (**resīdere**, *verb*), **resēdī**: sit down, settle

**resistō** (**resistere**, *verb*), **restitī**: oppose, make a stand

**resonō** (**resonāre**, *verb*), **resonāvī**: resound, echo respiciō (**respicere**, *verb*), **respexī**, **respectus**: regard, look at

respondeō (**respondēre**, *verb*), **respondī**, **respōnsus**: reply

rēte (**rētis**, *n.*): net, snare

retineō (**retinēre**, *verb*), **retinuī**, **retentus**: hold back, restrain, trap

retulī or rettulī, *see* **refero**

revertor (**revertī**, *deponent verb*), **reversus sum**: return, go back

rex (**rēgis**, *m.*): king

rictus (**rictūs**, *m.*): jaws, open mouth

rīdiculus, rīdicula, rīdiculum (*adj.*): silly, laughable

rīpa (**rīpae**, *f.*): bank, shore

rōdō (**rōdere**, *verb*), **rōsī**, **rōsus**: gnaw, chew

rogō (**rogāre**, *verb*), **rogāvī**, **rogātus**: ask

rosa (**rosae**, *f.*): rose

rostrum (**rostrī**, *n.*): beak

rota (**rotae**, *f.*): wheel

rubellus, rubella, rubellum (*adj.*): red, reddish

ruber, rubra, rubrum (*adj.*): red

rudō (**rudere**, *verb*): bellow, bray

rūgiō (**rūgīre**, *verb*): roar, bellow

rūgītus (**rūgītūs**, *m.*): roar, bellow

ruīna (**ruīnae**, *f.*): destruction, catastrophe

rūmor (**rūmōris**, *m.*): rumor, gossip

ruō (**ruere**, *verb*), **ruī**: rush, rush into

rūpēs (**rūpis**, *f.*): cliff, rock

rursum or rursus (*adv.*): on the contrary, again, in turn

rūs (**rūris**, *n.*): countryside, farm

rūsticus (**rūsticī**, *m.*): peasant, countryman

# S

sacer, sacra, sacrum (*adj.*): sacred, holy

sacrilegē (*adv.*): impiously, outrageously

saepe (*adv.*): often

saeta (**saetae**, *f.*): hair, bristle

saeviō (**saevīre**, *verb*), **saeviī**, **saevītus**: rage, rave

saginātus, sagināta, saginātum (*adj.*): fattened, well-fed

saltem (*adv.*): at least, except

saltus (**saltūs**, *m.*): leap, jump

salūs (**salūtis**, *f.*): health, safety

salūtō (**salūtāre**, *verb*), **salūtāvī**, **salūtātus**: greet, hail

sānē (*adv.*): truly, surely

sapiens (**sapientis**, *adj.*): wise

sarcina (**sarcinae**, *f.*): pack, bundle

satis (*adv.*): enough, satisfactory

satur, satura, saturum (*adj.*): well-fed, stuffed

satus, *see* **serō**

satyrus (**satyrī**, *m.*): satyr

saucius, saucia, saucium (*adj.*): wounded, injured

scandō (**scandere**, *verb*): climb, mount

scientia (**scientiae**, *f.*): knowledge, skill

scīlicet (*adv.*): of course, you know

sciō (**scīre**, *verb*), **scīvī**, **scītus**: know

sciscitor (**sciscitārī**, *deponent verb*), **sciscitātus sum**: ask, inquire

sē (*personal pronoun, also* **sēsē**): himself, herself, itself

sēcēdō (**sēcēdere**, *verb*), **sēcessī**, **sēcessus**: withdraw, secede

secundum (*adv.*): afterwards, a second time

secundus, secunda, secundum (*adj.*): second

sēcūrē (*adv.*): safely, unconcernedly

secūris (**secūris**, *f.*): axe, hatchet

sēcūrus, sēcūra, sēcūrum (*adj.*): safe, untroubled

secūtus, *see* **sequor**

sed (*conj.*): but

sedeō (**sedēre**, *verb*), **sēdī**, **sessus**: sit, stay

sēdō (**sēdāre**, *verb*), **sēdāvī**, **sēdātus**: allay, calm

sēdulō (*adv.*): carefully, attentively

seges (segetis, *f.*): field of grain, crop

segniter (*adv.*): slowly, lazily

segnitiēs (segnitiēī, *f.*): sluggishness, inertia

sēgregō (sēgregāre, *verb*), sēgregāvī, sēgregātus: remove, separate

sella (sellae, *f.*): seat, saddle

semel (*adv.*): once, on one occasion

sēmentis (sēmentis, *f.*): sowing, seeding

sēminūdus, sēminūda, sēminūdum (*adj.*): half-naked

semper (*adv.*): always

senecta (senectae, *f.*): old age

senectūs (senectūtis, *f.*): old age

senex (senis, *adj.*): aged, old

senior, senius (seniōris, *adj.*): older, elder

senium (seniī, *n.*): old age

sensus (sensūs, *m.*): awareness, sense

sentiō (sentīre, *verb*), sēnsī, sēnsus: perceive, feel

sentis (sentis, *m.*): thorn, briar

sequor (sequī, *deponent verb*), secūtus sum: follow, pursue

sermō (sermōnis, *m.*): speech, talk

serō (serere, *verb*), sēvī, satus: sow, plant

serpens (serpentis, *m.*): snake

sērus, sēra, sērum (*adj.*): late, too late

servō (servāre, *verb*), servāvī, servātus: preserve, save

servus (servī, *m.*): slave, servant, groom

sevērus, sevēra, sevērum (*adj.*): stern, unforgiving

sexiēs (*adv.*): on six occasions

sī (*conj.*): if

sībilō (sībilāre, *verb*), sībilāvī, sībilātus: hiss, whistle

sīc (*adv.*): thus, in this way

sīcut (*adv.*): like, just as

sileō (silēre, *verb*), siluī: be silent, keep quiet

silescō (silescere, *verb*), siluī: grow quiet, fall silent

silva (silvae, *f.*): woods, forest

silvānus (silvānī, *m.*): woodsman, forester

simplex (simplicis, *adj.*): simple, straightforward

simul (*adv.*): at the same time

simulō (simulāre, *verb*), simulāvī, simulātus: imitate, look like

sīn (*conj.*): if however, but if

sine (*prep.* + *abl.*): without

singulī, singulae, singula (*adj.*): separate, individual

sinō (sinere, *verb*), sīvī, situs: allow, permit

sinus (sinūs, *m.*): bosom, lap

sitibundus, sitibunda, sitibundum (*adj.*): thirsty

sitis (sitis, *f.*): thirst

situs, sita, situm (*adj.*): placed, positioned

smaris (smaridis, *m.*): picarel (tiny seafish)

societās (societātis, *f.*): alliance, company

socius (sociī, *m.*): ally, partner

sodālis (sodālis, *m.*): companion, associate

sōl (sōlis, *m.*): sun

soleō (solēre, *semi-deponent verb*), solitus sum: be in the habit of

sollertia (sollertiae, *f.*): skill, cleverness

sollicitō (sollicitāre, *verb*), sollicitāvī, sollicitātus: molest, annoy

sōlummodo (*adv.*): only, alone, just one

solvō (solvere, *verb*), solvī, solūtus: loosen, unbind, dissolve

somnus (somnī, *m.*): sleep

sordidus, sordida, sordidum (*adj.*): nasty, filthy

sors (sortis, *f.*): fate, lot in life

sortior (sortīrī, *deponent verb*), sortītus sum: win by lot, obtain

spatium (spatiī, *n.*): space, time

speciōsus, speciōsa, speciōsum (*adj.*): attractive, appealing

spērō (spērāre, *verb*), spērāvī, spērātus: hope, expect

spēs (speī, *f.*): hope

spīna (spīnae, *f.*): spine, thorn

spīnōsus, spīnōsa, spīnōsum (*adj.*): thorny, prickly

spīritus (spīritūs, *m.*): breath, spirit

splendeō (splendēre, *verb*): shine, be radiant

splendidus, splendida, splendidum (*adj.*): shining, brilliant

spoliō (spoliāre, *verb*), spoliāvī, spoliātus: rob, strip

spolium (spoliī, *n.*): spoils, booty

stabulum (stabulī, *n.*): stall, stable

statim (*adv.*): immediately, at once

statuō (statuere, *verb*), statuī, statūtus: establish, decide

stercus (stercoris, *n.*): manure, filth

sterquilīnium (sterquilīniī, *n.*): dung heap

stertō (stertere, *verb*), stertuī: snore

stō (stāre, *verb*), stetī, status: stand, stay

strāmen (straminis, *n.*): straw

strēnuus, strēnua, strēnuum (*adj.*): vigorous, energetic

struō (struere, *verb*), struxī, structus: build, construct

studium (studiī, *n.*): eager pursuit, dedication

stultitia (stultitiae, *f.*): foolishness, stupidity

stultus, stulta, stultum (*adj.*): foolish, stupid

suādeō (suādēre, *verb*), suāsī, suāsus: urge, exhort

sub (*prep.* + *abl.*): under, beneath

subeō (subīre, *irregular verb*), subīvī or subiī, subitus: go under, undergo

subitō (*adv.*): suddenly, quickly

subitus, subita, subitum (*adj.*): sudden, unexpected

sublactō (sublactāre, *verb*), sublactāvī, sublactātus: entice, dupe

subrīdeō (subrīdēre, *verb*), subrīsī, subrīsus: smile, grin

subveniō (subvenīre, *verb*), subvēnī, subventus: come to help, rescue

subvolō (subvolāre, *verb*), subvolāvī, subvolātus: fly up

succumbō (succumbere, *verb*), succubuī: collapse, lie down, succumb

succurrō (succurrere, *verb*), succurrī, succursus: run to help, assist

sudis (sudis, *f.*): stake, log

sūdō (sūdāre, *verb*), sūdāvī, sūdātus: sweat, perspire

sufflō (sufflāre, *verb*), sufflāvī, sufflātus: puff, blow

suggerō (suggerere, *verb*), suggessī, suggestus: furnish, supply

sum (esse, *irregular verb*), fuī: be

super (*adv.* and *prep.* + *abl.*): above, about, over and above

superaddō (superaddere, *verb*), superaddidī, superadditus: add on to, heap on top

superbiō (superbīre, *verb*): be proud, boastful

superō (superāre, *verb*), superāvī, superātus: overcome, outdo

supervolitō (supervolitāre, *verb*), supervolitāvī, supervolitātus: flutter over, fly above

supplicabundē (*adv.*): pleadingly, humbly

supplicābundus, supplicābunda, supplicābundum (*adj.*): pleading, entreating

supplicō (supplicāre, *verb*), supplicāvī, supplicātus: plead, beg

suprēmus, suprēma, suprēmum (*adj.*): highest, last

surgō (surgere, *verb*), surrexī, surrectus: rise up, get up

sūs (suis, *f.*): sow, swine

suspendō (suspendere, *verb*), suspendī, suspēnsus: hang

suspīrium (suspīriī, *n.*): sigh, deep breath

suspīrō (suspīrāre, *verb*), suspīrāvī, suspīrātus: sigh, utter with a sigh susurrō (susurrāre, *verb*), susurrāvī: whisper, mutter

suus, sua, suum (*adj.*): his/hers/its (*reflexive*)

# T

taceō (tacēre, *verb*), tacuī, tacitus: be silent, shut up

tacitus, tacita, tacitum (*adj.*): silent, quiet

taedet (taedēre, *impersonal verb*), taeduit, taesum est: it is wearisome, irks

taedium (taediī, *n.*): weariness, tedium

tam (*adv.*): so, so much, to such an extent

tamen (*adv.*): however, but, nevertheless

tandem (*adv.*): finally

tantillus, tantilla, tantillum (*adj.*): so small a quantity

tantum (*adv.*): only

tantummodo (*adv.*): only, merely

tantus, tanta, tantum (*adj.*): of such size, so great

tardigradus, tardigrada, tardigradum (*adj.*): slow-paced, limping

taurus (taurī, *m.*): bull

tectum (tectī, *n.*): roof, ceiling

temere (*adv.*): rashly, impetuously

tempus (temporis, *n.*): time

tēmulentus, tēmulenta, tēmulentum (*adj.*): drunken, tipsy

tendō (tendere, *verb*), tetendī, tēnsus: stretch, extend

tenellus, tenella, tenellum (*adj.*): tender, delicate

tentō (tentāre, *verb*), tentāvī, tentātus: attempt, try

tenuitās (tenuitātis, *f.*): slenderness, thinness

ter (*adv.*): three times, thrice

tergum (tergī, *n.*): back, rear

terminus (terminī, *m.*): end, boundary

terreō (terrēre, *verb*), terruī, territus: scare, frighten

territō (territāre, *verb*): frighten, intimidate

tertius, tertia, tertium (*adj.*): third

testūdō (testūdinis, *f.*): tortoise, turtle

tībiāle (tībiālis, *n.*): leg, shin

timeō (timēre, *verb*), timuī: fear, be afraid

timidē (*adv.*): fearfully, timidly

timor (timōris, *m.*): fear, dread

tolerō (tolerāre, *verb*), tolerāvī, tolerātus: bear, endure

tollō (tollere, *verb*), sustulī, sublātus: lift up, take away

torqueō (torquēre, *verb*), torsī, tortus: twist, torment

tot (*adv.*): many, so many

totiēs (*adv.*): as often, such a number of times

tōtum (*adv.*): completely, wholly

tōtus, tōta, tōtum (tōtīus, *adj.*): all, whole

trabēs (trabis, *f.*): tree-trunk, beam

trādō (trādere, *verb*), trādidī, trāditus: hand over, bestow

trahō (trahere, *verb*), traxī, tractus: drag, haul

trānō (trānāre, *verb*), trānāvī, trānātus: swim across

transfuga (transfugae, *m.*): deserter, renegade

trepidē (*adv.*): fearfully, anxiously

trepidō (trepidāre, *verb*), trepidāvī, trepidātus: tremble, fear

trepidus, trepida, trepidum (*adj.*): fearful, anxious

trēs, tria (trium, *adj.*): three

tribūtum (tribūtī, *n.*): tribute, contribution

tū (*personal pronoun*): you (*singular*)

tuba (tubae, *f.*): trumpet

tubicen (tubicinis, *m.*): trumpeter

tugurium (tuguriī, *n.*): cottage, hut

tulī, *see* fero

tum (*adv.*): then, next

tunc (*adv.*): then, at that time

turbō (turbāre, *verb*), turbāvī, turbātus: agitate, muddy

turbō (turbinis, *m.*): whirlwind, tornado

tūtus, tūta, tūtum (*adj.*): safe, secure

tuus, tua, tuum (*adj.*): yours (*singular*)

tyrannis (tyrannidis, *f.*): tyranny, regime

# U

ubi (*adv.*): where, when

ulciscor (ulciscī, *deponent verb*), ultus sum: avenge, punish

Ulixēs (Ulixis, *m.*): Ulysses, Odysseus

ultimus, ultima, ultimum (*adj.*): latest, last

ululātus (ululātūs, *m.*): howl, yell

umbra (umbrae, *f.*): shade, shadow, reflection

umerus (umerī, *m.*): shoulder, upper arm

ūmor (ūmōris, *m.*): liquid, fluid

ūnā (*adv.*): together

ūnanimis, ūnanime (ūnanimis, *adj.*): like-minded, in accord

unde (*adv.*): from where, whereupon, whence

undique (*adv.*): from all sides, on all sides

unguis (unguis, *m.*): claw, talon

ūnicus, ūnica, ūnicum (*adj.*): single, only

ūnītus, ūnīta, ūnītum (*adj.*): combined, united

ūnus, ūna, ūnum (ūnīus, *adj.*): one, sole

urbānus, urbāna, urbānum (*adj.*): urban, city

urbs (urbis, *f.*): city

urna (urnae, *f.*): pot, urn

ursulus (ursulī, *m.*): little bear

ursus (ursī, *m.*): bear

uspiam (*adv.*): anywhere, somewhere

usque (*adv.*): all the way, always

ūsus (ūsūs, *m.*): use, advantage, enjoyment

ut (*conj.*): as; so, so that

uter, utra, utrum (utrīus, *adj.*): which (of two)

uterque, utraque, utrumque (utriusque, *adj.*): each of two

utrimque (*adv.*): on both sides

ūva (ūvae, *f.*): grape

uxor (uxōris, *f.*): wife

# V

vacuus, vacua, vacuum (*adj.*): empty, empty-handed

vādō (vādere, *verb*), vasī: go

vae (*interjection*): alas, woe

vagor (vagārī, *deponent verb*), vagātus sum: roam, wander

vagus, vaga, vagum (*adj.*): wandering, unreliable

valedīcō (valedīcere, *verb*): say goodbye to

valeō (valēre, *verb*), valuī: be well, be strong

validus, valida, validum (*adj.*): strong, powerful

vānus, vāna, vānum (*adj.*): meaningless, useless

varius, varia, varium (*adj.*): different, diverse

vās (vāsis, *n.*): vessel, container

vehemens (vehementis, *adj.*): violent, vigorous

vehō (vehere, *verb*), vexī, vectus: carry, convey

vel (*conj.*): or

velle, *see* volō

vēlōcitās (vēlōcitātis, *f.*): rapidity, swiftness

vēlox (vēlōcis, *adj.*): rapid, swift

velut (*adv.*): just as, as if

vēnāticus, vēnātica, vēnāticum (*adj.*): for hunting, hunter's

vēnātiō (vēnātiōnis, *f.*): hunt, the chase

vēnātus (vēnātūs, *m.*): hunting

vendicō (vendicāre, *verb*), vendicāvī, vendicātus: avenge, claim

veneror (venerārī, *deponent verb*), venerātus sum: worship, revere

veniō (venīre, *verb*), vēnī, ventus: come

ventus (ventī, *m.*): wind

vēnum (vēnī, *n.*): something for sale

Venus (Veneris, *f.*): Venus (goddess of love)

vēr (vēris, *n.*): spring, spring-time

verber (verberis, *n.*): lash, whipping

verbum (verbī, *n.*): word

vereor (verērī, *deponent verb*), veritus sum: revere, respect

vērō (*adv.*): in fact, indeed

versicolor (versicolōris, *adj.*): changing color, varicolored

vertīgō (vertīginis, *f.*): dizziness

vērum (*adv.*): the fact is, truth be told

vescor (vescī, *deponent verb*): eat, feed on

vesper (vesperis, *m.*): evening

vespertīliō (vespertīliōnis, *m.*): bat

vester, vestra, vestrum (*adj.*): your, yours (*pl.*)

vestīgium (vestīgiī, *n.*): track, trace

vestīmentum (vestīmentī, *n.*): garment, clothing

vestītus (vestītūs, *m.*): clothing, clothes

vetulus, vetula, vetulum (*adj.*): aged, old

vexī, *see* vehō

via (viae, *f.*): way, road

viātor (viātōris, *m.*): wayfarer, traveler

vīcīnus (vīcīnī, *m.*): neighbor

victor (victōris, *m.*): winner, victor

victōria (victōriae, *f.*): victory

victus (victūs, *m.*): food, sustenance

videō (vidēre, *verb*), vīdī, vīsus: see

vigil (vigilis, *adj.*): alert, watchful

vīlescō (vīlescere, *verb*), vīluī: become worthless

vīlis, vīle (vīlis, *adj.*): cheap, worthless

vīlla (vīllae, *f.*): farm, country home

vincō (vincere, *verb*), vīcī, victus: conquer, defeat, win

vīnum (vīnī, *n.*): wine

violentus, violenta, violentum (*adj.*): violent, impetuous

violō (violāre, *verb*), violāvī, violātus: dishonor, outrage

vīpera (vīperae, *f.*): snake, viper

vir (virī, *m.*): man, husband

virga (virgae, *f.*): twig, rod

virgō (virginis, *f.*): virgin, girl

virtūs (virtūtis, *f.*): worth, excellence

vīrus (vīrī, *n.*): venom, poison

vīs (*abl.* vī, *acc.* vim, *pl.* vīrēs, *f.*): force, strength

viscera (viscerum, *n.*): entrails, vitals

vīsō (vīsere, *verb*), vīsī, vīsus: visit, go see

vīta (vītae, *f.*): life

vitium (vitiī, *n.*): fault, defect

vītō (vītāre, *verb*), vītāvī, vītātus: avoid, evade

vitreus, vitrea, vitreum (*adj.*): glass, glassy

vitula (vitulae, *f.*): heifer, young cow

vīvō (vīvere, *verb*), vixī: live

vīvus, vīva, vīvum (*adj.*): living, alive

vix (*adv.*): scarcely, hardly

vocō (vocāre, *verb*), vocāvī, vocātus: call

volātus (volātūs, *m.*): flight

volō (velle, *irregular verb*), voluī: want, will

volō (volāre, *verb*), volāvī, volātus: fly

volucris (volucris, *f.*): bird, winged creature

volvō (volvere, *verb*), volvī, volūtus: roll

vorābundus, vorābunda, vorābundum (*adj.*): voracious, gulping

vorō (vorāre, *verb*), vorāvī, vorātus: swallow, devour

vox (vōcis, *f.*): voice

vulnerō (vulnerāre, *verb*), vulnerāvī, vulnerātus: wound, hurt

vulpēcula (vulpēculae, *f.*): fox, vixen

vulpēs (vulpis, *f.*): fox

vulpīnor (vulpīnārī, *deponent verb*), vulpīnātus sum: be sly, play the fox

# GRAMMAR INDEX
## (including Latin words)

# V

verbal adjectives, see gerundives and
  participles
verbal nouns, see gerunds and supines
verbs
  frequentative 235; inchoative 279; parsing of *xv*; word list format *xii*
*vero* 239
vocative 167

# W

word boundaries 79; see also compound
  words
word order 23, 39, 147
word wraps 23

# LIST OF CHARACTERS

# GENERAL INDEX

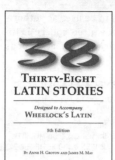

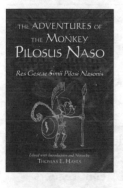

# ℬℭ LATIN Readers

**Series Editor: Ronnie Ancona**
*Hunter College and CUNY Graduate Center*

These readers, written by experts in the field, provide well-annotated Latin selections to be used as authoritative introductions to Latin authors, genres, or topics. Designed for intermediate/advanced college Latin students, they each contain approximately 600 lines of Latin, making them ideal to use in combination or as a "shake-it-up" addition to a time-tested syllabus.

## APULEIUS READER
*Selections from the*
*METAMORPHOSES*
Ellen D. Finkelpearl
xxxviii + 160 pp., 4 illustrations & 1 map (2012)
5" x 7." Paperback, ISBN 978-0-86516-714-8

## A CAESAR READER
*Selections from BELLUM GALLICUM*
*and BELLUM CIVILE, and from*
*Caesar's Letters, Speeches,*
*and Poetry*
W. Jeffrey Tatum
xl + 206 pp., 3 illustrations & 3 maps (2012)
5" x 7." Paperback, ISBN 978-0-86516-696-7

## A CICERO READER
*Selections from Five Essays and*
*Four Speeches, with Five Letters*
James M. May
xxxviii + 136 pp., 1 illustration & 2 maps (2012)
5" x 7." Paperback, ISBN 978-0-86516-713-1

## A LATIN EPIC READER
*Selections from Ten Epics*
Alison Keith
xxvii + 187 pp., 3 maps (2012)
5" x 7." Paperback, ISBN 978-0-86516-686-8

## A LIVY READER
*Selections from AB URBE CONDITA*
Mary Jaeger
xxiii + 127 pp., 1 photo & 2 maps (2010)
5" x 7." Paperback, ISBN 978-0-86516-680-6

## A LUCAN READER
*Selections from CIVIL WAR*
Susanna Braund
xxxiv + 134 pp., 1 map (2009)
5" x 7." Paperback, ISBN 978-0-86516-661-5

## A MARTIAL READER
*Selections from the Epigrams*
Craig Williams
xxx + 185 pp., 5 illustrations & 2 maps (2011)
5" x 7." Paperback, ISBN 978-0-86516-704-9

## AN OVID READER
*Selections from Seven Works*
Carole E. Newlands
xxvi + 196 pp., 5 illustrations (2014)
5" x 7¾" Paperback, ISBN 978-0-86516-722-3

## A PLAUTUS READER
*Selections from Eleven Plays*
John Henderson
xviii + 182 pp., 1 map & 5 illustrations (2009)
5" x 7." Paperback, ISBN 978-0-86516-694-3

## A PROPERTIUS READER
*Eleven Selected Elegies*
P. Lowell Bowditch
xliv + 186 pp., 5 illustrations and 2 maps (2014)
5" x 7¾" Paperback, ISBN 978-0-86516-723-0

## A ROMAN ARMY READER
*Twenty-One Selections from*
*Literary, Epigraphic, and*
*Other Documents*
Dexter Hoyos
xlviii + 214 pp., 7 illustrations & 2 maps (2013)
5" x 7." Paperback, ISBN 978-0-86516-715-5

## A ROMAN VERSE SATIRE READER
*Selections from Lucilius, Horace,*
*Persius, and Juvenal*
Catherine C. Keane
xxvi + 142 pp., 1 map & 4 illustrations (2010)
5" x 7." Paperback, ISBN 978-0-86516-685-1

## A SALLUST READER
*Selections from BELLUM*
*CATILINAE, BELLUM*
*IUGURTHINUM, and HISTORIAE*
Victoria E. Pagan
xliv + 159 pp., 2 maps & 4 illustrations (2009)
5" x 7." Paperback, ISBN 978-0-86516-687-5

## A SENECA READER
*Selections from Prose and*
*Tragedy*
James Ker
lvi + 166 pp., 6 illustrations & 1 map (2011)
5" x 7." Paperback, ISBN 978-0-86516-758-2

## A SUETONIUS READER
*Selections from the LIVES OF*
*THE CAESARS and the LIFE*
*OF HORACE*
Josiah Osgood
xxxix + 159 pp., 1 map & 7 illustrations (2010)
5" x 7." Paperback, ISBN 978-0-86516-716-2

## A TACITUS READER
*Selections from ANNALES,*
*HISTORIAE, GERMANIA,*
*AGRICOLA, and DIALOGUS*
Steven H. Rutledge
xlvii + 198 pp., 5 illustrations, 2 maps,
& 3 charts (2014) 5" x 7." Paperback
ISBN 978-0-86516-697-4

## A TERENCE READER
*Selections from Six Plays*
William S. Anderson
xvii + 110 pp. (2009)
5" x 7." Paperback, ISBN 978-0-86516-678-3

## A TIBULLUS READER
*Seven Selected Elegies*
Paul Allen Miller
xx + 132 pp., 2 illustrations (2013)
5" x 7." Paperback, ISBN 978-0-86516-724-7

## *Forthcoming*

## A ROMAN WOMEN READER
*Selections from the Second*
*Century BCE to the Second*
*Century CE*
Sheila K. Dickison and Judith P. Hallett
ISBN 978-0-86516-662-2

 **WWW.BOLCHAZY.COM**